Fighting on Two Fronts

FIGHTING ON TWO FRONTS

African Americans and the Vietnam War

James E. Westheider

NEW YORK UNIVERSITY PRESS

New York and London

NEW YORK UNIVERSITY PRESS
New York and London

Copyright © 1997 by New York University

Library of Congress Cataloging-in-Publication Data
Westheider, James E., 1956–
   Fighting on two fronts : African Americans and the Vietnam War /
James E. Westheider.
      p.   cm.
   Includes bibliographical references and index.
   ISBN 0-8147-9301-0 (alk. paper)
   1. Vietnamese Conflict, 1961–1975 — Afro-Americans.   2. United
States — Armed Forces — Afro-Americans.   3. United States — Race
relations.   I. Title.
DS559.8.B55W47   1997
959.704'3'08996073—dc21   96-45832
                                            CIP

New York University Press books are printed on acid-free paper,
and their binding materials are chosen for strength and durability.

Manufactured in the United States of America
10   9   8   7   6   5   4   3   2   1

For my mother,
Ruth Westheider

Contents

All photographs appear in the insert section following page 110

Acknowledgments

There are many people and institutions I wish to thank for their immense support and help in researching and preparing this book. I will always appreciate the courtesy extended to me by Harry Sommers, Randy Hackenberg, and the rest of the staff at the U.S. Military History Institute at Carlisle Barracks, Pennsylvania, and by Elaine Engst and her colleagues at Cornell University's rare manuscript collection and Vietnam War Veterans Archive. The staff at the Cincinnati and Hamilton County Public Library were always courteous and helpful, as were Sally Moffit and her staff at the Langsam Library at the University of Cincinnati. I would also like to thank Charles Anderson for his helpful comments and his permission to quote him directly from his wartime letters home.

My colleagues at the History and Geography Department at Northern Kentucky University deserve a very grateful mention. I will always remember their encouragement and enthusiasm, their willingness to help a young scholar, and their valuable suggestions. I will always appreciate the support and understanding extended me by the department chair, Michael C. C. Adams, and the director of Afro-American Studies, Michael Washington, as well as by Jeffrey Williams, James Ramage, John Metz, John Brenner, Bruce McClure, Robert Vitz, Bob Wilcox, Frank Steely, and the rest of this fine faculty. In particular, I would I thank the department's administrative assistants Alissa Ogle and Jan Rachford for all of their help and kindness and my friends and young colleagues Eric Jackson, Doug Knerr, and Scott Merriman for their support, both academic and moral.

At the University of Cincinnati, I am especially grateful to Daniel Beaver, not only for his support and guidance on this project but for all his help throughout the years. Most of all, however, I thank my mentor, Herbert Shapiro. My decision to work in African American history was sparked at least in part by his enthusiasm, wisdom, and love of the topic, and it was he who helped me turn an idea into a book. I will always be in both men's debt.

Acknowledgments

A special thanks to my brother David Westheider and to Tony Saupe, Jeff Witwer, Mike Kruse, Bill Brungs, and Beth Eline, all old friends who provided encouragement and moral support and helped me retain what little sanity I have left.

Four people deserve a very special mention, because without their help and support, this book might not have been written. I will forever be indebted to Linda Klaus-Legeza for her years of friendship and support, not to mention her invaluable technical skills. I am deeply indebted to my close friend and colleague Frederic Krome, not only for his friendship and Monday-night football games but also his advice and insight in preparing this manuscript. To Suzanne DeLuca I owe a very special personal debt for all of her love and support, and for seeing me through the long years. She stood with me throughout the process, and it was her encouragement, companionship, and advice, especially concerning the photographs used in this book, that gave me the strength to see this book to completion. And to my mother, Ruth Westheider: I don't think I can express in words how much her love and encouragement has meant to me. It was my mother and my late father, James E. Westheider, Sr., who taught me to treat all people with respect and dignity.

In some respects, I owe my deepest debt of gratitude to John K. Brackett, Henry Dority, James Hawkins, Jr., Clinton Hunt, Allen Thomas, Jr., Raymond Wells, and Alfonzo Wright, Jr., for sharing their lives and experiences with me and ultimately making this work possible. I have become a wiser and better person for knowing them, and for that I will always remain thankful.

Introduction

On 28 April 1966, President Lyndon Johnson awarded the Congressional Medal of Honor posthumously to army private first class Milton Olive III. Olive became one of the few African Americans to receive the nation's highest honor and the first from the Vietnam War. In presenting the medal to Olive's parents, Johnson stated, "By his heroic death, Milton Lee Olive III taught those of us who remain how we ought to live." The president added that unlike the previous seven black recipients of the Medal of Honor, "Pvt. Olive's military records have never carried the color of his skin or his racial origin—only the testimony that he was a good and loyal citizen of the United States."

Olive's heroic sacrifice had a deep symbolic meaning for President Johnson, but even more so for African Americans. Military service was, of course, not a new phenomenon in the black community; in fact, blacks had served in all of America's previous conflicts. But more often than not, they had done so in segregated units and were relegated to menial labor, detailed to be the haulers of ammunition, grave diggers, messmen, and cooks for the allegedly more capable white soldiers and sailors. Still they fought, believing that through blacks' military service, white America would eventually come to realize that its preconceptions were wrong and that African Americans were indeed worthy of equal citizenship in the United States.

It would be a two-hundred-year struggle to gain both opportunity and recognition. To this end, Cuff Whitmore and Salem Poor, along with more than five thousand other African Americans, fought in the American Revolution. To this end, more than 186,000 United States Colored Troops (USCTs) fought gallantly in the Civil War, not only securing freedom for their enslaved Southern brethren but also winning a permanent place in America's military establishment, albeit a segregated presence. After the war, blacks continued to serve, still in segregated units such as the Ninth and Tenth Cavalry, the famous Buffalo Soldiers stationed in the American Southwest. But despite the impressive records of the USCTs and Buffalo Soldiers—as well as the "Smoked Yankees" in the Spanish-American War and the Tuskegee Airmen in the Second World War—their contributions were largely ignored, and status as equal citizens was denied them. Furthermore, whites still harbored the belief that African Americans were naturally inferior soldiers to whites, and a number of critics pointed to the collapse of all-black units in both the Second World War and Korea as evidence that African Americans lacked the discipline, intelligence, and élan of white combatants.

Private Olive and other African Americans serving in Vietnam were finally destroying this myth of black inferiority. Vietnam was the first war since the American Revolution in which the armed forces were fully integrated from the very beginning, and the first in which blacks ostensibly had the same opportunities as whites to make the same contributions for the same rewards. Without the restraints imposed by segregation and limited opportunities, African Americans would acquit themselves well, proving themselves as pilots, as staff officers, as tank commanders, and in dozens of fields from which they had previously been excluded and winning a reputation as capable and patriotic warriors. What emerged early in the Vietnam War, then, was a new, albeit more flattering, stereotype of the African American in military service: that of the "good soldier."

The armed forces, for their part, were proud of their recent record of desegregation and minority advancement. At a time when African Americans and the Civil Rights movement were scoring impressive triumphs over segregation and prejudice, spokespersons for the armed forces often pointed out that the military's record in these areas since 1948 was better than that of any other segment of American society, and for the most part, it was. In the early phases of the Vietnam War, African Americans appeared to agree with this assessment. Military service was viewed not as an undue burden but as an opportunity, a chance for both social and economic advancement. Consequently, blacks joined the service in great numbers and reenlisted at over twice the rate of whites. Many black leaders around the nation lauded the military for its advances and held it up as a model for the rest of the nation to emulate.

Prior to 1968, little had occurred to tarnish the armed forces' favorable image. Incidents of racial violence or protests in the military had been isolated and sporadic and did not constitute a serious concern for those in command. Yet by 1968, a number of factors combined to shatter both the military's complacency on racial issues and its high status in the black community. The goodwill had largely evaporated, and the armed forces were faced with a growing internal racial problem. Blacks now charged the services with racism. Private Olive was no longer symbolic of a loyal black citizenry willing to pay the ultimate price; instead, he became an example to many of how the United States exploited blacks in a racist war for a racist nation that offered little or nothing in return for their sacrifices. Racial tension and dissatisfaction erupted in racial violence throughout the military and threatened to disrupt the armed forces' ability to perform its various missions, including its combat mission in Vietnam.

This book describes the factors and pressures that led to the racial problems that surfaced in the armed services in the period from 1968 to 1973. It further examines the effects of racism on black service personnel during the later stages of the Vietnam War.

Military authorities initially discounted the possibility that racist practices and attitudes within the armed forces contributed to the military's racial problems. The Department of Defense's Annual Report for 1968, for example, stated categorically that "equal treatment and opportunity be afforded all servicemen without regard to race, color, creed or national origin. The application of this principle, established in 1948, has officially eliminated racial discrimination in the armed forces." Instead, the authorities chose to believe that racial problems were caused by forces unleashed in civilian society—forces over which they had only limited control—and then brought into the military by new inductees. It was not racism but a handful of black "radicals and militants," mostly draftees, who were causing the problems and using racism in the military as an excuse.

In part, they were correct. These were the times of the classic Civil Rights and Black Power movements, and African Americans were openly and forcefully questioning American society and its institutions. Young blacks recruited into the service arrived with new, more aggressive attitudes and heightened expectations. Many entered the service already convinced that the armed forces were just as racist as civilian society, and they reacted against any real or, in some cases, perceived racism. In addition, many were reluctant draftees, ordered to fight and, possibly, die in an increasingly unpopular war in Southeast Asia.

But the problems were not solely the result of racial turmoil in the civilian world. The armed forces had, in fact, helped create their own problems. Despite their proud boasts about being on the cutting edge of racial integration and opportunity, the armed forces had originally been reluctant participants, forced to integrate by President Harry Truman's executive order of July 1948. Many white career military personnel would continue to harbor racist preconceptions and resent the services being used as a social laboratory, and the result would be the dogged perseverance of prejudicial policies and practices. Racism was endemic to the system and had a major impact on every aspect of the minority serviceperson's military career. From induction to discharge, the color of one's skin did matter, in training, assignments, promotion, and the administration of military justice; African Americans were always at a disadvantage, compared to their white counterparts.

It was as much the failure of the armed forces to admit to and deal with the issue of racism as it was the problems generated by American society as a whole that led to discontent and open violence. Though a few of the so-called militants could be considered professional dissidents, insofar as they either belonged to radical organizations or had joined the military to organize other service personnel and disrupt the various missions of the armed forces, most of the so-called troublemakers were not political radicals but simply young men and women rebelling against an unjust system and in many cases, just trying to get out of the military.

It was after 1968 that this new characterization of at least some black service personnel as "militants" crystallized. Many of the so-called or self-styled militants were not revolutionary in their orientation, but they were wary of any white power structure, and unlike most whites, they recognized that racism came in many forms and affected African Americans in many ways. It could be overt or subtle, intentional or accidental, real or perceived. For this study, I use and define the three distinct but interrelated forms of racism that affected African American service personnel.

The first is "institutional," or "systemic," racism, wherein an institution or organization contains inherent vestiges of racism, which leads to built-in disadvantages for racial minorities. Institutional racism is most often unintentional, subtle, and accidental and is often hard to detect for these reasons. The battery of tests given to every new inductee, the Armed Forces Qualification Test (AFQT) tests, are a good example of institutional racism. Because of educational disadvantages for blacks in civilian society and a Euro-cultural bias in the tests themselves, African American inductees tended to be concentrated in the lowest two educational and training categories—categories III and IV—and this relegated them most often to combat infantry training. Once categorized, it was virtually impossible to escape one's classification, meaning blacks could not receive training in or advance to the more lucrative technical fields, which were, in turn, usually dominated by whites. The lack of Afrocentric consumer goods at the post exchanges (PXs) and the practice of denying copies of the Koran to black Muslim inmates in military prisons are also examples of institutional racism.

When military leaders finally became convinced that institutional racism still existed despite their efforts to eradicate it, the armed forces did take steps to eliminate the problems. They also targeted and attempted to eliminate "intentional," or "personal," racism from the ranks.

Personal racism was endemic to the military; many white officers, non-commissioned officers (NCOs), and privates harbored a deep prejudice against African Americans. Despite official policies, they treated blacks as inferior and often provoked racial confrontations. After Dr. Martin Luther King's assassination on 4 April 1968, white service personnel at Cam Ranh Bay donned makeshift Ku Klux Klan outfits and paraded around the base. Throughout the Vietnam War, Confederate flags, a constant source of racial antagonism to black troops, were proudly and defiantly flown. Prejudiced white officers often bypassed deserving blacks for promotion, and white enlisted personnel scrawled racial slurs and graffiti, such as "I'd rather kill a nigger instead of a gook," on walls of latrines and enlisted-men's clubs. African Americans tended to believe that Southerners in the military were largely to blame for personal racism, but the problem does not appear to have been confined to Southern military personnel. Ironically, many Southerners in the military, particularly South Carolina native General William Westmoreland, were unstinting in their praise of blacks in the war.

The third form was "perceived" racism. In some cases, African Americans perceived racism where none intentionally existed. Many blacks entering the armed forces had lived in almost totally segregated environments. They had attended all-black schools and all-black churches and had grown up in all-black neighborhoods. The military was often their first direct exposure to a power structure directly controlled and dominated by whites. It was only natural that they viewed this system with the utmost suspicion and, on occasion, misinterpreted the actions of whites as racist. Many believed, for example, that their drill sergeants in boot camp were racist, but most eventually came to realize the harsh treatment meted out by the drill instructors (DIs) was not racially motivated but only part of the military's general dehumanizing training process.

Ignorance and misunderstanding also contributed to racial tension in the military. Whites considered the black soldiers' habit of going through extended "dapping," or ritualized handshaking, as elitist, aggressive, and done intentionally to aggravate whites. To blacks, it was not a sign of militancy but simply a symbol of solidarity in a hostile environment, and many dapped with friendly whites as well. Still, it remained a source of friction. In chow and beer lines, fights often broke out when whites grew tired of waiting for blacks ahead of them to complete lengthy and complicated daps.

African Americans serving in Vietnam were literally fighting on two fronts. Like their white comrades in arms, they were engaged in a war in Southeast Asia and trying to survive their tour of duty. The other front was unique to minorities requiring them to fight and, they hoped, to survive in a racist institution that still treated blacks differently and with more hostility than it did its white personnel. For black troops in Vietnam, racism was as real an enemy as the Communist-dominated People's Liberation Army, better known to most Americans as the Vietcong, and its ally, the People's Army of Vietnam (PAVN).

The military's priorities were obviously somewhat different from those of its black enlistees. It needed to identify the causes of racial violence in the military, correct them, and determine to what degree this dissension was affecting the military's ability to perform its combat mission in Vietnam. At the time, both the military and many civilians feared that the combination of racial violence, drug abuse, and antiwar activity would lead to the demoralization and eventual disintegration of the American military. In retrospect, it is clear that racial violence did not seriously impede the military's ability to prosecute the war effort. Racial conflict was very rare within combat units and seldom impaired fighting efficiency. Most of the problems occurred in rear, or support, areas, especially in settings where personnel from several different units congregated, such as mess halls, enlisted-men's clubs, and civilian bars and brothels. In addition, blacks and whites apparently tended to get into fights with blacks and whites from units, especially companies, other than their own. Primary group cohesion and identity, necessary to preserve the integrity and fighting ability of the military, therefore does not appear to have been seriously changed by racial violence.

In researching this book, two sources in particular have proven invaluable in reconstructing an accurate portrait of racial conditions in the armed forces during the Vietnam War era. The first is the Senior Officer Oral History of the U.S. Army Military History Institute, Carlisle Barracks,

Pennsylvania, a series of nearly nine hundred interviews conducted with company grade-officers who served in Vietnam. With typical military efficiency, each interviewee was asked about race relations in his particular unit and how the unit dealt with any problems.

Though these interviews were helpful and insightful, the vast majority of officers interviewed were white and thus provided only one perspective on the issue. To help redress the imbalance, I conducted my own (albeit more modest) series of interviews with African American veterans. The selection process for the interviews could best be described as random, as the interviewees were people I contacted through veterans' agencies, American Legion posts and Vietnam Veterans of America meetings, as well as personal acquaintances; two were even students in my classes. Each person was asked the same questions in the same sequence, and the interviews were tape-recorded to help ensure accuracy, but they were not conducted with any type of statistical analysis in mind. Rather, the key contributions of both sets of interviews are that they help put a human face on a complex and often confusing historical process and allow the participants to tell their own, unique experiences during one of the more important but volatile eras in American history.

By its very nature, this study focuses almost exclusively on the problems and experiences of African American service personnel during the Vietnam War. It would be a serious omission not to point out that other minorities—women, Hispanic Americans, and Asian Americans—also suffered from discrimination during their military service. These groups deserve their own, individual studies, and it would be an injustice simply to include these groups in this study as an afterthought, or addendum to the experiences of African Americans. In studying African Americans, or any other minority group within the military, for that matter, one can learn not just about the underside of the so-called American dream, a dream from which minorities have traditionally been excluded, but also about how a nation treats its own people differently in times of war as well as in times of peace.

1

"Good Soldiers"

African Americans and
the Right to Serve

A Sudden Visibility

African Americans often welcomed their assignment to Vietnam in the early days of the war. Historically, the black community had viewed wartime military service as a chance for social and economic advancement, as well as an opportunity to erase the myth that whites were superior fighting men to blacks. Frederick Douglass, writing one hundred years before American involvement in Vietnam, stated, "Let the black man get upon his person the brass letters U.S. Let him get an eagle on his button and a musket on his shoulder, and there is no power on earth which can deny that he has earned the right to citizenship in the United States."[1] Though African Americans had served in all of America's wars prior to Vietnam, with few exceptions they had done so in segregated units and usually were relegated to performing only menial labors. Their chance to earn equal citizenship was generally denied them. Vietnam would be different. It was the first war in which the armed forces were totally integrated, and the first in which African Americans ostensibly had the same opportunities as whites.

Many observers commented favorably on this new and expanded role for blacks. In the *Baltimore Afro-American* in 1966, Whitney Young, Jr., claimed that in Vietnam, for "all intents and purposes, race is irrelevant," and that "in spite of dangers and loneliness, the muck and mire of a war-torn land, colored soldiers fight and die courageously as representatives of all America." [2] Two years later, Daniel P. Moynihan noted that "the single most important psychological event in race-relations in the nineteen-sixties was the appearance of Negro fighting men on the TV screens of the nation," adding that "acquiring a reputation for military valor is of the oldest known routes to social equality." [3] Also in 1968, *New York Times* correspondent Thomas Johnson reported that African Americans were fully participating in every aspect of the Vietnam War. "Negroes in Vietnam," he wrote, "were unloading ships and commanding battalions, walking mountain ranges and flying warplanes. . . . The Negro fighting man has attained a sudden visibility—a visibility his fore-fathers never realized while fighting in past American wars." [4]

Even official military histories reflected this new theme. Marine Corps historians Henry I. Shaw, Jr., and Ralph W. Donnelly noted that in Vietnam, African Americans were fully integrated into the marines and it was impossible to gauge only the contributions of blacks to the "team" effort. But they added that African Americans were highly visible and important members of the team. "Squads, platoons, and companies were led in battle by black officers and NCOs. Responsible staff and support positions were held by blacks . . . black pilots flew close air support . . . and ranged north over the demilitarized zone." [5]

African Americans serving in Vietnam in 1968 echoed these sentiments and generally agreed with these observations. A black officer assigned as an adviser to the Army of the Republic of Vietnam (ARVN) remarked, "The brother does all right here. . . . You see it's just about the first time in his life that he finds he can compete with whites on an equal—or very close to equal basis. He tries hard in this kind of situation and does well." Army major Beauregard Brown agreed. He believed service in Vietnam represented the best chance for advancement, anywhere, for a black career officer. [6] One eighteen-year-old marine private put it more simply, proudly stating, "The brother is here, and he's raising hell. We're proving ourselves."

As they had in previous wars, African Americans once again were "proving" their proficiency in war in Vietnam. This time, however, the old myth of black inferiority finally was largely put to rest. But it was replaced by not one but two new stereotypes of African American military personnel.

The first stereotype was that of the "good soldier." This assessment of African Americans as disciplined, determined, and capable fighters did have antecedents in previous conflicts but emerged to replace the earlier, less flattering image of blacks only during the early years of American combat involvement in Vietnam. Good soldiers, black or white, just did their jobs to the best of their abilities and did not question too deeply the war itself or the basic fabric of American society. As late as 1967, Wallace Terry found that most black soldiers in Vietnam "roundly criticized" such leading African Americans as Dr. Martin Luther King, Jr., and Muhammad Ali for their opposition to the war.[7] Those who did question either the morality of the war or the racial policies of the military were derisively labeled "militants" or "black-power types" by more mainstream career military men, both black and white.

This second stereotype, that of the black militant in uniform, did not crystallize until the late 1960s. The militants would always be thought of by military officials as constituting only a small percentage of all minority service personnel, but they would wield an influence far out of proportion to their actual numbers and would eventually rock the armed forces with their charges of racism.

It was the image of the good soldier that prevailed in the military in the early years of the Vietnam War, and those in command positions noted the abilities and motivation of the black soldier. The commander in chief of the Military Assistance Command, Vietnam (MACV), General William C. Westmoreland, was lavish in his praise of African Americans under his command. In a 1967 speech in his native South Carolina, Westmoreland declared that "the performance of the Negro serviceman has been particularly inspirational to me. They have served with distinction. He has been courageous on the battlefield, proficient, and a possessor of technical skills."[8] Captain (later Major) Richard Torovsky, who led an infantry company in Vietnam in 1970-71, considered the "vast, vast majority" of African Americans in his unit to be "excellent soldiers."[9] Army Captain (later Major) John Ellis, who also commanded an infantry company in Vietnam in 1971, stated that he "had good soldiers that were blacks that did as well as any soldier out there." Ellis recalled two African American troopers in particular. One was his radio telephone operator (RTO), whom Ellis described as "dedicated" and "the finest young man I've ever met in the Army." The other was the company supply sergeant, Leon Caffey. Despite a minor heart condition that kept Caffey from going out into the field, the sergeant still "worked his tail off" and impressed Ellis with his "ability to deal with other black recruits."[10] First Lieutenant (later Major) Donald Dean referred to the African American first sergeant in his headquarters company as "very sterling," a high compliment in military jargon and an assessment of black noncommissioned officers shared by many officers, both black and white.[11]

Brigadier General Daniel "Chappie" James, Jr., the second black general in the United States Air Force, a Vietnam veteran of seventy-eight combat missions over North Vietnam and, for many, the epitome of the good soldier, spoke glowingly about "the young black GI, who is proudly out there leading his platoon through the jungle, destroying the enemy, and doing what he is supposed to do." But James also expressed concern that blacks seldom got the recognition they deserved for serving their country. "So many of them come home with a stack of ribbons and their pride intact," he said, "but you seldom hear about them."[12]

A High Price for Heroism

African Americans were coming home from Vietnam with medals and ribbons, and at least some were getting the recognition they deserved. On 28 April 1966, President Lyndon Johnson bestowed the Congressional Medal of Honor posthumously on army private Milton Lee Olive III. Private Olive, who was killed on 22 October 1965 while shielding four comrades from a hand-grenade blast, became the first African American to receive the nation's highest military award for service in Vietnam.[13] Marine Corps Private James Anderson, Jr., was killed in February 1967 also saving the lives of his fellow marines. Anderson and his platoon were caught in an ambush not more than twenty meters from the enemy's position when a grenade landed among them. Without hesitation and "with complete disregard for his own personal safety," the young marine pulled the grenade to his chest and wrapped himself around it, absorbing the blast. For his "personal heroism, extraordinary valor, and inspirational supreme self-sacrifice," Anderson became the first black marine ever to be awarded the Medal of Honor.[14] Of the 237 Medals of Honor awarded during the Vietnam War, 20 went to African Americans, as did 15 of 154 awards in the army and 5 of 56 awards in the Marine Corps.[15] In contrast, no African American received the Congressional Medal of Honor in either the First or the Second World War.[16]

African Americans, like their white comrades, paid a high price for their heroism on the battlefield. Army private Frederick Williams, who earned seven citations in Vietnam including the Bronze Star and the National Defense Service Medal, was killed in action.[17] So were all five marine recipients and ten of the fifteen army recipients of the Medal of Honor.[18]

Army sergeant James Rush, who considered himself a "pro and a damn good one," was forced to retire after fourteen years in the military when he lost his right arm in a mortar attack.[19]

A few were luckier. Staff Sergeant Arthur Westbrook returned home from Vietnam "without a scratch," having earned five meritorious commendations, including the Bronze Star.[20] Medal of Honor winner Specialist Fifth Class Dwight Johnson also returned from the war "without a scratch," despite "fighting his way through devastating fire . . . fully exposed to the enemy" and killing an enemy soldier with the stock end of his submachine gun.[21] Fellow Medal of Honor recipient Specialist 6 Lawrence Joel not only escaped Vietnam in 1965 without being wounded but also volunteered and returned for a second tour of duty in 1969.[22]

African Americans believed that the bravery and determination they displayed in Vietnam had finally destroyed the myth that they were inferior soldiers. Milton Olive, Sr., on accepting the city of Chicago's Medal of Merit for his deceased son, told Mayor Richard Daley and the audience that he was now convinced "that the service the colored soldier has given in Vietnam has erased for all time the disparaging statements made about him."[23] For some African Americans, even the high casualty rates among blacks in Vietnam offered vindication. Referring to the high death rate, Lieutenant Colonel George Shoffer, one of the highest-ranking blacks in the army in 1968, said, "I feel good about it. Not that I like the bloodshed, but the performance of the Negro in Vietnam tends to offset the fact that the Negro wasn't considered worthy of being a front-line soldier in other wars."[24]

Blacks were suffering disproportionately high casualty rates in Vietnam, and a growing number of critics did not interpret these deaths in the same favorable light as did Lieutenant Colonel Shoffer. Between 1961 and the end of 1967, African Americans accounted for more than 14 percent of American fatalities in Southeast Asia.[25] In 1965 alone, blacks comprised almost one out of every four combat deaths,[26] and they constituted 16 percent of those killed in action in 1966. The disproportionately high death rates so alarmed Pentagon officials that they ordered a "cutback in front-line participation by Negroes" in Vietnam. One general told *U.S. News and World Report* in 1966 that "we deliberately spread out Negroes in component units at a ratio pretty much according to the division total. We don't want to risk having a platoon or company that has more Negroes than whites overrun or wiped out."[27] The changing nature of American involvement in Vietnam from ground combat early in the war to primarily air power and support services in the later years was also a major factor, because as much just as ground units were disproportionately black, the more technically oriented units were overwhelmingly white.

For whatever reason, the black casualty rate did begin to drop after 1967. In 1968, African Americans accounted for 13 percent of those killed in action, but they comprised only 9 percent in 1970[28] and reached a low of only 7.6 percent in 1972. Between 1961 and 1972, 47,244 U.S. service personnel were killed in action. Of this number, 5,711, or about 12 percent, were African Americans.[29] Among all of the armed services during the war, blacks suffered 7,241 deaths, or 12.6% of the total deaths of U.S. military personnel serving in Southeast Asia. Since African Americans comprised, on average, about 9.3 percent of the total active duty personnel assigned to Vietnam, the death rate for blacks was roughly 30 percent higher than the death rate for U.S. forces fighting in Southeast Asia.[30]

Volunteering for Vietnam

The problem was not that African Americans were overrepresented in Vietnam. In 1964, blacks comprised 8.7 percent of the U.S. armed forces. Though this figure would rise slightly during the war, to almost 10 percent in 1968 and 11.1 percent in 1972, African Americans averaged between 9 and 10 percent of military personnel assigned to Vietnam.[31] Of the 448,000 marines who served in Vietnam between 1965 and 1973, for example, about 41,000 African Americans.[32]

The problem was that African Americans tended to be concentrated in combat, as opposed to support, units and thus were far more likely to see fighting. In 1968, *Ebony* reported that African Americans made up 60 to 70 percent of some combat units.[33] Blacks did, in fact, constitute more than 20 percent of the combat infantry personnel assigned to Vietnam that year,[34] down from 31 percent in 1965.[35] The 173d Airborne, considered by many observers to be the best brigade in the war, was, in the words of Thomas Johnson, "heavily Negro."[36] Specialist 4 James Edward Hawkins, who served in the 173d in 1968, recalls that his company was over 40 percent black.[37] Private First Class Henry Dority claims that he and other African Americans made up nearly two-thirds of his airborne unit.[38] E-4 Clinton Hunt served in the First Air Cavalry, which was "about 50 percent" African American.[39] Captain (later Major) Bruce B. Cary, a white officer who served his tour of duty in 1970–1971, said his "company was about fifty-fifty" black and white. Other units in the same battalion, he recalled, "were probably seventy-five to eighty percent black."[40] Another white officer, Captain (later Major) Henry Parker, stated that 60 percent of his company and 95 percent of NCOs were African Americans.[41]

There were several reasons that African Americans were more likely to serve in combat units. As noted in the next chapter, lack of educational opportunities and a Euro-cultural bias in the military's AFQ tests often kept blacks out of the more technical fields in the armed forces. In addition, many either were draftees or had been recruited under Secretary of Defense Robert MacNamara's "Project 100,000," in both cases, blacks were usually assigned to the infantry. Arthur Westbrook and Clinton Hunt, for example, were both drafted and ended up in combat in Vietnam, as did Allen Thomas, Jr., who received his induction notice "the morning of my eighteenth birthday." Thomas eventually served three combat tours in Southeast Asia.[42]

African Americans also volunteered in large numbers for combat units. Service in one of the more elite branches, such as airborne or ranger units, offered young blacks a status and prestige they were unlikely to acquire as civilians. Henry Dority volunteered for the air cavalry, and James Hawkins for the airborne. Hawkins, like many of his fellow African Americans, had mixed reasons for his choice. He was proud of the brigade's elite status: "We were a bastard brigade," he states with a touch of pride, "the only one in Vietnam completely jump-ready." But he also volunteered to avoid being drafted and given a less desirable but equally dangerous assignment.[43]

Money was also a motivating factor. Many African Americans joined the military in the first place because of limited job opportunities in the civilian sector. They reenlisted for the same reason. The armed forces at least offered decent pay and job security. "I know a lot of brothers who will stay in the Army," stated Private James Williams in 1968, "because they're afraid to get out and face what's out there." Staff Sergeant Charles Donald reenlisted in 1966 for six more years because "if I got out, I would have to take my chances," adding that there were no jobs in his native South Carolina available to blacks that would pay as well as the military.[44] Unlike a lot of returning veterans in his hometown of Baltimore, Maryland, Seaman First Class Alfonza Wright found a good job at Armco Steel after he left the Navy. But Wright eventually decided that the military offered more security and chance for advancement than did the civilian sector, so he reenlisted, this time in the army.[45] Charles Cato really liked his job as a jeweler's apprentice and felt he was learning a good trade, though he only made fifty-five dollars a week in 1965. After serving in the army for three years and a tour of duty in Vietnam, Cato left the military and returned to civilian life, only to find his old job was unavailable. He was reduced to living off thirty-three dollars a week in unemployment insurance.[46]

In contrast, an E-4, a rank most recruits could expect to obtain after three years of service, cleared sixty dollars a week, with no expenses for room, food, basic clothing, or medical needs. Serving with an elite unit, such as the paratroops, would add another fifty-five dollars per month in "jump pay."[47] A tour of duty in Vietnam added yet another sixty-five dollars per month in "hostile fire" pay; married military personnel received even higher allowances for food and living quarters.[48] Reenlistment bonuses during the war were especially extravagant. First-time reenlistees could net between nine hundred and fourteen hundred dollars in cash bonuses, depending on rank and occupational skill. In the words of one African American reenlistee, "That's an awful lot of money to a young black cat who's never had more than one hundred and fifty dollars at one time in his life." Reenlistment may have brought monetary rewards, but it almost always meant a tour, or a second tour, in South Vietnam.[49]

Patriotism as well as career concerns influenced some African Americans to seek combat assignments in Southeast Asia. Like many of their white counterparts, black career officers and NCOs viewed Vietnam as a vehicle for quick promotion. A combat assignment in the war was known in military parlance as "getting your ticket punched" and was often a prerequisite to obtaining a higher rank and a choice assignment. Future chairman of the Joint Chiefs of Staff General Colin Powell is a prime example. Powell served two tours of duty in Vietnam: first in 1962, as a captain and an adviser to an Army of the Republic of Vietnam (ARVN) infantry battalion, then in 1968 as a major and battalion executive officer. Powell earned eleven medals in Vietnam, including a Purple Heart and a Bronze Star. By 1973 he had commanded a battalion in Korea and was on the "fast track" for promotion. But most career military personnel, like Powell, also believed quite strongly that it was their patriotic duty as soldiers to seek a combat assignment. Medal of Honor recipient Lawrence Joel voluntarily served a second tour of duty in Vietnam as a combat medic, because "I want to do what I can here, to serve my country as best I can."[50] James H. Scott, who served a tour of duty in 1967, stated at the time that he did not think either Dr. Martin Luther King, Jr., or Student Nonviolent Coordinating Committee (SNCC) leader Stokely Carmichael was right in protesting against the war. "They live in a free country," Scott said, "and somebody has to pay for it."[51]

Black women, of course, also considered it their patriotic duty to serve in Vietnam, even if they were not allowed combat assignments. (Consequently service meant less to women's career advancement.) Sergeant Doris "Lucki" Allen was already a seventeen-year army veteran when she volunteered for duty in Vietnam in 1967.[52] Sergeant Pinkie Hauser turned down a choice public relations job at the Pentagon, four different opportunities to go to Germany, and a comfortable assignment at Fort Knox, Kentucky, and had to reenlist for six years just so she could volunteer for Vietnam. "I just wanted to be there in the war," Hauser explained. "I felt like I wasn't serving my country enough by being at Ft. Knox."[53]

Despite a sincere desire to serve their country, many African Americans, especially high-ranking officers, had to fight the white establishment before they could fight in Southeast Asia. White officials still demonstrated a tremendous reluctance to trust blacks with senior command positions. Major General Frederic E. Davison, the first African American battalion commander in Vietnam, had to wage a bitter struggle with the military just to get a combat assignment: "I wanted to go very badly. There was no plan to take me." Davison recalled that the struggle even affected his personal life, stating, "And I God damn nearly lost my family—lost my family because they couldn't see why the hell I had to volunteer to go to Vietnam."[54]

General Davison's family was not alone in questioning why Davison and other African Americans needed to volunteer for a war that was killing them in disproportionately high numbers. As early as March 1966, an editorial in the moderate *Baltimore Afro-American* referred to the high death rate among blacks as "disturbing" and suggested that race might be a contributing factor.[55] The editors of the *Black Panther* were, as usual, far more blunt in their accusations. The headline of a typical article, which ran in the 26 October 1968 edition of the party newspaper, stated that "Black Marines Die Needlessly" and blamed white racist "glory-seeking" generals for the high casualty rates among blacks.[56] But by 1968 many African Americans, and not just self-styled radicals such as the Black Panther Party (BPP), were alarmed over the large number of black war dead. It was recognized that many factors contributed to the concentration of minorities in combat units and the consequent high casualties. But many critics began to suggest that this was just one manifestation of a larger problem confronting African American military personnel—the problem of racism. The issue was no longer whether black Americans would be allowed to do their "fair share" in their country's wars but rather if they were being asked to carry a disproportionate load of the fighting and dying, and all for a nation that still treated them essentially as second-class citizens.

As American commitment to the war in Southeast Asia expanded, so did the size of the armed forces. By 1968 there were nearly five hundred thousand Americans serving in Vietnam, and the military needed ever-increasing numbers of recruits and draftees to fill the ranks.[57] But many of the young African Americans now entering the service were far more sensitive to racism and less likely to tolerate it than their predecessors had been. Many were also reluctant draftees. In addition, the armed forces had failed to keep pace with the rapid changes occurring in civilian society. The Armed Forces were no longer being held up by black leaders as a shining example for the rest of the nation of race relations and equal opportunity. The goodwill of the late 1950s and early 1960s was rapidly evaporating. Young African Americans were now suspicious of the military's racial policies, and for good reason. What they discovered confirmed their suspicions. Race and racism were major influences in virtually every aspect of their military service. And it all began with their induction into the armed forces.

2

"I'm Not a Draft Evader . . .
I'm a Runaway Slave"

African Americans and the Draft

Reasons for Resistance

On 6 January 1966, John Lewis, an official of the Student Nonviolent Coordinating Committee, issued a statement condemning American participation in the Vietnam War and the use of the draft to raise the manpower needed in the conflict. Lewis stated that SNCC was "in sympathy with and supports the men in this country who are unwilling to respond to a military draft which would compel them to contribute their lives to United States aggression in Vietnam . . . in the name of the "freedom" we find so false in this country."[1]

In the following weeks, SNCC's stance on the draft would gain support from other black leaders, notably Georgia state representative elect Julian Bond[2] and Eldridge Cleaver. Dr. Martin Luther King, Jr., would not yet go so far as to endorse SNCC's antidraft policy, but he did urge all those opposed to the draft to seek conscientious objector status and expressed the hope that the Selective Service System would consider civil rights work as an acceptable alternative to military service.[3] In addition, in the spring of 1996 Representatives Adam Clayton Powell and John Conyers would both question the fairness of the draft in regard to African Americans,[4] reflecting in somewhat more moderate terms a position taken earlier by Malcolm X. On New Year's Eve 1964, in a speech at McComb, Mississippi, Malcolm X stated that the U.S. government was the most "hypocritical since the world began," because it "was supposed to be a Democracy, supposed to be for freedom," but "they want to draft you . . . and send you to Saigon to fight for them" while blacks still had to worry about getting "a right to register and vote without being murdered."[5]

In early 1966, however, the vast majority of African Americans apparently did not share these beliefs. A Gallup poll conducted for *Newsweek* that year found that three out of every four black Americans supported the draft and believed the present Selective Service System was fair to minorities. But as the war in Vietnam escalated and increasing numbers of young African Americans were drafted and sent to Southeast Asia, where many of them would be killed, opposition to both the war and the draft grew in the black community. In June 1969 another *Newsweek* survey found that almost half of all African Americans thought the draft was racially biased.[6]

Many African Americans in the antidraft movement held a position similar to that of most of the whites who opposed the draft on philosophical, legal, and moral grounds. They argued that the Vietnam War was illegal and immoral and that it was wrong to force anyone to participate in the conflict against his will.[7] But most blacks had their own, different reasons for opposing the system. Many, in fact, did not necessarily oppose either the war or the use of the draft but felt the present system was unfair and simply wanted the inequities corrected. They pointed out that the numerous exemptions and deferments all favored middle- and upper-class whites, thus leaving African Americans to be drafted and sent to Vietnam in disproportionately high numbers. Army colonel John Thomas Martin, National Association for the Advancement of Colored People executive secretary Roy Wilkins, and Detroit congressman Charles C. Diggs all questioned the draft on these grounds, as did white *New York Times* reporter Hanson Baldwin. Baldwin stated that the problems facing African Americans stemmed from inequities in American society and that these were problems "which the draft can't cure and for which it should not be blamed." Martin, who was then one of the more senior black army officers, believed that the draft could be beneficial to young black males in that it rescued them from the ghetto and provided them with educational and economic opportunities.

But Martin was reflecting the viewpoint of an older generation, one that had generally benefited from military service during the relatively peaceful 1950s. Most young African American leaders, growing up in the more turbulent 1960s, held a far more critical view of the draft than did officers such as Martin, and like John Lewis, they opposed it on both philosophical and political grounds. They argued that since African Americans were not accorded the rights and privileges of citizenship, they were not obligated to fight, and possibly die, for the United States. "White people intellectualize," explained University of California-Berkeley student and black militant Leonard Henderson in 1968. "We have a different reason for not going. We haven't enjoyed the benefits of this society. The whites are resisting as citizens. We resist on the grounds that we aren't citizens. He who has no country should not fight for it."[8] One young African American who avoided the draft by going to Canada put it more succinctly: "I'm not a draft evader," he explained, "I'm a runaway slave. I left because I was not going to fight white America's war."[9]

To many of the young radicals, the draft was viewed as simply one cog in an overall conspiracy to use African Americans to fight white America's "racist" war against the Vietnamese people. Young blacks were being channeled into the military, either indirectly by the lack of economic opportunity in the civilian sector that forced them to seek employment in the armed forces, or directly by the more coercive draft. Once they were forced into the military, a racially biased system of testing, training, and promotion worked to keep most blacks out of the more lucrative and rewarding technical fields and concentrated them in combat units. Consequently, a young African American was far more likely to be drafted, sent to Vietnam and killed, than a young white male. Some radicals even expressed the view that the draft was actually a sinister attempt systematically to murder young African Americans. Walter Collins, a SNCC spokesperson and activist, expressed these concerns when he denounced the draft as "a totalitarian instrument used to practice genocide against black people,"[10] a theme often reflected in the pages of the *Black Panther* and the *Black Liberator* newspapers.[11]

Though the U.S. government was not using the draft systematically to exterminate young African American males, blacks had good reason for believing the selective service system was inherently racist and placed an undue burden on minorities. African Americans were being drafted in disproportionately high numbers. Between 1965 and 1970, the height of American involvement in Vietnam, blacks constituted slightly over 11 percent of the draft-eligible population, aged nineteen to twenty-six, but represented 14.3 percent of all draftees.[12] During the 382,000-man draft of 1966, over 47,500, or 13.4 percent of the inductees were African American. The following year, 37,000 blacks were drafted, representing over 16 percent of the total. As late as 1970, with both the draft and American involvement in Vietnam winding down, African Americans still accounted for 16 percent of the inductions.[13]

The Selective Service and African Americans

The high percentage of black inductees during the Vietnam War followed a historical pattern first established in 1917. African Americans made up almost 10 percent of the draft-age population when the United States entered the First World War, but the 367,710 black inductees constituted 13.08 percent of all draftees between 1917 and 1919. African Americans had less opportunity to enlist at the beginning of the war because the U.S. Army had only four black regiments, and high reenlistment rates meant relatively few openings for new recruits. In fact, only 4,000 African Americans were accepted as volunteers, compared with 650,000 whites.[14] But racism was also a factor in the high draft calls. Most local draft boards made it a practice to have eligible blacks tear off a corner of their selective service form, making them easier to identify and draft.

In the Second World War, pressure from African American leaders led President Franklin Roosevelt to implement a less racially biased selective service system. The Selective Service Act of 1940 prohibited discrimination based on race or color, and military officials attempted to ensure that the percentage of blacks drafted was roughly equal to their proportion of the overall population, slightly more than 11 percent. Between January 1940 and September 1945, 2,438,831 African Americans were drafted, comprising 10.7 percent of all inductees.[15]

After World War II, Congress allowed the Selective Service Act to expire in March 1947, eventually replacing it with the Selective Service Act of June 1948. The new law did not specifically rule out either racial quotas or a segregated draft, but both were officially ended after President Harry Truman issued Executive Order 9981 on 26 July 1948. Truman's directive did not explicitly outlaw segregation but called for "equality of treatment and opportunity for all persons in the Armed Services without regard to race, color, religion, or national origin." A month later, in late August 1948, a spokesperson for the Selective Service announced that in response to the president's order, racial quotas would no longer be a factor in the draft. The armed forces also announced an end to limits on black enlistments.[16]

The Korean conflict was the first war to be affected by Executive Order 9981. Though the United States would enter the war with a still largely segregated military, the demands of combat would lead to rapid integration, especially in the combat units. In several key aspects, Korea would foreshadow the African American experience in Vietnam. As in the First World War and Vietnam, blacks would be drafted in disproportionately high numbers. Between 1950 and 1954, more than 1.7 million men were drafted and 219,128, or 12.8 percent of the total were African Americans. In both Korea and Vietnam, African Americans would also enlist in large numbers. By mid-1951 nearly one in four of the army's new recruits was black, and whether draftee or volunteer, he was more likely than the average white soldier to see combat and become a casualty, just as in Vietnam.

The Selective Service Act of 1948 would have a great influence on the African American experience in Vietnam in yet another way. After the Korean War ended in July 1953, the armed forces continued to rely on the draft for some of its manpower requirements. The problem now facing the military was that they did not need, nor could they possibly absorb, all of the eligible inductees. To solve the problem, they limited the size of the potential manpower pool by instituting and expanding a complicated system of deferments, allowable under the 1948 draft law. College deferments that began during Korea were expanded to include graduate work and became virtually automatic, as did a wide variety of occupational deferments. Fathers were not inducted, and married men were placed in a lower priority category. The minimum mental and physical standards for induction were also raised. Not only would the armed forces be guaranteed the requisite number of new recruits each year, the civilian economy and society were less likely to be disrupted because those deemed to be the most "productive," middle- and upper-class whites, were likely to be spared service.[17]

Since relatively few African Americans qualified for either the college or occupational deferments in this era, they would continue to be overrepresented in the draft calls throughout the 1950s and early 1960s. But the number of inductions each year was generally low, there was not an unpopular war causing American casualties, and African Americans generally held a positive view of military service. Serving in the armed forces, whether through voluntary enlistment or through the draft, was not seen as an unfair burden but as a chance for advancement. In this respect, Allen Thomas, Jr.'s experience was typical. Drafted in 1957, he decided to remain in the army and make a career out of it before the end of his first tour of duty. "I was brainwashed," he added; but like many young blacks of his era,

Thomas found both a home and a career in the military, and ultimately, his decision to remain in the service was voluntary.[18]

Beginning in 1965, however, things began to change. When the United States escalated its efforts in Vietnam, a greater percentage of eligible draftees were called up, and it became increasingly difficult for an eligible but unwilling African American to avoid induction. Blacks now began seriously to question the racial fairness of the draft, and one of the main grievances was the granting of college deferments.

Technically, the deferment system did not racially discriminate against minorities, because it was just as easy for a black student to get a college deferment as it was for a white.[19] Future associate justice of the Supreme Court Clarence Thomas was a student at Holy Cross in Massachusetts during the war and received a deferment, to cite just one example. But the Selective Service System was inherently biased along class and economic lines and clearly favored those who could afford the cost of a higher education. Most black families could not. In 1967 the median income for the average white family was $8,274 a year. For African American families it was only $5,141 a year. Only one in five urban black families earned more than $10,000 a year,[20] and more than 30 percent of all African American families were at or below the poverty line.

Many African Americans were also kept out of college because of a substandard precollege education in underfunded and segregated schools, which did little to prepare them for university admission. White families could often afford to hire a tutor or to shop around for a school with lower entrance requirements. Black families seldom had this kind of economic flexibility or these options.

Economic, class, and educational levels were often interrelated and were very important determinants as to who was or was not drafted. A 1977 sociology study of 380 war dead from the state of Wisconsin found a very strong correlation between socioeconomic status and mortality in Vietnam. The lower the economic class, the higher the death rate. More than 87 percent of the war dead from Wisconsin came from either poor or working-class families.[21] A 1980 study by the Veterans Administration reached similar conclusions based on education levels. The Veterans Administration claimed that education was a more important factor than race in determining who was drafted; those with lower than a high school education were three times as likely to be drafted as those with a college education.[22] College deferments were such a safe haven from the draft that Stewart Alsop wrote in 1970 that

"Yale, Harvard, and Princeton to cite three obvious examples, have graduated two — repeat two young men in the whole course of the war, who were
drafted and killed in action in Vietnam."[23]

But in America, race is often a key determining factor of one's socioeconomic class and educational level. The economic and educational biases
inherent in the system may not have constituted overt racial discrimination, but they clearly represented a case of systemic, or institutional, racism. It is interesting to note that though both blacks and whites were active
in the antidraft movement, the fairness of college deferments was never a
major issue among the white activists, many of whom either were still in
college or were recent graduates.

Racism and the Local Draft Board

If the selective service's college deferment policies represented a form of
institutional racism, the actions of many of the local draft boards were
often classic examples of overt personal racial discrimination. There were
more than 4,080 local draft boards in the United States, and they held a
great deal of power in determining one's fate. It was up to the local boards,
for instance, to grant or deny occupational, hardship, and conscientious
objector deferments.[24] The composition of each board was supposed to be
representative of the local community, but this was rarely the case. Even in
areas where African Americans comprised a large percentage of the population, they were almost always underrepresented on the local draft boards.
In 1966 there were only 230 African Americans sitting on local draft boards,
a mere 1.3 percent of the total local draft board composition.[25] In 1967
there were only 278 blacks out of a total of 17,123 local board members, and
still no African Americans at all on boards in seven Southern states.[26] The
situation was so bad in the South that in 1968 Charles Evers, executive
secretary for the NAACP in Mississippi, sued Governor John Bell Williams
in federal court, in an attempt to force the governor to appoint blacks to
the boards in that state. Evers stated that "Negroes were tired of having
their sons and husbands sent off to Vietnam by all white draft boards."[27]
In South Carolina, the NAACP and the American Civil Liberties Union
(ACLU) filed a class action suit to halt the drafting of African Americans,
based on the absence of blacks on that state's draft boards. In Georgia,
SNCC activist Cleveland Sellers and the ACLU successfully fought Seller's
induction on the same grounds.

The lawsuits seldom had the desired effect, but several Southern states eventually gave in to pressure from the director of the Selective Service, General Lewis B. Hershey, and appointed a few African Americans to local draft boards. The state of Arkansas had no African Americans serving on local boards in 1966 but had appointed thirty-five by early 1968. Louisiana, which also had none in 1966, appointed thirty-three in the next two years. But other Southern states made token appointments at best. By 1968 there were fifteen African Americans on local boards in Georgia, only six in South Carolina, three in Alabama, and still none in Mississippi. Nationally, some progress was made.[28] By late 1970 there were 1,265 African Americans, or 6.6 percent of all members, on local boards, but throughout the war African Americans continued to be underrepresented on the boards, particularly in the South.

The situation was just as bleak at the state level, where there were no African Americans serving as state directors. By 1968 there were only two blacks serving in the equivalent post of territorial director, Colonel Joseph A. Christmas in the Virgin Islands and Colonel John Thomas Martin for the District of Columbia.[29]

The typical local board member throughout the Vietnam War tended to be white, male, conservative, over forty, and a veteran of either World War II or Korea.[30] Some were admitted racists. Jack Helms, the head of the largest draft board in Louisiana, Local 42 in New Orleans, was a Grand Dragon in one of the state's Ku Klux Klan organizations. Helms served as chairman of Local 42 from 1957 to April 1966, when pressure from the NAACP finally convinced Hershey to suspend him. Helms, voicing an opinion shared by many whites, denounced the NAACP as a "communist inspired anti-Christ, sex-perverted group of tennis short beatniks whose sole purpose is to cause strife in our beloved land." He also denounced Hershey as a "terribly misinformed" and "senile" man.[31]

Though many white board members did not quite share Helms's assessment of either Hershey or the NAACP, they seldom displayed much sympathy or understanding for African Americans. Edward Neal, from Tehula, Mississippi, was denied a hardship deferment by his local board even though he worked two jobs and was the sole supporter of his mother, disabled father, and eight siblings.[32] Luther Wilson's application for an exemption was also denied, even though his father was dead and his mother was dying of sickle-cell anemia.[33] In contrast, actor George Hamilton was granted a hardship exemption by his local board in California because he was the sole supporter for his widowed mother, who lived in a "modest" mansion.[34]

Another area in which local boards tended to discriminate against African Americans was in the granting of conscientious objector (CO) or I-O deferments. Prior to Vietnam, one usually had to belong to a traditionally pacifist sect, such as the Amish or the Mennonites, to qualify for CO status. During the Vietnam War, the Selective Service realized the controversial nature of the conflict and recognized that many eligible young men objected to service on moral grounds. Many local boards granted CO status based on guidelines established in a 1965 Supreme Court decision, *U.S. v. Seeger*, which indicated that conscientious objector status could be based on either religious or moral grounds, "a given belief that is sincere and meaningful" and "occupies a place in the life of its possessor parallel to that filled by the orthodox belief in God of one who clearly qualifies for the exemption."[35] Some civil rights activists were initially granted conscientious objector status and given alternative service, based on their religious and moral opposition to military service.

But African Americans were often denied CO status because of racial preconceptions shared by many white board members. In 1968 a spokesperson for the Chicago draft board frankly remarked that his board had found "few Negro boys who are true conscientious objectors. They say they object to going because of religious reasons ... they pretend to believe in God and say I don't want to kill anybody, then right afterwards they go out in the streets and cut some person's throat."[36]

These preconceptions deeply affected African Americans who sought religious exemptions but did not belong to a mainstream Christian sect. One group in particular, the followers of the Nation of Islam (NOI), or Black Muslims, found it nearly impossible to get CO exemptions based on religious grounds. Nation of Islam member Stanley L. Garland refused to take his preinduction physical in 1965 because of religious objections and after two years of court battles lost his case and was sentenced to three years in a federal prison.[37] Many whites simply refused to accept the Nation of Islam as a real religion, and many urban police departments considered the Muslims to be criminals and militants. Furthermore, the Justice Department had ruled that the Nation of Islam did not meet the criteria of a traditionally pacifist organization because they "only objected to certain wars under certain conditions"; they were allowed to fight only if a conflict was deemed a holy war, or "jihad," by Islamic religious leaders.[38]

In its brief history, the Nation of Islam had established something of a pacifist tradition. By the 1960s, its members had refused to serve in either

World War II or Korea. During World War II, more than eighty Black Muslims were sent to federal prison on charges of draft evasion and interfering with the draft. In 1942, the leader of the NOI, Elijah Muhammad, was given a six-year sentence for interfering with the draft and disrupting an induction center.

During the Vietnam War, the most highly publicized dispute between the Nation of Islam and the Selective Service involved then heavyweight boxing champion Muhammad Ali. In February 1964, the boxer publicly embraced the Nation of Islam and, at the direction of Elijah Muhammad, changed his name from Cassius Marcellus Clay to Muhammad Ali. In the next two years, Ali twice took the Selective Service's preinduction intelligence test and both times failed to achieve the necessary minimum score. The boxer was classified I-Y and considered mentally unfit for service.[39]

But the armed services were becoming desperate for manpower, and in April 1965 they lowered the minimum physical and mental standards for induction. Ali was now considered eligible for induction, and in February 1966 his local board in Louisville, Kentucky, sent him his draft notice. Ali then filed for a conscientious objector deferment, citing his Black Muslim faith.[40]

On 28 April 1967, Ali's application for a religious deferment was rejected, and he was ordered to report for induction at Houston, Texas. Ali refused, and on 20 June 1967 he was convicted and sentenced to five years in prison for draft evasion.[41] The World Boxing Association had already stripped him of his heavyweight title in April. Four years later, on 28 June 1971, the Supreme Court overruled Ali's conviction on a technicality.[42] Other followers of Elijah Muhammad were not as fortunate. Nearly one hundred Black Muslims served federal prison sentences for draft evasion during the Vietnam War.[43]

Other favorite targets of the local draft boards, especially in the South, were civil rights workers and "militants." Cleveland Sellers, national program director for SNCC, claimed that local draft boards were trying to "wipe out" the organization by drafting all of its members.[44] In fact, the draft was often used as a weapon against any politically active or outspoken young African American. In late January 1966, the Selective Service announced it would review the CO status of SNCC spokesperson John Lewis because of his recent antiwar and antidraft statements. The authorities cited in particular his admiration for "draft card burners."[45] In 1968 the chairman of Atlanta's draft board publicly referred to Georgia state representative Julian Bond as "this nigger" and bitterly complained that the draft board had "missed him." "I've always regretted that," the board chairman added.[46]

The Atlanta board may have "missed" Julian Bond, but other local Southern boards were more successful, especially in Mississippi. A local draft board turned down civil rights activist Bernie Tucker's application for conscientious objector status, because "he caused nothing but trouble," with his civil rights work. Robert James was originally granted a CO deferment by his local board in Mississippi, but soon after the board became aware of his civil rights activities, they ordered him to perform alternative service in a distant town. James refused and was eventually convicted of refusing induction and sentenced to five years in a federal prison. Activist Hubert Davis was drafted immediately on declaring his intention to run for mayor in a small Mississippi town.

In Louisiana, authorities could not draft New Orleans civil rights leader Jeanette Crawford, but within a week after she refused to appear before the Louisiana House Committee on Un-American Activities, induction orders were issued for her three sons. Authorities then charged Crawford's oldest son, James, with failing to register for the draft, despite the fact he was a thirteen-year army veteran presently stationed in Germany. James Crawford's situation was quickly resolved, but his youngest brother, Warren, was not as lucky. The younger Crawford refused induction and was eventually given six concurrent five-year prison terms, the most severe sentence given to a nonviolent draft resister during the war.[47]

Harsh prison sentences for black draft resisters were common. SNCC activist Walter Collins refused five straight induction notices from his Louisiana draft board; he was convicted of draft evasion and sentenced to five concurrent five-year sentences.[48] African American draft resisters were generally given longer prison sentences than white resisters, five years on average for African Americans as opposed to three to four years for whites. African American resisters also tended to serve nearly a year longer in prison than did fellow whites.[49]

Between 1967 and 1971, the Selective Service instituted a series of reforms aimed at eliminating apparent racial and class discrimination in the system. Undergraduate, graduate, and occupational deferments were phased out, as were exemptions for fathers. Selective Service officials also instituted a new way of choosing inductees, the lottery system, based on one's birthday. Each day of the year was chosen at random and assigned a number from 1 to 365. The lower the number of one's birthday, the greater the likelihood of being called up. But reform came slowly. Graduate school deferments were eliminated in 1967, but Congress did not finally grant the president authority to end underclass college deferments until September 1971. This effectively protected the graduating class of 1972 from the draft.[50]

Avoiding Induction

Even without the deferments, there were still many ways one could avoid induction, and they still tended to favor middle- and upper-class whites. One way was service in the National Guard or the reserves. Guard and reserve units were, of course, liable for service in Vietnam. In Korea, for example, between 1950 and 1954 more than seven hundred thousand guardsmen were eventually called up for federal service. But President Lyndon Johnson did not want to risk disrupting the economy by mobilizing the guard and the reserve, and so only thirty-eight thousand National Guardsmen were called into federal service during the Vietnam War. Only fifteen thousand National Guardsmen were sent to Vietnam, all in 1968, during the height of American combat involvement.

The National Guard quickly became viewed by the white middle class as a relatively honorable and safe alternative to active military service. Future vice president J. Danforth Quayle, who chose to serve in a headquarters unit of the Indiana National Guard during the war, was typical of his class and generation. A 1966 Pentagon study found that nearly 71 percent of all guard enlistments appeared to be draft-motivated. In 1970, James Cantwell, president of the National Guard Association, believed that 90 percent of all guard enlistments were draft-motivated; the guard had a waiting list of over one hundred thousand applicants that year, the vast majority of them white.[51]

Each state controlled its own guard organization and its own appointment process, which was often subject to political pressure, corruption, and local considerations. Having an influential ally in state government, for instance, could move one's name up the appointments list.[52] In the South, local considerations often meant having virtually no African Americans in a white National Guard. Mississippi, a state in which blacks constituted 42 percent of the population in 1969, had only one black guardsman out of a state total of 10,365. In Alabama, in which 30 percent of the population was black, there were only ten blacks among 15,030 National Guardsmen.[53] The Maryland National Guard had no black officers, even though many eligible African Americans were on its waiting list.[54]

This situation was not just in the South. In most states the guard was composed largely of white, middle-class college graduates. As the draft calls increased, black representation in the guard would decrease, from 5,184 black guardsmen in 1967 to only 4,944 in 1968, only 1.15 percent of the total guard strength. The problem would have been worse if not for a new, experimental "overstrength" program ordered by the Pentagon. The New Jersey National Guard recruited 527 African Americans under this program, in which the Pentagon allowed and supported a 5 percent "overstrength" in its normal quota to attract eligible African Americans.[55] Because of such overstrength programs and pressure from both the Pentagon and many civil rights leaders, the African American presence in the guard steadily increased. By June 1971 there were officially 16,792 African Americans in the guard. By 30 September 1972, the number had increased 70 percent, to 28,472. But by then, both the war and the draft had dwindled in significance, and the guard no longer had a waiting list. Blacks still comprised only 3.1 percent of total guard and reserve strength.[56]

Many who did not want to serve in either the active forces or the reserves sought medical deferments. Being diagnosed with a non-life-threatening ailment, such as ulcers or a severe allergy, usually would keep one out of the service. But again, whites tended to benefit most from this policy. African Americans often lacked adequate medical care, and a condition likely to keep them out of the draft usually would go undiagnosed. A white was more likely to have the money and resources to find a doctor willing to perform enough tests to find a deferrable ailment. Some physicians, either for a fee or because of genuine opposition to the war, were reputedly willing to fake a certificate attesting to a medical condition. Every new inductee was given a medical examination by a military doctor, but these physicians were generally overworked and their departments understaffed. It was far more expedient simply to defer to the civilian doctor's diagnosis than to waste time reexamining the inductee. The standard examination given to a potential inductee was often fairly routine and cursory, and most ailments likely to keep an African American or poor white out of the service again would go undiagnosed. That these practices favored whites is evidenced by the fact that in 1966 the Selective Service found that a mentally qualified white inductee was 50 percent more likely than a mentally qualified African American to fail his preinduction physical. In 1970, more than one in every three whites but less than one in four blacks failed his preinduction physical.[57]

Many draft resisters successfully fought induction through the legal system. Selective service law was complicated and full of potential loopholes and legal precedents. One of the most popular and successful defenses used by lawyers was known as the "order of call" defense. Under the law, one had to be inducted in an orderly fashion, and all had to be called up in the same order in which their names appeared in the draft rolls. If a lawyer could prove that someone had been called up before everyone ahead of him on the list, this invalidated the induction orders. Since draft rolls often contained tens of thousands of names, a persistent lawyer could usually find at least one, and usually many more, call-ups that had been missed. The attorney for black militant Leroy Thompson was able to get all charges against his client dropped based on the order-of-call defense.

Lawyers specializing in selective service law also became very adept at challenging deferment decisions made by the local draft boards, by appealing to the state board and, if that failed, to federal courts. The process took years and effectively kept one out of the service. The federal courts often proved to be somewhat less biased and arbitrary than the local draft boards, and at least in a few cases, they proved to be far more sympathetic toward resisters. The nation's first African American U.S. attorney, Cecil Poole, was not very enthusiastic about prosecuting draft resisters in the San Francisco area. Poole treated draft resistance the same way he treated other "victimless" crimes, by giving consideration to local community standards. Since antiwar sentiment was prevalent in the Bay Area, he did not vigorously pursue draft resistance cases. In fact, Poole's office declined to prosecute nine out of every ten draft cases referred to his office.[58] Another federal judge was known to sentence draft resisters to only one day's probation, and in one case, one hour's probation. Most prosecuting attorneys and judges were not as lenient, but they found that draft resistance cases were usually difficult and time-consuming to prosecute, factors that worked to the advantage of the defendant. Many federal law officials, especially late in the war, often found it more convenient to drop a case based on a technicality than to prosecute vigorously. The attorneys were so successful that an expert in selective service law could usually guarantee a client noninduction for around twenty-five hundred dollars.[59] A few individuals, such as Muhammad Ali, could afford the cost, and some, like Cleveland Sellers, had the resources of the ACLU backing them; but for most African Americans, the legal fees were prohibitive and free help often unobtainable.

There were some free alternatives. Many religious organizations, such as the American Friends Service Committee and the Catholic Peace Fellowship, and professional organizations such as the leftist-oriented National Lawyers Guild and the Vietnam Veterans Against the War/Winter Soldier Organization (VVAW/WSO), provided free draft counseling and, in many cases, legal aid to resisters. These organizations were effective, and the religious groups in particular had a high success rate early in the war.[60] The main problem was not money this time; it was that the groups these organizations sought to help, African Americans, Hispanics, and poor whites, rarely sought counseling. Even at predominantly black Fisk University, it was usually middle-class whites who showed up for help at the draft counseling office. In Chicago, one medical clinic provided counseling and medical examinations to whites only if they brought along one draft-eligible African American.[61] The white-controlled organizations usually had little success in attracting African Americans. Blacks did not know these programs were available or simply did not trust whites or believed these organizations were not responsive to their needs. A 1973 report issued by the Vietnam Veterans Against the War/Winter Soldier Organization blamed racism, even among the more radical white groups, for the failure to reach and work effectively with African Americans. The VVAW/WSO concluded that such projects failed because they "were run by whites with little understanding of the struggles of minority peoples."[62]

Fighting the Draft

There were some black organizations actively involved in the antiwar and antidraft movements, most notably the Black Panther Party, the Student Nonviolent Coordinating Committee, and the National Black Antiwar Antidraft Union, founded in February 1968. Like many of the more radical white antiwar groups—the Students for a Democratic Society, (SDS) and the VVAW/WSO, for example—these organizations tended to prefer direct action, such as mass demonstrations and raids on draft offices, to counseling and passive resistance. On 18 August 1966, SNCC organized a demonstration in front of an Atlanta induction center.[63] On 31 March 1967 the Spring Mobilization for Peace, a biracial organization led by noted civil rights activist the Reverend James Bevel, staged a protest and sit-in at Selective Service headquarters in Washington, D.C.[64] In October 1967 the Black Panther Party staged a "Stop the Draft" week at the Oakland Induction Center.[65] In Chicago in September 1969, fifteen members of the Black Antiwar Antidraft Union temporarily disrupted selective service call-ups in that city by breaking into the Sixty-third Street Selective Service office and burning the 1-A, or draft-eligible, files.

All of the militant black organizations opposed the draft because they believed it was racist and an attempt to commit genocide against African Americans. Linda Quint, spokesperson for the self-styled Chicago Fifteen who raided the Sixty-third Street offices, said their actions were "designed to free African Americans from the draft and to highlight the connection between racism and the military." Quint added, "Most whites stay at home and argue about the immorality of the war while the minorities are sent off to fight."[66] Members of the Black Union, SNCC, and the Black Panther Party, however, usually resisted induction and refused to be "sent off to fight." Between January and May 1967, fifteen members of SNCC refused induction, and National Chairman Stokely Carmichael announced he would refuse to go to Vietnam if drafted.[67] Carmichael was spared a confrontation with the Selective Service because in March 1967, his draft board in New York City classified the rights leader 4-F, or unfit for duty, after he failed his medical examination.[68]

Members of the Black Panther Party were explicitly forbidden to fight in "colonial wars of aggression" and were supposed to resist induction. Rule 6 of the party's bylaws stated that "no party member can join any army or force other than the Black Liberation Army."[69] But it was often far more difficult for rank-and-file members of the Black Panthers, SNCC, or one of the other "militant" groups to successfully avoid induction than it was for their leadership. David Bell, a SNCC official, spent two years in the Danbury Federal Correctional Institute for resisting the draft.[70] Black Panther and American Servicemen's Union (ASU) member Isaac Baar finally ran out of options and appeals, just two days before his twenty-sixth birthday, and was promptly drafted.[71]

In an October 1968 editorial, the *Black Panther* proudly claimed that "the Black Liberators strong opposition to U.S. imperialism's aggressive war against Vietnam was sharply highlighted by the refusal of many young Black Liberators to be drafted. They burnt their draft cards and drove away draft officials."[72] Many young African Americans did burn their draft cards and refuse induction; but the vast majority, faced with the option of a prison sentence for refusal, accepted induction. Some did so reluctantly. Billy Dean Smith originally resisted but eventually went into the army to please his family.[73]

Others had no hesitation about reporting. Clinton H. Hunt, for example, believed he was fulfilling an obligation to his country.[74] A University of California study of urban African Americans released in 1967, found that nearly 90 percent "indicated a willingness to fight for the United States." Because the interviews for the study were first conducted in 1964, when the war still had support among most Americans, the findings released in 1967 were probably somewhat dated.[75]

But many did enlist willingly, influenced at least in part by the draft. The navy and air force were not as directly involved in combat as were the army or marines, so draft-eligible young men often enlisted in one of these branches first. John Brackett chose to enlist in the navy to avoid being drafted into the army.[76] Before the Vietnam War, African Americans had constituted only about 5 percent of the enlisted personnel in both the air force and navy. By 1972, African Americans were 7.3 percent of the Navy's enlisted strength and 12.6 percent of the air force's.[77] Some also joined the army, in hopes of avoiding Vietnam by securing a better occupational choice. James Hawkins volunteered because he was about to be drafted.[78] Anthony Preston also volunteered because he was likely to be drafted. He could not find a decent job, and he just "began roaming the streets, getting into trouble." He decided the army was a better alternative than winding up in jail.[79]

Some young men were literally given this choice. During Vietnam, the military allowed local judges to present convicted offenders with the option of military service or jail time. The practice was known as "punitive enlistment." The enlistee had to obtain a waiver consent form from both military and civilian authorities and be guilty only of relatively minor offenses.[80] James Hobson was a leader of a Chicago street gang, the Vice Lords, and had served jail time for forty-three offenses, including burglary and battery, before Judge Paul Epton gave him the choice of a state penitentiary or military service. Sergeant Hobson was one of the lucky ones. He returned to Chicago after a tour in Vietnam wearing two Bronze Stars, having earned a presidential commendation, and with a new "perspective" on his gang days.[81] The results were seldom this successful. The activist Clyde Taylor referred to punitive enlistment as "a kind of modern Shanghai recruitment,"[82] and General William Westmoreland was clearly unhappy with the practice. He referred to these recruits as "wrong-doers" and "troublemakers, some with criminal backgrounds." In March 1972, the armed forces ended the practice of punitive enlistments and sent letters to numerous civilian judges and prosecutors, asking them to stop offering military service as an alternative to a prison sentence.[83]

Punitive enlistments provided few recruits, and the armed forces needed to find a new source of manpower to augment the draft and volunteer enlistments. The result was Project 100,000 announced in August 1966, by Secretary of Defense Robert McNamara. Project 100,000 was publicized as a military version of President Lyndon Johnson's "Great Society" domestic reform program. Under the program, 100,000 young men who could not meet the military's minimum standards on the mental aptitude test would be enlisted annually in the army. These men were to be given training and educational opportunities they would not ordinarily have been able to get as civilians.[84] Between October 1966 and June 1969, 246,000 men were recruited into the military under Project 100,000, and 41 percent of them were black.[85] Less than half of the project's recruits had high school diplomas, and more than a third could not read at the fifth-grade level. Not surprising, thirty-seven percent of them were assigned to combat arms and more than half would eventually end up in Vietnam.[86] Far from receiving educational opportunities, most of the "new standards" men, as they were called, were not even allowed to reenlist because they were still unable to make the minimum test scores.[87]

Failure to make even the minimum score on the military's aptitude tests kept many African Americans out of the draft. The same substandard education also prevented many from enlisting. In one key respect, the draft-eligible African American differed from his white, working-class counterpart: whites with potential for great success in civilian life could normally avoid the draft; in the black community, those with the least chance for success were least likely to be drafted. The draft drained the most intelligent and physically fit from the community—as Whitney Young described them, "the cream of the crop," the "potential forces of leadership . . . in the battle cry for freedom at home."[88] An eligible African American had a 30 percent chance of being drafted, compared to only an 18 percent chance for an eligible white, according to a 1964 Pentagon study.[89] By 1967, with the military rapidly expanding, almost one-third of eligible whites were being drafted, but the figure for African Americans had risen to nearly 64 percent of those eligible.

Whether a reluctant draftee or a volunteer, the average young African American recruit by 1968 was more sensitive to racism and more aggressive in defending his rights than his predecessors had been. "The Black soldier has begun to find his new found black pride," wrote the journalist Wallace Terry in 1970.[90] Black cadets at the Air Force Academy informed their superiors at Wing Staff that "the black fourthclassman learns to do without many . . . things, but he will not give up his newly found black identity."[91] Command Sergeant Milton White, founder of the Malcolm X Society among black airmen, spoke of the "younger black airmen just entering the military system, fresh from the revolutionary civilian society outside."[92] In testimony before Congress, white army lieutenant Joseph H. Hall stated that "the current nineteen year olds have less patience and interest in waiting, and this is true of both blacks and whites."[93] What was true was that many young African Americans were entering the armed forces expecting racism and unequal treatment, and often their expectations were confirmed.[94]

But the military contended officially that discrimination no longer existed in the armed forces. It had been outlawed. The Department of Defense's *Annual Report for Fiscal Year 1968* clearly stated that "Defense manpower policy has long required that equal treatment and opportunity be afforded all servicemen without regard to race, color, creed, or national origin. The application of this principle, established in 1948, has officially eliminated racial discrimination in the Military Services and led to major breakthroughs in advancements in rank based on merit alone."[95] But contrary to the assertions of the Pentagon, the problems of racism ran deep in the fabric of the armed forces, and blacks entering the services would be deeply affected by institutional racism in testing, training, assignment, promotion, and the military justice system.

3

"A Bonus for Growing Up White"
The Problem of Institutional Racism

Testing and Placement

Institutional, or systemic, racism has been defined by the Department of Defense as "policies or practices which appear to be neutral in their effect on minority individuals or groups but which have the effect of disproportionately impacting upon them in harmful or negative ways."[1] Unlike the overt discrimination practiced by the armed forces before 1948, institutional racism is far more subtle, often unintentional, and therefore much harder to detect; but it still posed major problems for African Americans in the services during the Vietnam War, particularly in the areas of testing, training, assignment, and the administration of military justice.

During the Vietnam War, every recruit was tested at induction to determine his or her general intelligence and aptitude. The standard exam given by all branches of the military was the Armed Forces Qualification Test (AFQT), which was similar to a standard civilian intelligence quotient (IQ) test. In addition to the AFQT, other exams were administered to determine a recruit's potential for specialized training, such as the Army Qualification Battery (AQB), used by both the army and marines; the navy's Short Basic Test Battery (SBTB), and the Airman Qualifying Examination (AQE), in the air force. A recruit's performance on these exams largely determined his or her career options in the military.[2] Those with high scores could enter the more prestigious and rewarding "hard-core" specialties, generally the intelligence and technical fields. A recruit needed a minimum score of forty on the AQE to qualify for enlistment in the air force, for example, but to qualify for electronics training, one needed to score at least a sixty on the exam.[3] The army used the AFQT and the AQB to place recruits in one of five categories (I, II, III, IV and V). Those in either category I or category II could basically choose an occupational specialty. Those who tested in III or IV were placed in a "soft-core" area, meaning service and supply or combat training. Those in V were generally disqualified from service.

African Americans often scored poorly on these tests and as a result ended up in soft-core areas. In 1965 and 1966, 40 percent of the African Americans taking the exams ended up in category IV.[4] In 1971 the Department of Defense reported that blacks had "markedly lower" AFQT scores than did whites. Among army personnel with between nineteen and twenty-four months service, roughly one out of four whites had a score of thirty or lower on the exam, placing the individual in category IV. For African Americans, the number was nearly three out of four.[5] Though African Americans represented slightly over 12 percent of the total enlisted strength, fewer than 5 percent of the military's electronics equipment technicians were black, and African Americans constituted only 7 percent of the armed forces communications and intelligence specialists. In contrast, blacks represented 16.3 percent of enlisted personnel assigned to combat specialties and nearly 20 percent of the service and supply troops.[6] In the air force, probably the most technically oriented branch of the service, African Americans were generally concentrated in five areas: administration, air police, food service, supply and transportation. As late as 1972, blacks represented one-quarter of the air personnel assigned to administration and 37.7 percent of those assigned to service and supply units.

There were two explanations for why African Americans usually failed to achieve higher test scores and consequently were assigned to soft-core occupational specialties. The first and most widely accepted explanation was that blacks did not have the same educational opportunities as whites before entering the service.[7] The schools blacks attended were too often segregated and underfunded and did not stress the science and advanced mathematics courses needed to score well on the technical exams. As one black sergeant bitterly explained, "When you come in, you take the AFQT.

If you haven't had a good background and a good high school or college education, or experience in electronics, into Supply and Transportation you go. I graduated from high school in 1955. I got substandard education, compared to the white NCOs my age."[8]

The other explanation was more controversial. Many critics charged that the examinations were culturally biased in favor of whites. Like the civilian IQ tests, the AFQT reflected not just how intelligent a person was but how much he or she accepted and articulated Eurocentric culture and values.[9] In a 1968 interview with *Ebony*, sociologist Donald F. Hueber characterized the AFQT as "a measure of the individual's participation in the culture,"[10] and in 1971 the NAACP reported that black servicemen considered the higher scores whites achieved in the exams as "a bonus for growing up white."[11]

The military should have been aware of these problems. As early as 1949, the "President's Committee on Equality of Treatment and Opportunity," more commonly known as the Fahy Committee after its chairman, Charles M. Fahy, noted that even if the military did not openly pursue racist policies, African Americans enlisting in the armed forces would be affected by two preconditions: first, "that whites did not normally associate" with blacks, and second, that "through no fault of their own" African Americans "do not have the skills or education required for many of the Army's occupational specialties."[12] But throughout most of the Vietnam War, the armed forces would do little to redress the racial imbalance prevalent in most occupational specialties. First, the military usually could find enough recruits with technical ability. What they needed during Vietnam were more combat troops, not electricians. As army chief of staff in 1972, General Westmoreland wrote that "because the fundamental purpose of a military force is to engage the enemy in combat, the premium is on manpower for the combat arms. Failure to recognize or accept this premise created problems for many inductees."[13] Second, the armed forces as an institution has traditionally stressed an ethos of achievement and overcoming the odds, so there existed an inherent reluctance to "lower our standards to the street level," according to the deputy assistant secretary of defense for public affairs, air force brigadier general Daniel "Chappie" James, himself an African American. Brigadier general James added, however, that "we have to keep our standards high, but also we must make sure there is a vehicle for the young black and other minority members to be able to compete for these positions. And that is what we are doing."[14]

And in fact, some progress was made during the Vietnam era to ensure that minorities had greater opportunities to enter the more rewarding intelligence and technical fields. In his final report to Congress in 1973, Secretary of Defense Melvin Laird could claim that "after an analysis revealed that racial imbalances among occupational specialties could be corrected without the lowering of standards, each service initiated an intensive management program to insure more equitable distribution of racial and ethnic groups among them."[15] The percentage of African Americans in the army's military police increased from 8 percent in 1968 to 15 percent in 1972, and the number of black data-processing machine operators increased 6.7 percent between May 1971 and June 1972. Officials admitted that out of a total of 225 service specialties in the army, racial imbalances—meaning less than 13 percent minority participation—had existed in 169 specialties, but by 1972, improvements had been made in 137 occupations.[16] Also in 1972, the army replaced the AFQT with a new exam, the Army Classification Battery (ACB), which was designed to be more culturally neutral than the previous exam. The change to use of the ACB led to a rise from 33 percent of African Americans testing in category I-III in 1972, the last year for the old AFQT, to more than 42 percent in 1973, with white scores remaining virtually the same.[17]

But these reforms came late in the Vietnam War and consequently had little effect on the vast majority of African Americans who served during the conflict. The reforms also neglected to address certain deficiencies in the military's training and educational programs. Most of the military's educational programs, for example, were remedial in nature, geared more toward helping a serviceperson pass a high school diploma equivalency test than toward providing the training needed for the more technical occupations.[18] It was also difficult to transfer from one military occupational specialty (MOS) to another, a procedure known as "lateral" or "cross-training" in military parlance.[19] Even when cross-training was available, it was usually from one low-level, soft-skill occupation to another. Consequently, most felt trapped by a "military training system which all too frequently assigns Blacks, Chicanos, and Puerto Ricans to truck driving, supply work, cooking, in short the jobs nobody else wants."[20]

The problems African Americans encountered with institutional racism in the military were often compounded by the actions and beliefs of white recruiters and instructors. One black specialist four testified before Congress that he had been flunked out of a technical course by a racist instructor in a "deliberately planned act to hold him back because he was black." He was then counseled by another white to transfer from his basic infantry MOS to another occupation, only to discover later that his new area terminated promotion at E-4, leaving him no opportunity to advance.[21] Master Sergeant Donald Duncan, a recruiting agent in California for the Special Forces, was told by his captain, "Don't send me any niggers. Be careful, however, not to give the impression we are prejudiced in the Special Forces. You won't find it hard to reject them. Most will be to [sic] dumb to pass the written test. If they luck up on that and get by the physical testing, you'll find that they have some sort of criminal records."[22]

Assignment and Promotion

Most African Americans were convinced that not only one's initial occupational classification but also one's subsequent job assignments and chances for promotion were affected by racism. Clinton Hunt believed that both assignment and promotion policies were unfair to African Americans, and Alfonza Wright was once denied the chance for promotion when a racist white petty officer "from the South" refused to recommend him for promotion.[23]

There were a number of ways a biased officer could affect someone's chance for promotion. Air force sergeant Crispus Bosworth, a fourteen-year veteran, told the *Baltimore Afro-American* that white officers used biased performance reports to prevent blacks from being promoted.[24] Another tactic was to withhold information from African Americans concerning the time and location of promotion exams and review boards. Allen Thomas, Jr., was not notified about a pending promotion board until eleven o'clock the night before it was scheduled to meet, and he was stationed at a remote firebase at the time. An all-night truck ride through the dark and dangerous back roads of central Vietnam failed to get him to the meeting on time. "Racism was rampant," he recalled, "and had a lot to do with the lack of promotions" for African Americans. Private Raymond Wells claimed that promotion depended "on who you knew, and the color of your skin";[25] and Lionel Anderson, in a letter to the *Black Panther,* complained that "Black people are the last to be promoted as far as rank goes."[26]

Another common, valid complaint was that whites were promoted faster than blacks. Many whites were immediately promoted from E-2 to E-3 after arriving in Vietnam, but blacks often spent nearly their entire tour before being promoted to E-3. Specialist Four Victor Hall claimed that "a Negro has to give two hundred percent where a white man just has to keep his nose clean to make sergeant." Nearly 64 percent of the African Americans in Vietnam who were surveyed by journalist Wallace Terry believed that whites were promoted faster than blacks.[27]

Throughout much of the Vietnam era, African Americans were, in fact, promoted at a lower rate than whites and concentrated in the lower pay grades. By 1972, only 7 percent of the E-9s and 14 percent of the E-8s, the two highest pay grades in the army, were black, though African Americans made up over 17 percent of enlisted strength. The situation was worse in the other services. In the marines, African Americans accounted for only 4.4 percent of E-9s and only 6.5 percent of E-8s, with similar numbers for the air force. The navy had the lowest number of blacks in the top two enlisted grades: only 2.3 percent of the E-9s and 3.5 percent of the E-8s were black. African Americans made up only slightly more than 6 percent of the navy's enlisted strength but represented nearly 17 percent of all E-1s and 12.3 percent of E-2s, the two lowest pay grades. In the army, blacks made up around 18 percent of the lowest pay grades.[28]

African Americans were correct in believing that both institutional and personal racism affected their chances for a good job assignment or promotion. But there were other factors in addition to racism. Blacks were concentrated in infantry, administrative, and service and supply units, and these areas needed fewer noncommissioned officers than did the technical fields. During Vietnam, a logjam occurred in which there was a surplus of qualified blacks, competing largely against each other, in some cases, for only a few promotions in their specialty each year. One African American serviceman told an NAACP committee that was investigating military racism in Germany that "on a promotional exam for the few slots that do open up in my field—which is top-heavy with black and white NCO's—I have to score damn near perfect. In fact, I must be perfect to even meet the 'cutoff' for consideration for promotion. In the administrative field, which I am in, my score has got to be phenomenal, or I am out of it, in terms of promotion. That is what is killing us."[29]

Another reason African Americans were underrepresented in the top pay grades had to do with length of service. Attaining the rank of E-8 or E-9 was as much a function of seniority as it was of job performance; and because segregation and racial quotas ended only in 1948, few blacks had been in the service long enough to qualify for the most senior rankings. "It's my observation that outstanding men get promoted," stated Lieutenant Colonel Hurdle L. Maxwell, the first African American to command a marine battalion, adding, "I'm sure there have been isolated instances where serving men don't get promoted. But it's only in the extreme higher grades that you got great disparity between the proportion of blacks in grades."[30] It was true that there were relatively few African Americans in the highest two pay grades, but blacks were, in fact, overrepresented in the mid-level pay grades, E-5 to E-7. In the army in 1970, 16.6 percent of all E-5s were black, quite close to their 17 percent total enlisted strength, and African Americans comprised almost 24 percent of all E-6s and 19.6 percent of E-7s. But in the navy, air force, and marines, African Americans were still slightly underrepresented in the mid-level pay grades, compared to their percentage of enlisted strength. The disparity, however, was small.[31] Marine Master Sergeant Thomas A. Roberson, a veteran by 1968 of twenty-two years in the corps, claimed charges of promotion discrimination were unwarranted. Roberson said, "A lot of times we get our butts chewed out and we need a crutch to fall back on. Prejudice."[32]

But prejudice was an important factor, and for African Americans serving in Vietnam, discriminatory promotion and assignment policies could literally affect one's chances for survival. Blacks made up a disproportionate share of the combat troops and believed, with some justification, that they were given the most dangerous assignments. One black private first class stated in 1968, "When it comes to patrols, operations and so forth, we are first," a complaint echoed by many African Americans.[33] David Parks, who served in Vietnam in 1967, wrote in his diary about a racist sergeant who "fingered only Negroes and Puerto Ricans" for a dangerous assignment, adding, "I think he's trying to tell us something . . . everytime he comes I get the feeling that I should have been born white."[34]

Blacks were being promoted in Vietnam, but again, a double standard existed. When a white soldier was promoted, he was often given a support job in a rear area, especially toward the end of his one-year tour of duty. A black under similar circumstances could also get promoted, to squad leader for example, but he still found himself in combat. John R. White, stationed at Lai Khe in 1968, said at the time that whites "don't like to see the Black man out of the 'woods.' Most of us have to lie our way out of the 'woods' because these white dogs won't give us a real job."[35] Both Allen Thomas, Jr., and Henry Dority believed that a double standard existed in Vietnam, wherein both blacks and whites were promoted but African Americans remained in combat while whites were transferred out.[36]

Even many whites agreed that discrimination existed in promotions and assignments. Cheryl Rankin, a civilian Red Cross worker in Vietnam in 1970–71, recalled that as far as she "could see, the blacks were not treated

fairly or equally. For one thing, they were given a lot of the shit details."
Dennis Camire, a white soldier, said "Percentage-wise, I believe blacks do
get more dangerous duty," and a white sergeant, Dan G. Miller, stated that
"I think you have to honestly say that the black man in our brigade receives
less consideration than his fellow white soldier. He has almost no chance
of getting a support job."[37]

But many white officers who served in Vietnam defended their assignment and promotion policies and denied that racism factored into their
decisions. Captain (later Major) Richard Bevington recommended an African American in his unit for promotion to E-5 "on several occasions." The
man was "certainly qualified for promotion, but whenever he went before
the board he got tongue-tied" and, as a result, was not promoted. He
blamed Bevington and racial prejudice by the promotions board for "his
own failure, his own inadequacies, by saying that the world was against
him." Bevington had another black enlisted man who thought his transfer
from mess duty to a forward firing base was racially motivated, and
according to Bevington, "he managed to interpret this to his buddies that I
was trying to get him killed."[38] Captain (later Major) Henry L. Parker was
told by one black enlisted man that he and "his entire chain of command"
were racist, which Parker found a bit amusing with "eighty-five percent of
the chain of command being black."[39]

Some black noncommissioned officers also believed that the charges of
racism in assignments were somewhat overrated. Marine sergeant Roberson dismissed charges that blacks were deliberately put "on point," a
dangerous position in front of the main body. If "a man is an outstanding
squad leader point man, he'll be on the point every time, black or white,
some guys have a sixth sense about finding the enemy. . . . I've never seen a
man who asked to be taken off point who wasn't taken off. If he's asking to
be taken off, he's not a good point man anymore."[40] Specialist Four James
Edward Hawkins, Jr., was a bit more philosophical. Though he hated the
NCOs "with a passion," he said, "all they [the officers and NCOs] saw was
body counts. . . . A lifer is a lifer. . . . They were unfair to everybody,"
regardless of race.[41]

Many officers did admit to using assignments and transfers to get rid of
militants and troublemakers, and many who they felt belonged in these
categories were black. When Captain (later Major) Parker assumed command of his company in Vietnam, he established "discipline" and a "chain
of command," and "a lot of people that I replaced and got transferred out
of the unit were black."[42] Captain (later Major) Thomas Cecil "farmed out

... four or five troops" who were "instigators" to frontline units. The soldiers believed it was an attempt to get them killed, but Cecil maintained that he had originally requested only that they be transferred out of the battalion; it was the battalion commander who decided to send them into combat.[43] Airman Yusef Sudah was not sent into combat but found himself assigned to such lowly tasks as dandelion picking and latrine cleaning as punishment for his militant activity.[44]

Transfers were also used by those in command to rid themselves of African Americans who expounded militant or revolutionary doctrine to their fellow servicepersons. Private Joseph Daryl Miles, an activist and member of the radical, multiracial GIs United, was transferred from Fort Jackson, South Carolina, to a remote outpost in Alaska, where his superiors believed he could do little harm.[45] In Vietnam, blacks who were considered militants or troublemakers were often transferred to active combat units. Private Morocco Coleman wrote in 1968 that when a black "speaks out against the unequal treatment imposed upon us, he is most assuredly 'railroaded' to the D.M.L., An Khe or some other extremely dangerous area,"[46] and for the "slightest provocation," black marines stationed in I Corps were threatened with transfer to the northernmost, and most dangerous, bases in the corps.[47]

Military Justice

The institutional racism manifested in unequal testing, assignment, and promotion policies was a powerful factor in negatively affecting the service careers of black military personnel during the Vietnam War era, but it was not the most important one. The greatest source of systemic racism in the armed forces, and the greatest focus of complaints regarding discrimination, was in the administration of military justice.

In the armed forces, justice is administered at two distinct levels. Serious transgressions, such as felony offenses or desertion, are adjudicated by courts-martial, which are similar in most respects to a civilian court trial. Lesser offenses—being late for a work assignment or a uniform code violation, for example—are subject to a procedure known officially as nonjudicial punishment (NJP). Nonjudicial punishment, which was more often called an "Article 15" in the air force and army and a "Captain's Mast" in the navy and marines, has no real parallel in the civilian legal system. Perhaps the closest civilian analogy to NJP would be the ability of an employer to discipline employees for company infractions, such as tardiness or petty theft, with penalties ranging from a written warning to dismissal.[48]

An enlisted person could be written up for an Article 15 by any officer or senior NCO, but guilt and any subsequent punishment would be determined by the enlisted person's company commanding officer or ship's captain in a hearing. The accused was allowed a "personal representative," but this was often just another officer or NCO, and counsel was seldom a trained lawyer.[49] Few enlisted personnel took advantage of this right. Many did not even know it existed. Others simply distrusted anyone in the chain of command or felt the charge was too petty and the penalty too light to warrant making an issue of the matter. In addition, it was generally believed by the rank and file that guilt was predetermined, and fighting back might result only in a more severe punishment.[50] Except on board a ship at sea or under extreme circumstances, an enlisted person has the right to refuse nonjudicial punishment and demand a court-martial. But because the maximum penalties are much greater if convicted at court-martial, most simply accept NJP.

Under nonjudicial punishment, the maximum penalty an officer can impose is thirty days of correctional custody in the stockade, forty-five days of extra duty, or sixty days of restriction and forfeiture of half a month's pay for two months. In addition, any of the above can be accompanied by a reduction to the lowest enlisted grade, E-1, for E-4s and below. A serviceperson with an E-5 ranking or higher can be reduced only one grade under NJP. But punishment can also be as minor as a written reprimand in one's official record. In contrast, conviction by court-martial can lead to years in prison, reduction to the lowest enlisted grade, forfeiture of all pay and privileges, and a dishonorable discharge on completion of sentence. A death sentence can be imposed for treason, mutiny, rape, murder, and "misbehavior before the enemy."[51]

Throughout the Vietnam War era, African Americans received Article 15s in greatly disproportionate numbers relative to their overall percentage in the armed forces.[52] Typical were the numbers reported by the equal opportunity officer, United States Army Retentions' Services Officer (USARSO), for the 193d Infantry Brigade stationed in West Germany. Between 1 June 1970 and 31 July 1971, African Americans received 39 percent of the Article 15s in that unit but comprised only 27.5 percent of the brigade's assigned strength.[53] And in Berlin in 1971, blacks made up only 15 percent of the command but received over one-third of the Article 15s.[54]

The reason for this disparity was simple. Because an officer or NCO had a great degree of discretion in issuing Article 15s, a double standard often developed in which blacks were routinely written up and punished for many infractions for which whites were not. Black service personnel were well aware of the existence of this racially based double standard.[55] Clinton Hunt, who received an Article 15 for returning late from leave at Fort Lee, Virginia, said that blacks definitely faced "prejudicial ignorance" and consequently had more "racially motivated" Article 15s.[56] Raymond Wells also got an Article 15 at Fort Lee, "by a racist white NCO, for being fifteen to twenty minutes late," and one in Vietnam, for missing morning formation, even though his NCO knew he had just been relieved from guard duty. Protesting his nonjudicial punishment led to Wells's temporary incarceration in Long Binh Stockade outside Saigon.[57] A special NAACP investigative team, led by Nathaniel R. Jones, that examined charges of racism among American forces stationed in Germany reported that "two types of non-judicial disciplinary action—Article 15 and pretrial confinement—represent a major source of grievance among black servicemen," and that black soldiers were "convinced that white soldiers are not punished for behavior which, on the part of a black, would bring an Article 15 action. Whites, they said, were not dealt with for wearing long hair while blacks were punished for long hair. There seemed to be two sets of rules: one for whites and the other for blacks."[58] And the Congressional Black Caucus stated in their 1972 report on military racism that "no military procedure has brought forth a greater number of complaints and evidences of racial discrimination than the administration of non-judicial punishment."[59]

As they had with their assignment and promotion policies, many white officers defended their use of nonjudicial punishment and denied it was motivated by racial prejudice. Major Harry Fancher, a spokesperson for the United States Army, Europe's (USAREUR's) Judge Advocate General (JAG) Division, stated in 1968, "We often hear complaints that a Negro soldier believed he has received an Article 15 or court-martial for an offense that a white soldier would only have been slapped on the wrist for. . . . It is bad that many people believe this and it hurts the Army's image." He added, "Most of the time there is no validity to complaints of racial inequity in the military justice system."[60] Major Bruce B. Cary, a company commander in Vietnam, had to resort to nonjudicial punishment on occasion but claimed he could not "remember a court-martial or even an Article 15 that was racially related."[61] Henry L. Parker, a captain in Vietnam in 1969–70, said that "even though an Article 15 was justified," he "had to deal with a number of people when I was only giving an Article 15 to one," because many African Americans under his command wrongly assumed his actions were racially motivated.[62] Thomas Peoples inherited a company in Vietnam that was overwhelmingly composed of African Americans, most of whom had just recently been released from the Long Binh Stockade. In his first three months at his new command, Peoples presided over fifty-four Article 15 hearings and four courts-martial, but after that, he had "very little discipline problems."[63] Peoples had very few racial problems in his company and apparently earned the trust and respect of his men, both black and white. He handled the dispensation of justice with an even hand, and his company understood that his purpose in issuing nonjudicial punishments was not to punish an individual but to instill discipline and make that person a better soldier.

In fact, most of the white officers who did not believe their actions were racially motivated echoed Peoples's sentiments concerning the purpose of nonjudicial punishment: it was simply a tool for instilling discipline and not necessarily punitive in nature. The key to avoiding misunderstanding was communication between officer and enlisted personnel. The officers who were capable of maintaining an open dialogue or who at least attempted to be fair to both black and white seldom had double standard problems in their commands.

Not all African Americans believed the system was biased along racial lines. John Brackett, who had no great love for the navy and considered the service to be extremely racist, believed it was "just as easy . . . black or white" to get a Captain's Mast in the navy. The problem was that most enlisted personnel did not understand the system and were usually not informed of their rights. Consequently, it was difficult to prove successfully that an Article 15 was racially motivated or unjust.[64] Colonel Willard C. Stewart, an inspector general stationed at army headquarters in Heidelberg, Germany, and one of the very few African Americans to hold high rank in the military justice system, claimed complaints concerning racial discrimination were unwarranted. "Unfortunately, the colored soldier bases his complaints on his race too frequently," Stewart told *Ebony* in 1968. "He uses it as a crutch."[65]

Undoubtedly, some did use claims of discrimination as a crutch, and there were many competent and fair officers like Peoples and Cary. But the situation varied from company to company, and the wide discretion officers had in dispensing nonjudicial punishment meant the system was ripe for abuse by racist officers and NCOs. Some officers did not intentionally discriminate, but they held racial beliefs that virtually guaranteed a double standard and discrimination. One black enlisted man testified before Congress that he was given fourteen days' restriction and fourteen days' extra duty for wearing a "slave bracelet," a small bracelet usually woven out of bootlaces and worn by African Americans as a sign of solidarity.[66] Whites defended the practice of citing African Americans for wearing slave bracelets or carrying "black power" canes because these were uniform code violations and considered signs of "militancy." But whites were almost never written up for wearing fraternity rings or peace symbols; both were technically uniform violations, and one could easily argue that a peace symbol was a far more "subversive" symbol, given the role of the military, than were black-power canes and slave bracelets.[67]

Ignorance of and lack of respect for African American culture certainly contributed to the double standard and the inordinate numbers of Article 15s given minority personnel. One member of the Nation of Islam was given numerous Article 15s for refusing to eat the mess-hall food on certain days because of his religious beliefs.[68] On at least one occasion, a Muslim held in military confinement was refused a copy of the Koran, but it was standard practice to allow Christian and Jewish prisoners copies of their respective Bibles.[69]

Unintentional discrimination and ignorance contributed to the creation of a racially based double standard, but overt and intentional racism lay at the heart of the problem. One white officer, Major Michael F. Colacicco, a company commander stationed near Bien Hoa, South Vietnam, in 1971, reported a case of blatant discrimination: "One sergeant, who had been my platoon sergeant, I had to relieve because I started to get a string of people coming before me for Article 15s for failure to make work call formations. . . . They were all black. Of course, in conducting the Article 15 investigations, I found out it was because the platoon sergeant was going through and waking up white soldiers and not waking up the black soldiers. He would pick on particular black soldiers and particular people he didn't like, who all happened to be black."[70] Captain Thomas Culver, an attorney for the air force's Judge Advocate General Division, along with NAACP general counsel Nathaniel Jones, were given permission in 1970 to examine the files of a brigade in Europe in conjunction with an NAACP study on military racism. They found documented evidence of a racially based double standard. Culver, in a statement read before the Congressional Black Caucus, elaborated:

So I looked at his file. In the file was a lengthy list of misconducts by white GIs. Billy Jones was late to work four days out of the month of August. Tom Smith hit so and so on such and such a day. Nothing was done. One black GI did the same thing, he was late. He got an Article 15. Another black GI was involved in a fight. He got an Article 15 or a court-martial. Here . . . is where I feel the greatest racism comes out. It is in the discretionary use of military justice. When the white soldier commits an offense, this offense is excused. When the black soldier commits the same offense, he is dealt with harshly.[71]

Several investigations were conducted into the problem and causes of racial discrimination in the administration of military justice in the later Vietnam era, and all reached the same conclusion: institutional and personal racism in the administration of military justice severely affected African American service personnel and led to a racially based double-standard. The Congressional Black Caucus and the NAACP found that racially based nonjudicial punishment damaged black service careers. The Congressional Black Caucus report on racism in the military stated that "Article 15 punishments administered at the discretion of individual commanders for 'minor' offenses, has without doubt resulted in irreparable damage to the service careers of blacks vastly out of proportion to black enrollment in the military."[72] The NAACP in its report urged the military to institute immediate reforms in the system. Jones stated that it was clear that in the administration of military justice, "immediate and sweeping steps must be taken by the Department of Defense and the United States Army to make the system of justice eliminate the glaring as well as subtle inequities."[73]

The Department of Defense and the various branches of the military reached essentially the same conclusions in their own, independent investigations. An air force study conducted under orders from Lieutenant General George B. Simler of the Air Force Air Training Command confirmed the existence of a racially based discriminatory pattern. The fifteen-man Human Relations Team, which included four African Americans and two Hispanics, reported that "unequal treatment is manifested in unequal punishment," and "double-standards in enforcement of regulations."[74] In September 1970 the newly appointed deputy assistant secretary of defense for equal opportunity, Frank Render II, launched an investigation into race relations and conditions in the European theater. In three and a half weeks Render, the highest-ranking African American at the Pentagon, accompanied by a multiracial Defense Department team comprised of officers, enlisted personnel, and civilians, visited numerous American military bases in Germany, Spain, Italy, and Great Britain. They found substantial evidence of racism and discrimination in many phases of the military experience, including the administration of military justice, and urged the Pentagon to adopt reforms immediately, especially in the use of nonjudicial punishment.[75]

The Department of Defense's own Task Force on the Administration of Military Justice, a racially mixed team of civilians and military personnel, found discrimination to be endemic to the system. The task force's 1972 report states that the authors "became convinced that the black or Spanish speaking enlisted man is often singled out for punishment by white authority figures where his white counterpart is not. There is enough evidence of intentional discrimination by individuals to convince the task force that selective punishment is in many cases racially motivated."[76]

African Americans faced discrimination not only in the administration of nonjudicial punishment but in virtually every aspect of the military justice system during the Vietnam War era. One of the worst instances was the frequent use of pretrial confinement. Under military law, a serviceperson can be held in confinement for up to thirty days without formal charges being filed and, in special cases, even longer, if the officer exercising general court-martial jurisdiction deems it warranted. There is no procedure allowing the incarcerated serviceperson to appeal the officer's decision or to request bail; and the defendant and defense counsel usually are not even notified of the decision or the reasons for continued confinement.

The use of pretrial confinement is discretionary and can be ordered by the defendant's commanding officer or provost marshal under the following conditions: to ensure the defendant's presence at trial, because of the serious nature of the alleged offense; and if the defendant is considered disruptive or dangerous.[77] But many commanding officers in the Vietnam era used pretrial confinement to serve their own purposes, such as eliminating a "militant" influence from their unit or as unofficial punishment for some trivial offense.[78] In Da Nang, Vietnam, for example, some African Americans spent between fifteen and thirty days in pretrial confinement for having long hair. Often the serviceperson was then released without any formal charges being filed. This type of situation was typical. In West Germany in 1970, to cite just one example, nearly a third of the blacks held in pretrial confinement were eventually released without ever having formal charges brought against them.[79] Even when charges were eventually preferred, blacks often had to spend an inordinate amount of time in jail before the military justice officials decided on a course of action. White prisoners averaged twenty-nine days in pretrial confinement, but black prisoners averaged thirty-four and a half days in jail before release or trial, more than five days longer than their white counterparts.[80] Billy Dean Smith, accused of murdering two lieutenants in March 1971 at Bien Hoa Army Base in Vietnam, spent nearly eighteen months in confinement before the military brought him to trial. Smith was eventually found not guilty on both counts of murder.[81]

Though Smith's length of confinement was exceptional, a discriminatory pattern in the use of pretrial confinements against African Americans was both widespread and apparent. In 1970 nearly forty percent of blacks facing absent without leave (AWOL) charges were held in pretrial confinement, whereas only 15 percent of whites facing similar charges were incarcerated. The 1971 Department of Defense study on the administration of military justice found similar percentages for blacks and whites held for more serious offenses, such as alleged felonies or challenging military authority.[82] Though African Americans constituted only slightly less than ten percent of the army's enlisted strength in West Germany, they constituted roughly 50 percent of all prisoners held in pretrial confinement. Of 1,136 servicemen held in pretrial confinement at selected bases in 1971, the Department of Defense found that though blacks made up only 15.8 percent of the population at the selected installations, they made up 21.2 percent of all those in pretrial incarceration.[83]

Courts-Martial

African Americans generally fared no better if and when their cases came to trial, and they were more likely than whites eventually to receive punishment or a court-martial. The Defense Department study concluded that "of particular note is that whites are over twice as likely to be released without subsequent disciplinary or judicial action."[84] In 1970, for example, a "race riot" at Goose Bay Air Force Base, Labrador, Canada, led to the court-martial of five black airmen, but several whites equally culpable in the violence were never charged.[85] The Defense Department task force also found that of 1,441 servicemen court-martialed at the bases they studied, 34.3 percent were black.[86] At one installation, Camp Casey, Vietnam, blacks accounted for 57 percent of all general courts-martial.

The Department of Defense also found a disparity in the types of offenses whites and black were charged with committing. African Americans were charged with felonies or major military offenses, such as willful refusal to follow orders or attacking an officer, at a greater frequency than whites. More than 41 percent of black defendants were charged with these infractions. But whites were far more likely to commit drug-related offenses, nearly three-fourths of all class 2, or drug-related, offenses, were charged to whites. There was, however, one similarity between black and white military offenders: their level of education. Regardless of race, a serviceperson with a lower than a high school education had a much greater chance of being court-martialed. Over two-thirds of the accused in the army did not have a high school diploma, while only 16.5 percent of army personnel had fewer than twelve years of education.[87]

Though an African American was more likely to be court-martialed, and for a more serious offense, than was the average white offender, it also appears that it was more likely for a black than for a white to be acquitted. But regardless of race, beating the charges in a military court was a difficult feat to accomplish; in the Defense Department study, the accused was found guilty of at least one offense in more than 93 percent of the cases. But 9.5 percent of the blacks who contested the charges were acquitted, whereas only 5.8 percent of whites who contested the charges were found not guilty. In 512 cases reported to the task force by the army, blacks who contested the charges were successful 47.8 percent of the time, or twice the rate for whites. In the air force, whites and blacks had similar numbers: 27.4 percent for blacks and 24.2 percent for whites. In the Marine Corps, however, only one-quarter of the blacks who contested the charges received acquittal, compared to 15 percent of whites. The problem was that most offenders, both black and white, failed to contest the charges against them by entering a "not guilty" plea. Fewer than half of African Americans charged and only a third of the whites entered "not guilty" pleas in the army. In the marines, fewer than one in four African Americans challenged his indictment in court, and this was higher than the small number of whites, only 16.7 percent of whom defended themselves in court.

There were many reasons why a serviceman might choose not to contest the charges against him in court. Many were guilty and the evidence against them overwhelming, while others were simply ignorant of their rights. Others believed or were told they would receive a lighter sentence if they did not contest the charges. But many African Americans had yet another reason for not fighting back in court. Blacks did not trust white officers and did not believe they could receive a fair court-martial in a military justice system that was both composed of and controlled by white officers. A Department of Defense survey found that two-thirds of the white inmate population believed they had received a fair trial, but for black inmates, the figure was only around 50 percent.[88]

Both the prosecution and defense specialties were overwhelmingly white, with blacks accounting for only 2 percent of the judge advocate general's office during the Vietnam era. Virtually all of the full- and part-time military judges were white. Out of forty part-time military judges in Europe in 1970, only one was black, as was only one of the six full-time judges. The situation among military lawyers was much the same. In 1971 there were only forty-five black and thirty Hispanic judge advocates on active duty. There was only one African American judge advocate, Captain Curtis Smothers, out of 123 captains assigned to the JAG offices in West Germany. As late as 1972, only fifteen out of seventeen hundred active-duty military lawyers, or about 1 percent of the total, were black. The lack of black lawyers was deemed so critical a problem by the Defense Department that it "intensified efforts to recruit African-American lawyers" and studied the "feasibility of contracting with minority law firms" and organizations such as the NAACP and the National Urban League to address the shortage.[89]

The need for black lawyers was apparent to both the accused and the Defense Department, and both understood why: white JAG officers had "zero credibility" with black service personnel. According to the NAACP study on military justice, "Black servicemen suspect that JAG lawyers are neither independent of military influence nor free from racist attitudes." One black noncommissioned officer told the investigative team that he did not "want anything to do with a military lawyer. . . . I have been in the service fourteen years and I have never seen a white JAG lawyer do anything that great for a black man." African Americans stationed within the continental United States could occasionally retain a qualified black civilian lawyer to defend them, but this option was unavailable to African Americans stationed in Europe or Southeast Asia. Those who hired white civilian lawyers in Europe usually regretted it later. The NAACP investigative team reported that "a frequent complaint among black inmates of the Mannheim Stockade centered on paying a high price for legal fees for a civilian lawyer and then failing to hear from him over long periods of time." One white JAG lawyer characterized it as a "disgrace that the soldiers are paying money for the civilian lawyers," stating he would "welcome any program that would save the three hundred and fifty dollars which the soldier is now 'sending down the drain' for civilian counsel in Europe." Many of the German civilian lawyers gave their clients only a half-hearted effort at best. Some displayed their own racist preconceptions at the trial by asking the jury for leniency because their client's "natural animal instincts" were to blame.[90]

Another problem facing a black defendant in a court-martial was the composition of the trial board. In the military, enlisted personnel are not usually tried by a jury of their peers. The accused has the option of having either the presiding military judge or a trial board composed mostly of officers decide his or her guilt or innocence.[91] Because African Americans constituted only about 2 percent of the officer corps during the Vietnam era, there were usually no blacks available for trial duty.[92] In 1968, for example, twenty-seven out of thirty-two soldiers tried at general court-martial at one army division headquarters in West Germany were black, but according to Ebony's investigative reporter Curtis Daniell, "old timers could not recall when a black officer had been appointed to the jury."[93]

Even when black officers were appointed to trial boards, it did little to raise the confidence of the accused. Black enlisted personnel considered most black officers to be "Uncle Toms," and as one sergeant stated, "Uncle Tom is a friend of the [military] family."[94] These officers were viewed as unwilling to jeopardize their careers to help out a fellow African American. Billy Dean Smith had two black officers on his trial board, but critics claimed they were "hand-picked" accommodationists and were placed on the board only to give it the outward appearance of being fair, since Smith's was a highly publicized case.[95]

African Americans who lacked the notoriety of a Billy Dean Smith often had to contend with a "lily-white" court-martial, and because of racism and racial misconceptions, this placed them at a distinct disadvantage. One prominent but unnamed JAG lawyer bluntly told Daniell:

> A guy walks in the court-room walking his "soul walk," and talking his "soul" talk and it's three strikes against him already. He may know his weapon better than any white boy in the platoon, but you get some Kentucky Colonel on the board and he automatically figures he's a bum. . . . It is especially difficult to defend a Negro soldier in, say, a 212 elimination proceeding where there are no rules of evidence anyway. . . . Look, a Negro GI is accused of raping a German prostitute. O.K. I admit that a prostitute can be raped. But even if evidence shows she was willing, some court members will vote to convict just because they can't see a Negro trooper sleeping with a white woman.[96]

Punishment and Incarceration

Once convicted, African Americans received much harsher punishments than did convicted white offenders. The average prison sentence for blacks was three years but for whites only two and a half years. This disparity apparently had little to do with the nature of the offense for which either was convicted. Roughly 75 percent of all military prisoners served time for purely military offenses, such as willful disobedience, being absent without leave, or insubordination, none of which is considered a crime in civilian society.[97] But when only serious or felony convictions are considered, resulting in a sentence of hard labor, blacks still received longer sentences than did white offenders. An African Americans convicted of such a crime spent an average of 2.88 years at "hard labor," compared to less than 2 years for a white.[98]

African Americans considered by military officials to be militants often were dealt with harshly by the court system. In 1969 two black marines, Lance Corporal William Harvey, Jr., and Private First Class George Daniels, were given sentences of six and ten years respectively, at hard labor, for antiwar activity in 1967. During a break in field exercises at Camp Pendleton, California, on 27 July 1967, the two Black Muslims had called the African Americans from their company together under the shade of a large tree and held a spontaneous "rap" session, specifically to discuss "going over there and fighting the Vietnamese and coming back here and fighting the white man." Both had made statements against the Vietnam War to fellow marines, claiming it was a "white man's war" and blacks should not fight in it. They urged African Americans to protest assignment to Vietnam and the morning after the rap session, led an unsuccessful attempt by more than a dozen black marines to speak to their commanding officer about their grievances. When refused permission to see their captain, the men quietly disbursed and returned to their duties. Harvey and Daniels were never disorderly and never refused to obey a direct order, yet Harvey was convicted of violating provisions of the Uniform Code of Military Justice and Daniels of violating the 1940 Smith Act, a law originally passed to combat Nazi spies, which made it a felony to "cause insubordination, disloyalty, mutiny or refusal of duty." Though no overt act of disobedience had been committed, both men were given the maximum possible sentence.[99]

Because African Americans were more likely than whites to be court-martialed, and, if convicted, to receive longer sentences, blacks made up a disproportionately high percentage of the military prison population throughout the war years. In 1971, African Americans made up slightly less than 32 percent of all army confinements, 21 percent of marine prisoners, and over half—53.17 percent—of the air force prison population. In the navy, blacks represented only 16.2 percent of regular confinements, but this was still more than twice the percentage of blacks in that branch of the service.[100] In 1972, 37.8 percent of all military confinements were black.[101] These high numbers persisted throughout the Vietnam War era and were typical for most military confinement facilities. In 1968, 190 out of 512 inmates at USAREUR's seven stockades in West Germany, or 40 percent, were black.[102] In 1969, at the army's infamous Long Binh Stockade, usually called Long Binh Jail (LBJ) by its inmates, outside of Saigon, half of the prisoners were African Americans; James Hawkins stated that during his term there, nearly 70 percent of the prisoners were black.[103] At the main marine confinement facility in Vietnam, the Da Nang Brig, blacks on average made up 30 to 40 percent of the prison population and "around ninety-five percent" in the maximum security "cell blocks."[104]

Stateside bases were no better. In 1971, 16 percent of the personnel stationed at Fort Hood, Texas, were black, but African Americans accounted for 31 percent of the stockade population. African Americans were also 16 percent of the personnel assigned to the marine base at Quantico, Virginia, but represented nearly half of the stockade inmates at that facility.[105] At the U.S. Army Correctional Training Facility at Fort Riley, Kansas, just under 36 percent of the 3,448 enlisted personnel sentenced there were black. The air force also operated a "retraining facility," the 3,320th Retraining Group located at Lowry Air Force Base, Denver, Colorado. Between 4 June 1971 and 30 May 1972, blacks accounted for 43.2 percent of the 784 airmen entering that program.

The retraining programs in all of the services were designed to rehabilitate, retrain, and return military offenders to regular duty, and African Americans more often than not successfully completed retraining and went on to productive service careers. At Lowry, nearly 74 percent of the blacks, but only 66 percent of the whites, successfully completed the program and returned to active duty.[106] But most military stockades were not considered to be retraining facilities; they existed primarily to isolate and punish military offenders, with little consideration for rehabilitation. Lieutenant Charles Anderson, the executive officer at Da Nang Brig in 1968, ran an educational program for the inmates geared toward helping them earn a high school equivalency diploma. Anderson also helped inmates with difficult personal problems, such as the nineteen-year-old black inmate who needed a divorce from his wife of three years.[107] But it wasn't prison officials but fellow inmates at Long Binh who helped Raymond Wells kick his heroin habit. He credits black Muslims and his conversion to Islam, not the military justice system, for his rehabilitation.[108]

Anderson's and Wells's experiences tended to be exceptions to the rule, and the average stay in a military prison tended to be a dismal one, with little chance for either help or rehabilitation. Many military prisons were more like Mannheim Stockade than the retraining facilities. *Time* magazine in 1971 characterized Mannheim as "almost a carbon copy of the worst civilian prison facilities in the U.S.," adding, "Few if any prisoners at Mannheim are rehabilitated."[109] At the Da Nang Brig, black "hard-core riot leaders" and other dangerous prisoners were confined in grim, cold, dungeonlike cement cell blocks that measured only seven feet by seven feet.[110] Overcrowding was also a chronic problem. Vietnam's Long Binh Stockade was designed to hold about five hundred prisoners, but by 1968 it had nearly 740. In some stockades, prisoners also had to endure brutal guards. James Hawkins described the guards at LBJ as being "nasty" and "on a power trip" and claiming "they actually hated us." At the marine stockade at Camp Pendleton, California, guards were known to hog-tie and beat troublesome inmates.[111]

Punitive and Dishonorable Discharges

In addition to longer prison terms, African Americans were more likely than whites to receive punitive discharges as part of their sentence. In 1947 the armed forces adopted the five-tiered discharge system that would be in use during the Vietnam era: (1) honorable, (2) general, (3) undesirable, (4) bad conduct, and (5) dishonorable.

Honorable discharges were given to personnel who had faithfully executed their duties and completed their enlistment or who had been wounded and medically discharged. Most general discharges were also under "honorable" conditions and were given to those who could not complete their enlistments for medical, personal, or emotional reasons. Undesirable discharges were used to eliminate personnel with characteristics considered unsuitable for service in the armed forces, including chemical dependencies, radical activities, sexual "deviances" (most often homosexuality), and those who just could not adjust to military life and discipline. Bad conduct and dishonorable discharges were both classified as "punitive" discharges, and were given either in conjunction with or in lieu of a prison sentence. Bad conduct discharges were given for accumulated minor infractions, felony-type offenses, and serious breaches of the code of military justice. Dishonorables were issued only for the most serious of crimes or transgressions against the code of military honor, such as cowardice or attempting to desert to or aid the enemy.[112]

Throughout the Vietnam era, an overwhelmingly large percentage of both blacks and whites successfully completed their military careers and received honorable discharges. In 1968 and 1969, more than 96 percent of all discharged personnel received honorables.[113] In 1970, 95 percent of all African Americans and 97 percent of whites received either honorable or "general under honorable conditions" discharges.[114] In 1972 only 90.3 percent received honorable discharges, the lowest for any year during the war, but another 5.1 percent received general discharges.

Undesirable discharges were the most widely used of the less-than-honorable discharges, especially in the later stages of the war. In 1971 undesirables accounted for 2.9 percent of all discharges, and 4.1 percent in 1972. Dishonorable discharges were the rarest of all. There were only 34 in 1968, or .35 percent of the total; 356 were given in 1972, but this was still out of a total of 804,470 discharges that year.[115]

Yet again, reflecting the problems blacks had with the draft, with nonjudicial punishment, and with the use of pretrial confinement, African Americans constituted a disproportionately large percentage of those who received either general or less-than-honorable discharges. In 1970 blacks received 3,607, 18 percent of all, army discharges under less-than-honorable conditions, including 65, or 26 percent of all, dishonorable discharges that year. Though African Americans constituted only 6 percent of the navy's enlisted strength, they accounted for 141, or 8.1 percent of all, less-than-honorable separations and nearly 17 percent of that service's dishonorables. In the air force, almost 29 percent of those given undesirable discharges or discharged for the "convenience of the government" were black.[116] In the army in 1972, African Americans made up more than one-fifth of the bad conduct and nearly one-third of the dishonorable discharges. The ratio of blacks to whites receiving less-than-honorable discharges was 1.5:1 in the navy and 1.8:1 in the army. An Urban League Study confirmed that African Americans in the air force received dishonorable discharges at a rate three and a half times greater than that for airmen in general.[117]

The problem was not that blacks were less suited than whites for military life or more inclined to criminal activities. White brigadier general

Harley Moore, provost marshall of the U.S. Army in Europe, stated in 1968 that the African American soldier was "no better and no worse behaved" than the Caucasian.[118] Education was not a factor. The Department of Defense's own 1972 study on racism and the administration of military justice found that "in all services, blacks receive a lower proportion of honorable discharges and a higher proportion of general and undesirable discharges than whites with similar educational levels and aptitude. Thus, the disparity cannot be explained by aptitude or lack of education." The problem was institutional racism, the same problem that affected blacks throughout the military justice system. According to the NAACP's own study on military justice, "The system of administrative discharges operates as punitively for black soldiers as Article 15, pretrial confinement, and other discretionary discipline measures." One disgruntled black NCO told the NAACP investigative team that the "military's strategy for blacks" was "either jail them or get them out of the service. Or jail them, then cut them loose." [119]

The military did, in fact, often use general and less-than-honorable discharges to rid the armed forces of blacks who were perceived to be militants and troublemakers. The NAACP study heard complaints from younger black soldiers who "were convinced that these policies were designed to 'rid the Army of militants.' " [120] Admitted black radical Billy Dean Smith may have been acquitted on both counts of murder, but the army still reduced him to the rank of private and gave him a bad conduct discharge. Another black activist, Lionel Anderson, proudly told the *Black Panther* in 1969, "I was released under a bad conduct discharge for failure to comply with ruling class rules." Airman First Class Yusef Sudah was discharged by the air force because of his militant activities,[121] and Thomas Tuck was court-martialed and expelled from the army for organizing a black antiwar group at Fort Knox, Kentucky.[122] Privates Joseph Coles and José Rudder spent sixty-one days in the stockade for organizing militant activities but successfully resisted the army's attempt to discharge them as "unfit for duty." [123]

Unlike Coles and Rudder, few blacks chose to contest their discharges. A punitive discharge can be given only at court-martial, and those facing either a general or an undesirable discharge have the right to request a hearing by a special discharge board. In addition, a soldier had to voluntarily request certain general or undesirable discharges, such as a Chapter 10 discharge, given either for "unsuitability" or "for the good of the service." But many blacks complained about officers who harassed them "until they signed" a voluntary "request for discharge," and others were told that they would be released from the stockade only if they requested a discharge.[124] Many were also told—wrongly—that it would be relatively easy later to get a general or undesirable discharge upgraded to an honorable one. And many were just eager to get out of the military and did not realize what problems a "bad paper" discharge could later cause them in civilian life. In many instances such as Coles's and Rudder's, the military's case against the defendant was relatively weak and probably would not have stood up against the scrutiny of a review board or court-martial. But again, African Americans either distrusted the advice of their JAG-appointed white lawyer or were not informed of their chances of winning an acquittal. As a result, 95 percent of the soldiers who received some sort of administrative discharge waived their rights to either a review board or a court-martial.[125]

It was only later, when they were out of the military, that many blacks began to understand the consequences of accepting or receiving either an administrative or a punitive discharge. "On behalf of President Nixon," White House special assistant Robert J. Brown assured the Black Legislators' Association on 25 August 1971 that

> the services have been making a special effort to communicate to enlisted personnel the difficulty of having any other than an honorable discharge changed to honorable after separation from the service. Furthermore, it is an established policy that all persons subject to these discharges be informed of the adverse effect that an other than honorable discharge can have upon them in civilian life. The services have investigated the allegation that men were advised that they could easily change their other than honorable discharge status after leaving the service and were induced in this fashion to waive their right to an administrative board hearing. No substantial cases of any such actions have been uncovered.[126]

Despite Brown's emphatic denials, many blacks did accept administrative discharges believing they could later get them upgraded to honorables. The NAACP investigative team heard complaints about white "junior officers who encouraged those in their command to believe this myth,"[127] and the Defense Department's own study thought the problem so serious that it recommended a "prospective dischargee" be "fully advised as to the potential consequences of the receipt of a discharge other than an honorable discharge, with an accurate and realistic appraisal of the possibility that such discharge would never be changed to a discharge of more creditable nature."[128] Many blacks and whites were undoubtedly told they could upgrade their discharges because procedures did, in fact, exist to handle appeals and upgrades. Under *U.S. Code,* volume 10, section 1553, each armed service was empowered to establish review boards that could "change a discharge or dismissal, or issue a new discharge," the only exception being a discharge resulting from a general court-martial. An applicant did not have to appear personally before the review board, though he or she could make a direct appeal, and the applicant had up to fifteen years from the date of discharge to request a review. But the procedure was lengthy, often taking years, and was seldom successful.[129] Maurice Anthony received an undesirable discharge from the army in 1970 and spent two years going "about it the right way. By that I mean, going through the procedure, getting my papers filled out, waiting, hearing something like a, oh yeh, Anthony, here is a letter, next week we are going to send you some papers to fill out. . . . I am tired of filling out papers." Like those of virtually all the applicants, Anthony's appeal to upgrade his discharge was denied. In 1970, 95 percent of all applications for an upgrade of discharge to honorable status were turned down.[130]

Others mistook an "exemplary rehabilitation certificate," issued by the secretary of labor after 1966, for an official upgrade. It was not. The certificate was issued to former service personnel with punitive or general discharges after "at least three years of successful rehabilitation and exemplary conduct in civilian life." The Labor Department had no influence or jurisdiction over the military's discharge policies and provided the certificate simply to help less than honorably discharged veterans find gainful employment.[131]

Another problem was that there were "considerable differences" among the various branches of the armed forces regarding the conditions and reasons for issuing a specific discharge. In the army, for example, fewer than 10 percent of the personnel separated for "character and behavior disorders" received honorable discharges, but in the navy, more than 77 percent of the personnel separated for those reasons received honorable discharges. In the air force and marines, the percentages were 63.5 percent and 49.6 percent respectively. Many others given general discharges were told that they could be upgraded to honorable and that it would not affect their postmilitary, civilian careers or their ability to qualify for veterans' benefits. Complicating the issue was the fact that one's discharge papers, Defense Department form 214, carried what was known as a separation program number (SPN) detailing the exact nature and type of discharge, an honorable having a different code than a general or a punitive discharge. Though most general discharges were issued under honorable conditions, few potential employers, even government agencies, recognized the distinction, and therefore they tended to consider all but honorable as "bad paper" discharges.[132]

As a result, veterans with less-than-honorable discharges were stigmatized and found it difficult to find jobs. One black veteran with an administrative discharge bitterly remarked, "I have friends who've robbed liquor stores who can get jobs easier than I can." Maurice Anthony testified before Congress that he had been told, "There are no jobs for you. And with an undesirable discharge, there is nothing going to happen because you don't qualify, you aren't good enough." He added, "As long as I am out, I have to live and eat just like you … and if I cannot work in order to support myself, I am going to rip somebody off. And it doesn't make any difference who. And if it means taking a life, I will take it. It doesn't mean anything."[133]

Faced with chronic unemployment, many less than honorably discharged black veterans also discovered they were disqualified from most veterans' benefits, and at a time when many needed medical and emotional assistance. Anthony, like many, found he did not qualify for either unemployment compensation or welfare. Anthony simply lied about his discharge status to find work, but many, with few or no real alternatives, turned to crime. Several studies conducted in the early and mid-1970s found that a high percentage of veteran inmates in American prisons had received less-than-honorable discharges. A Federal Bureau of Prisons report in June 1973 stated that 32 percent of the nation's federal prisoners were veterans and that nearly 57 percent of them had received less-than-honorable discharges. According to the 1976 Veterans Administration's study of forty-four thousand inmates at 325 major state and federal prisons, veterans comprised a quarter of the prison population, with blacks accounting for 50 percent of the veteran total. In 1975, 44 percent of the prisoners in the Oregon state penitentiary system were veterans, and between 40 and 50 percent of those had less-than-honorable discharges; in Arizona, veterans made up nearly one-third of the prison population, and 42 percent had bad paper discharges; in South Carolina, veterans comprised only 13.8 percent of the state's inmates, but again, 40 percent had less-than-honorable discharges. Pennsylvania had one of the lowest totals; fewer than 17 percent of its veteran inmates had received other-than-honorable discharges. But in the District of Columbia, where veterans made up 13.2 percent of the total prison population, 99 percent were black and 54 percent had less-than-honorable discharges.[134]

Military officials were aware of these disparities in the administration of justice in the armed forces, and some reforms were instituted. Under the Military Justice Act of 1968, legal counsel would be provided by the military at the accused's request. The army provided for special courts-martial to adjudge bad conduct discharges, "thereby providing another forum for those accused of less serious crimes," according to Army chief of staff General William Westmoreland.[135] Additional restrictions were placed on the use of pretrial confinements. In Germany, USAREUR officials even assigned Captain Curtis Smothers, one of the very few black JAG lawyers, as a "troubleshooter" because, as Smothers said, his superiors finally "realized that I can get to those men in a way they can't."[136]

But many white officers and noncommissioned officers were reluctant to enforce fully the new regulations and reforms, and there were too few black JAG lawyers like Captain Smothers to make much of a difference. Even Smothers admitted that he only "occasionally manages to correct injustices." The armed forces were too preoccupied with prosecuting the war in Southeast Asia, as well as maintaining force levels in Europe, to listen to black complaints. Besides, most junior and senior officers and officials believed the military's equal opportunity programs and antidiscrimination policies were both just and adequate, if not always properly enforced. They considered the real problem to be a handful of whites who refused to follow the program and hard-core black militants who sought to incite trouble and rebellion among otherwise patriotic and disciplined black soldiers.[137]

But the problem obviously run much deeper, and as the war progressed, more and more African Americans became disillusioned by both the institutional and the personal racism they encountered in the armed forces. Some ran afoul of the military justice system and were imprisoned or discharged. Others deserted. Many, though disgruntled, still believed life in the military was better than what civilian society offered and remained silent. Others, however, did not, and resistance to racism began to take several forms among black service personnel. At Camp Lejeune Marine base in North Carolina and at the Air Force Academy in Colorado, for example, African Americans sought to work through the system and petitioned their commanding officers for relief. Some sought more militant solutions, and at numerous military bases—from Fort Hood, Texas, to Cam Ranh Bay, South Vietnam—African Americans either organized or joined such radical groups as the Movement for a Democratic Military (MDM), the American Servicemen's Union, the Black Mau Maus, the Blackstone Rangers, or the Black Panthers.

Despite the variety of responses, one very powerful force did begin to emerge as a constant from the black military experience during Vietnam: solidarity among African American service personnel. Complete with its own rhetoric and symbols, black solidarity would provide some sense of security and belonging to blacks in the armed forces, and many would adopt at least the outward manifestations of radicalism and black power, such as Afros and slave bracelets. Many whites would react with suspicion, fear, racial violence, and a racial polarity that would rock the very foundations of the American military establishment.

4

"My Fear Is for You"
The Rise of Black Solidarity in the Armed Forces

Boot Camp

Basic training, or "boot camp," was the one common experience shared by all of the 8.6 million men and women who joined the armed services during the Vietnam War era. Whether one was destined to be officer or enlisted, a combat infantryman in Southeast Asia or a clerk-typist in North Carolina, all had to complete the six- to ten-week basic training course.

Though the actual routine varied from branch to branch, the purpose of basic training was essentially the same throughout the services: to convert undisciplined civilians into disciplined soldiers, sailors, and airmen. This process entailed both a physical and a psychological transformation of the recruit. Of the two, the physical training was the easier task for both the trainee and the military. Despite the alleged difficulty of the marine obstacle course, for example, it was designed so that the average recruit possessing normal physical abilities could pass.[1]

The psychological training was far more important and far more difficult to accomplish. Its purpose was to instill in the recruit a sense of teamwork and esprit de corps. Studies conducted during and since the Second World War have demonstrated that a person may be motivated to join the armed forces out of a sense of duty and patriotism but they are far less likely actually to fight and die for an abstract principle or ideology. The most important influence on one's behavior in a combat situation tends to be the soldier's own comrades in arms. An individual fights to preserve his own life and honor and that of the others in his unit. Teamwork is essential, and a soldier has to care about and trust his or her comrades for a squad, platoon, or even a battalion to be effective in combat. In military parlance this bonding process is known as "unit cohesion," and it implies both a reliance on the individuals within the unit and a pride in the unit's collective accomplishments. In a larger sense, it means that an individual feels a sense of belonging to the organization, a belief that all are comrades in arms, whether in the marines, navy, air force, or army.[2]

Given the nature of the war in Vietnam, its increasing unpopularity in the United States after 1968, and the fact that many of the recruits were reluctant draftees, it is not surprising that the basic psychological training failed to instill these concepts of bonding and belonging in many of the trainees. This was especially true for African Americans who entered the military in this period. Many entered the service prepared to find racism and unequal treatment. Lieutenant Joseph Hall, in testimony before the Congressional Black Caucus, told Representative Ronald Dellums (D-California) that "the current nineteen year olds have less patience and interest in waiting, and this is true of both blacks and whites,"[3] and marine private Allen E. Jones echoed these sentiments when he told a reporter from the *Baltimore Afro-American,* "They say I am just a Marine, but how can I forget eighteen years of being black and all that being black means in this country?"[4]

Factors within the military also contributed to a sense of alienation among black military personnel. They increasingly felt isolated and out of place in what they considered to be essentially a white institution. Blacks were grossly underrepresented in the officer corps and held few real positions of responsibility, and their cultural needs and amenities were largely ignored by the command structure. This lack of cultural recognition, coupled with both institutional and personal racism, did eventually produce a cohesion and solidarity within the ranks, but not the type the military had intended. African Americans responded by closing ranks and developing a black culture, based on racial solidarity and racial pride, within the military, and they would openly display the symbols of this new culture, such as slave bracelets, black-power canes, and black-power flags.

Islands of Integration

Initially, however, life at a military installation was often seen as a haven from a hostile, segregated civilian world. Sociologist Charles C. Moskos, Jr., once described stateside military bases as "islands of integration in a sea of Jim Crow," an opinion shared by many African Americans in the armed forces. Master Sergeant William B. Tapp claimed that his first days in the army amounted to one of the happiest experiences in his life. Tapp, originally stationed at Fort Campbell, Kentucky, recalled, "It was the first time I had ever been treated like an individual. I could feel the difference again as soon as I stepped off base. So I didn't see any reason to leave the base and I still don't except to shop with my wife and two kids, who are being raised on the base in an atmosphere that doesn't preach fear or hate." David Llorens wrote in *Ebony* in August 1968 that "Negroes find the Armed Forces just about the most productive, rewarding, and racially congenial experience that they can have."[5]

One did not have to go very far off base to find literal signs of racism. A large billboard at Smithfield, North Carolina, between Raleigh and Camp Lejeune Marine Base, welcomed people to "Klan Country."[6] Another billboard outside Fort Bragg, North Carolina, proudly read "Welcome to Fayetteville, Home of the Ku Klux Klan. Fight Communism and Integration."[7]

In the Southern United States, black service personnel faced discrimination and hostility at most public recreational facilities. Being in uniform was no deterrent to racism. Raymond Wells would not wear his uniform off base when he was stationed at Fort Lee, Virginia, because it seemed to provoke white civilian racism.[8] Henry Dority, while in uniform, was refused service at a roadside diner in Georgia.[9] Louis Callender had just returned from a tour of duty in Vietnam with the 101st Airborne, wearing his uniform and medals, only to have the proprietor of a roadside cafe near Fort Bragg refuse him service. Callender was told the diner was a "private" club. When the Vietnam veteran asked the owner, "Why don't you just say you don't serve black people?" he was rudely told, "O.K., we don't serve niggers."[10]

Colin Powell recalled a similar incident in the 1960s when he was stationed at Fort Benning, Georgia, and he attempted to order a hamburger in a nearby Columbus, Georgia, restaurant. Powell was asked by the server if he were either an African student or a Puerto Rican, and when he answered no, he was told he would have to go to the back door for carryout service only. As late as 1970, Colonel Daniel "Chappie" James, on the promotion list for brigadier general, and recently named deputy assistant secretary of the air force for public affairs, was refused service at Hornes Torch Lounge in Pensacola, Florida. James, in Pensacola to receive the local Kiwanis "Man of the Year" award, was told by lounge owner Jack Horne that "it's always been a custom with us" not to serve blacks.[11] "Brother Omar" and two other black Vietnam veterans, one missing a leg, were reluctantly served ice-cream sodas in a Washington, D.C., drugstore, but the clerk refused to handle their money physically. The three wounded and decorated veterans were told to put their money on a napkin, and they received their change the same way.[12]

Black female military personnel were also treated with disrespect. Pinkie Hauser remembered a bigoted salesgirl in a shop near Fort Knox, Kentucky: "They were very prejudiced, I'd go to these stores, like in a shopping mall, and she'd take the money out of my hand when I paid for something, but when she gave me back my change she'd lay it on the counter." In his final report as chief of staff, dated 30 June 1972, General William Westmoreland admitted, "While discriminatory practices were forbidden on military installations, they existed in varying degrees in adjacent communities where many of our servicemen were obliged to reside." The chief of staff then warned that "discrimination in these communities was perhaps one of the chief factors in the demoralization and frustration of the Army's minority groups."[13]

African Americans stationed at overseas military installations found that stateside patterns of discrimination and racism had also been exported and were adopted by the local populations. Americans "imported racism into Germany," according to Allen Thomas, Jr.; "segregated bars, restaurants, clubs . . . just like in Georgia. . . . It happened everywhere there was a U.S. presence, Germany, Thailand, the Philippines."[14] Of course, some of the discrimination was due to local prejudice and superstition. Some landlords in Germany refused accommodations to African Americans because they were afraid the "color would rub off" on their bed linens.[15] In most cases, however, discrimination was practiced to please a white military clientele.[16] In Germany, Vietnam, and South Korea, it was often white GIs who enforced the "whites only" policy in drinking establishments.[17] The problem was particularly acute in the Federal Republic of Germany and throughout the Far East. An NAACP investigative team in 1970 stated that blacks found "that the extent of discrimination they face is even more overt and complete than it is in the United States. White only and 'membership' only bars abound." In Germany, conditions apparently worsened as the war in Vietnam progressed. In 1965 nearly two-thirds of all African Americans stationed in Europe said that Germany had more racial equality than did the United States, but by 1973 only one-third believed things were better in Germany.[18]

Off-Base Housing Discrimination

In Germany and in the United States, the most serious and frustrating off-base problem for African Americans was housing discrimination. Stateside, black service personnel for the most part encountered overt discrimination in restaurants, theaters, and other public accommodations only in the South; but housing discrimination was prevalent throughout the United States. In the early 1960s the Marine Corps did not assign African Americans to installations located in areas as diverse as Bridgeport, California; Charleston, South Carolina; and Hawthorne, Nevada—and before 1962 would not assign black women to Camp Lejeune—because minority service persons could not find decent off-base housing in these locations. In 1967 the Department of Defense estimated that only 3 percent of twenty-three thousand housing units within commuting distance of Andrews Air Force Base near Washington, D.C., were integrated. Many blacks stationed at Fort Meade, Maryland, had to travel as far as forty-eight miles from the base to find adequate living facilities.[19] Overall, the Defense Department found that only about 22 percent of nearly 1.2 million rental units located within commuting distance of military installations were listed as integrated.[20]

Germany was much the same. Private Elvin Williams and his wife could not find an off-base apartment in 1968 in Germany, even in army-approved housing, because he was black. Williams's case was not unusual.[21] That same year, Frankfurt real estate agent Wilfried Vollmerhaus estimated that "at least eighty percent of the landlords who want me to find them a tenant say 'no colored please.' "[22] In 1970 an NAACP investigative team found that more than 85 percent of the landlords with rental properties listed with the Family Housing Office for the Heidelberg area practiced racial discrimination.[23]

Military officials were aware of the problem and did take more positive steps than simply not assigning African Americans to certain areas. As early as July 1963, Secretary of Defense Robert MacNamara established the Office of the Deputy Assistant Secretary of Defense for Civil Rights and ordered the services to designate segregated housing units as "off-limits" to military personnel. A year later, in July 1964, the Office of the Secretary of the Navy banned navy and Marine Corps participation in or association with events or organizations that practiced racial segregation and discrimination. In July 1967, MacNamara issued a directive establishing housing referral offices at stateside defense installations, and two months later he issued more explicit orders, declaring all segregated housing near any stateside military base officially off-limits.[24] Congress, in the spring of 1968, made housing discrimination illegal throughout the United States with the Civil Rights Act. As a result of this new federal law, the Department of Defense issued yet another directive, dated 20 June 1968, stating, "Effective August 1, 1968, no member of the Armed Forces stationed at a base in the United States will be authorized to enter into a new lease or rental arrangement if the owner of the housing unit follows a discriminatory policy toward servicemen." Base commanders were also urged to notify the proper civilian authorities when federal antidiscrimination laws were violated. Two years later, in June 1970, USAREUR was finally granted authority to declare discriminatory housing units in Europe off-limits to service personnel.[25]

As early as the end of 1968, Department of Defense officials considered their antidiscrimination policies to be a success, declaring that nearly 83 percent of all apartments and trailer courts located near defense installations were now listed as "open."[26] But this figure appears to have been an overly optimistic assessment. Two years later, in 1970, the Congressional Black Caucus uncovered widespread housing discrimination around Fort Monmouth, New Jersey. Witnesses told the caucus that "specific cases in the Fort Monmouth area were discovered where minorities are grouped together in segments of apartment complexes. Officers were located who experienced difficulty in obtaining housing in predominantly white neighborhoods." The witness added that "attitudes of landlords varied from subtle tactics to general indifference to outright hostility."[27] At Quantico, Virginia, in 1971, black marines also complained about off-base housing discrimination, specifically citing the reluctance of local landlords and real estate agents to sell or rent "higher priced houses" to minorities.[28] Pentagon officials also concluded that housing discrimination remained a major problem. A 1972 Department of Defense study reported that the existing policies and practice of base commanders were "not effectively coping with the problems of segregated housing."[29] That year, in his final report to Congress, even Westmoreland admitted that after years of attempts by commanders "to persuade the adjacent communities to treat all servicemen and their families alike," little of substance had been accomplished. He referred to the implementation of the military's antidiscrimination policies as "a very difficult assignment that has achieved less than spectacular results."[30]

In some respects, base commanders *were* faced with a very difficult assignment. Despite the clear language in the strongly worded directives, military officials had no real authority to enforce regulations outside the confines of the military installation. They could punish military personnel who sought accommodations in segregated units, but this was about their only recourse—and this one the service personnel at no fault could easily circumvent with assistance from discriminatory landlords willing to backdate leases for whites, indicating they had rented the property before the directive was issued.[31] After passage of the Civil Rights Act of 1968, base commanders also could notify federal authorities when local landlords practiced discrimination, but again, there was no direct action the commanders themselves could take. Instead, they were reduced merely to urging local landlords to end housing discrimination voluntarily. If local real estate agents and landlords refused to halt such practices, the last recourse officials had was to remove discriminatory housing agencies from their base's housing referral listings. The net result was "that when the housing referral list is exhausted, the soldier finds himself dealing with the agency which practices discrimination."[32]

Compounding the problem was the reluctance of many local commanding officers to enforce the existing regulations. In 1971 an NAACP investigative team charged military officials with ignoring the issue and, "until recent[ly]," failing "to actively intervene to protect the rights of black servicemen." A year later, the Defense Department admitted that "command concern comes pretty late in the day, now that the original segregation has already taken place." Even when commanders found discrimination they rarely acted. Despite the directive issued for the USAREUR in 1970 and the widespread discrimination practiced in Germany, army commanders in Germany declared only four establishments off-limits during the first eight months of 1970.[33] With good reason, African Americans assumed that many base commanders were racists and acted in sympathy with the local white landlords. In its report to Congress, the Congressional Black Caucus was forced to conclude that

> while each branch of the service has issued numerous guidelines and directives aimed at assuring compliance with open housing regulations, the

experiences of black servicemen adequately point up the military's dismal record of acquiescence to local practices. It would not be an overstatement to suggest that local commanders often expend more of their energy conspiring with local agents in an effort to circumvent open housing regulations, than they spend in the effort to obtain decent accommodations for minority personnel.[34]

Even in death, African Americans faced discrimination. In at least two separate incidents, African Americans killed in action in Vietnam were refused burial in all-white cemeteries. The first was a nineteen-year-old Special Forces paratrooper, Private First Class Jimmy Williams, who was sent to Vietnam in February 1966, only to be killed by a hand grenade blast three months later on 19 May. Despite Williams's being the first one from his hometown of Wetumpka, Alabama, killed in Vietnam, local white officials did not even bother to contact the family and offer condolences. The insult was not totally unexpected, because the Williams family had recently been involved in efforts to desegregate the small community of twenty-five hundred whites and fifteen hundred blacks, and three of Jimmy Williams's, siblings had begun attending the town's newly integrated school. One result of these activities was that Williams's mother, a practical nurse, was unable to find employment. Another was quite possibly the treatment of her son.

Private Williams was returned home for burial, accompanied by Lieutenant Robert L. Kraselsky, the military survivor's assistant assigned by the army to aid the Williams family. The burial party was told by local elected officials that the black sections of the town's two-hundred-year-old cemetery were full and they could not bury Williams in the whites-only section. The best Wetumpka could offer its war dead was a pauper's grave. "The colored section was full," explained Mayor Demp Thrash, "and we aren't going to dig up slave graves for anybody." Mrs. Williams angrily refused the offer, explaining, "He was not fighting a second class war and did not die a second class death. . . . My son was not a shoeshine boy like his father. He was a soldier, a paratrooper in the Green Berets. . . . My son died fighting on the front for all of us. He didn't die a segregated death and he'll not be buried in a segregated cemetery." She kept her vow, but her son was not laid to rest in Wetumpka. Instead, in June 1966, Jimmy Williams was buried with full military honors one hundred miles from home in the Andersonville (Georgia) National Military Cemetery. It was the nearest integrated site.[35]

The case of twenty-year-old Bill Terry, Jr., would at least end with a bit more satisfaction. On 3 July 1969 the young private from Birmingham, Alabama, was killed while on a search-and-destroy mission. Before leaving for Vietnam, Terry had told both his mother and his sixteen year old wife, Margaret Faye Terry, of his desire to be buried at Elmwood, a local all-white cemetery near where he grew up. Terry's body was taken to Elmwood with a full military escort, but the cemetery refused to sell the family a grave site because it did not accept African Americans. Lacking any immediate alternatives, the family temporarily interred the body on 19 July 1969 at nearby all-black Shadow Lawn cemetery. Six days later, with the backing of the NAACP Legal Redress Committee, the Terry family, along with a Mr. Blevin Stout who, in an unrelated incident, had also tried to buy a plot and was refused, filed a class action suit in federal court against the cemetery.

The case quickly received national attention. A group of Catholic priests, led by Father Eugene Farrell, called on President Nixon to speak out on Terry's behalf, and they staged a prayer vigil in Washington, D.C., as part of a campaign to convince Elmwood to change its racially exclusive policy. A similar prayer vigil was staged in Birmingham, and a former Alabaman living in California, Albert Griffen, graciously offered his plot at Elmwood to the Terry family, but cemetery directors refused to allow the transfer.

On 22 December 1969 the Terry family won its case against Elmwood when U.S. district court judge Seybourne H. Lynne handed down a seventeen-page ruling striking down racial restrictions in any cemetery as "void" and of "no legal effect" and ordering the graveyard to sell plots to anyone who applied, regardless of race. Elmwood agreed not to contest the ruling, and on a Saturday morning in January 1970, after services at Our Lady of Fatima Catholic Church in Birmingham, Terry was finally laid to rest at Elmwood. More than a thousand people, singing "We Shall Overcome," accompanied the body to its final resting place and listened as Father Farrell observed, "We, the white race, have a lot of atonement to make to this young man, for we have discriminated against him from the cradle to the grave. . . . When he had done his best for his country, his country was still doing its worst for him."[36]

A Color-Blind System

If black military personnel felt racism and hostility off base, they were usually confronted with an official ambivalence to their needs and desires on base. This lack of cultural recognition stemmed partly from the military's own equal opportunity policies and the increasingly prevalent viewpoint of the command structure that a soldier was a soldier regardless of race. The system prided itself on being officially color-blind. The standard line in the Marine Corps, for example, was that there were no white marines and no black marines, just green marines. But this attempt to view all enlisted personnel as the same meant that black cultural needs were usually ignored in favor of white cultural needs. Despite the fact the services were integrated, they were still essentially white-controlled and -dominated institutions and invariably reflected white society and culture. Major General Frederic E. Davison remarked that the white corps commander he served under was "the type of person in combat I don't think you could have beaten. I think he is totally fair as he sees it, but I think he sees the Army as green and the people in the Army as green and that insofar as he was concerned there would be equal treatment with the setting of standards. And therein, of course, you have the quintessence of institutional discrimination."[37] Lieutenant Colonel Hurdle L. Maxwell, one of the highest-ranking African Americans in the marines, bitterly commented that "the Corps says it treats all men just one way—as a Marine. What it actually has done is treat everybody like a white Marine."[38]

Blacks were constantly surrounded with reminders that they served in a white military. At Camp Lejeune, examples of acceptable haircuts for white marines decorated the walls of the base's barbershops, but none illustrated regulation hairstyles for blacks, a problem common on most military posts. Even had there been examples, it might not have made much of a difference, because few military barbers were trained to cut black hair.[39] Since no one was quite sure what constituted a permitted black hairstyle, African Americans were often singled out for disciplinary action. In Vietnam, where hair guidelines seldom mattered anyway, one black GI complained, "The brothers over here are being made to cut their natural hair style in combat where hair is not the major issue, when the pigs are wearing extremely long hair as if they were the Beattles [sic] or something." There were pictures of white Medal of Honor winners in the mess halls at Lejeune, but none of the black recipients. In West Germany there were few commemorations to African American military heroes, but a barracks was named after Robert E. Lee. Recreational facilities at most installations were geared to whites in general but white officers in particular. As one black marine private ruefully observed, "You don't see many of the brothers out on the skeet range."[40]

Probably the two major grievances African Americans had with the system were the lack of black-oriented products in the post exchanges (PXs) and the lack of black music at the enlisted men's (EM) and noncommissioned officer's clubs. In the PXs black hair-care products, magazines, and clothes, among other items, were usually in short supply or nonexistent.[41] Stateside, blacks could shop off base for these amenities, but in Vietnam this was seldom the case, and in a combat situation, the little things acquired much greater meaning and importance. In 1968 a black army private in Vietnam thanked *Ebony* magazine for its concern for black soldiers, writing that "everytime a soul brother over here gets an *Ebony* or a *Jet* magazine, there is a waiting line of at least 30-50 soul brothers throughout our troop waiting to read it. The black people back in the U.S. don't know what it means to a black soldier to have magazines such as *Ebony* and *Jet* to call their own."[42] More radical publications, such as the *Black Panther* newspaper, were often very difficult to find and in many instances were banned by base or company commanders. One commander in Southeast Asia even banned the recorded speeches of Malcolm X and pressured local merchants into removing them from their shops.[43]

African Americans also complained about the lack of black "soul music"—artists such as James Brown, Otis Redding, and Aretha Franklin—at the base NCO and EM clubs. The NAACP found that "base clubs, never the favorite serviceman's hangout in any case, were viewed as alien and often hostile places for blacks." One Vietnam veteran mentioned that the music played at his NCO club had a white bias; soul music was played only during weekdays, while prime off-duty weekend time was reserved for country and western.[44] The issue of whether soul or "white" music— almost always country and western—would be played was a serious one and was the catalyst for many of the racial fights and incidents that would plague the military during the Vietnam War. Most of the recruits were young, usually between the ages of nineteen and twenty-two, and the popular music of the day—soul for blacks and rock for whites—had a particularly profound influence on their lives. Especially in Vietnam, the right to listen to the music of one's generation and culture was jealously guarded. According to Wallace Terry, African Americans in Vietnam believed that "if blacks can account for up to twenty-two percent of the dying they should at least have twenty-two percent of the juke box or the music on Armed Forces radio."[45] It is interesting to note that both rock and soul were the musical expressions of the younger recruits, and that when trouble broke out over music, it almost always involved not rock but country and western, the music favored by the older, career-oriented personnel—men of a different generation as well as race.[46]

The military, as it became aware of the problems, did attempt to address more fully the cultural needs of black personnel. More black music was programmed for the club jukeboxes, and black bands were hired for dances and mixers. More black entertainers, including James Brown, Miss Black Utah, and Miss Black America, performed for the troops in Vietnam. Black-oriented products, from Afro-Sheen to African-style dashikis, began to appear at post exchanges. More books on African American history and culture began to appear on base library shelves, and by 1973, barbers had been trained specifically in cutting blacks' hair and had been dispatched to stateside bases.[47] African American contributions to the American military tradition were also being recognized. In January 1970 a barracks at Quantico, Virginia, was named after the first black marine recipient of the Medal of Honor, Private First Class James Anderson, Jr.[48] On 19 April 1974 at Camp Lejeune, Camp Gilbert H. Johnson was activated, named after Sergeant Major Gilbert H. Johnson, one of the first blacks ever admitted into the Corps.[49] But as was the case with many of the other racial reforms instituted by military officials, these came in the later stages of the war and had little impact on most blacks who served in the armed forces during this era. As late as 1971, African Americans stationed at such diverse bases as Groton, Connecticut; Fort Monmouth, New Jersey; and in Germany and Southeast Asia still felt that the military slighted their cultural needs.

African Americans often had problems communicating their just grievances to their commanding officers because they felt out of touch with the command structure. They were underrepresented in the officer corps, averaging only about 2 percent of the total throughout the Vietnam War era, and most professional occupations, such as law and medicine, were also heavily white.[50] A young black seeking counseling in Vietnam, for example, had to "go to a white sergeant for permission to see a white officer for permission to go to a white psychiatrist." Blacks, especially from the South, were not accustomed to trusting whites to act in their best interests, and often the command structure confirmed these suspicions. In the air force, African Americans with sickle-cell traits were prohibited from gaining flying status, but despite repeated entreaties from blacks, the military never bothered to research the condition to see if it indeed affected one's ability to fly aircraft. Another condition far more likely to affect blacks than whites was pseudofolliculitus, more commonly known as "shaving bumps." It was a skin condition that could lead to facial scars if someone afflicted with it continued to shave regularly. Growing a beard was the only simple and effective way of dealing with pseudofolliculitus, but military regulations allowed personnel to stop shaving only for medical reasons and only for up to three months. Again, officials would not listen to the pleas of black servicemen and amend the regulations, leaving African Americans the choice of shaving and risking scarring themselves for life or facing disciplinary action.[51]

Disillusionment

Most African Americans had entered the armed forces believing that the services offered more opportunity and less discrimination than did civilian society. But by 1968, blacks were increasingly disillusioned with life in the military. Faced with repeated examples of both personal and institutional racism and the command structure's obvious apathy and failure to deal with these problems, African Americans came to consider the military to be more, not less, racist than civilian society. In October 1968, Major Lavell Merritt, a twenty-year army veteran then serving in Vietnam, publicly denounced the army as a "racist organization . . . that denied equality and justice to its black personnel." In January 1969, Zalin B. Grant wrote in the *New Republic* that "past favorable publicity about integration of U.S. troops" in Vietnam "has shimmered and disappeared like paddy water under a tropic sun."[52] Private Thomas Tuck considered the army "at least as racist as the rest of America. Yes it's even more of an oppressive institution than we experience in the ghetto."[53] Private Joseph Daryl Miles agreed, calling the army "the most racist institution I've seen," adding, "We got a whole lot of freedom on the battlefield, a whole lot of democracy in the foxhole, a whole lot of equality to die."[54] Petty Officer Third Class John Brackett, who served in Vietnam in 1968-69, referred to the navy as "the best example of institutional racism" he had ever seen.[55] Another black GI in Vietnam put it more bluntly, telling the *Pittsburgh Courier* that the "Army is the most racist pig organization you ever seen. . . . It's set up by dudes for dudes. Nothing for the brothers except trouble."[56]

African Americans responded to this changing perception of the military in a variety of ways. Many simply left the military after their enlistments were up. Over the course of the war, the black reenlistment rate dramatically dropped. In 1966 more than two-thirds of the blacks in the armed services chose to reenlist; by 1970, those reenlisting were fewer than 13 percent.[57] Some did not want to wait until their time was up and deserted, and they often cited racism as the reason. Deserter Don Williams, co-chairman of the Afro-American Deserters Committee in Stockholm, Sweden, stated in 1968 that "the main reason—and I cannot stress this enough—for my own defection is the injustices committed against my people in the U.S." One black, identified as "Frenchy" and as living in Paris, France, blamed army racism for his leaving his unit in Germany and told the *Black Panther* that "blacks in the army have more reason to leave than whites." Terry Whitmore deserted the army after serving in Vietnam and cited both racism and opposition to the war as his reasons for leaving.[58] By 1971 in Vietnam, at least one hundred black deserters were living on Saigon's "Soul Alley" near Tan Son Nhut Airport, and many of these also cited racism as being a primary factor in their defections.[59]

All told, nearly 20 percent of the deserters from the army during the Vietnam War were black.[60] For the vast majority, however, racism was not the primary reason for desertion. In fact, the profiles of the typical white and the typical black deserter were strikingly similar. White or black, those who chose to leave before their service time had expired almost always did so for purely personal reasons or because of repeated conflicts with military authority. Most had been young, usually nineteen or younger, when they entered the service; they had usually been usually enlistees, not drafted; and they had less than the equivalent of a high school diploma. Only twelve percent deserted because of the war, and only 3 percent actually did so in Vietnam; the vast majority deserted from duty assignments in the United States. Though many were influenced to desert as a political statement protesting discrimination and racism, the typical African American was more likely to leave because of a failing marriage, sickness in the family back home, or personal conflicts with his sergeant.[61]

Others remained in the services but protested unfair treatment by working slowly or by refusing to complete duty assignments. This was particularly true if blacks felt the duty assignment was racially motivated. White Captain (later Major) Gary L. Tucker reported that in his mechanized infantry company in Vietnam in 1970, "if the black guys didn't like what was going on, then they chose sometimes not to do it."[62] Captain (later Major) Thomas Cecil had, by his estimates, "only forty percent of the people doing one hundred percent of the work" in his ammunition supply company.[63]

In Vietnam, protesting discrimination often took the form of combat refusals. Major Richard Torovsky, Jr., reported that "there were a couple of very small incidents [in] which people tried to use supposed bias as, I guess, an excuse for not wanting to do field duty."[64] But combat refusals, especially later in the war, were not uncommon for both blacks and whites, even though many commanding officers tended to single out blacks. By 1970 it was such a widespread problem that one American stationed at Cu Chi casually remarked that "if a man is ordered to go to such and such a place, he no longer goes through the hassle of refusing; he just packs his shirt and goes to visit some buddies at another base camp."[65] James Hawkins would go absent without leave "once in a while . . . unauthorized R and R" and would just be sent "back into the jungle," as if he had never left, when he returned.[66]

Sometimes entire companies were involved. Later in the war, many units out on search-and-destroy missions would display red bandannas, signaling to the Vietcong and North Vietnamese that they would fight only if attacked. In mid-1969 a company of the 196th Light Infantry Brigade refused orders and sat down, despite their commander's pleas. As portrayed on a CBS TV news broadcast in late 1969, another company from the First Air Cavalry Division "flatly refused" to advance down a dangerous road.[67]

The refusal to perform one duty in particular was however, racially motivated. Many blacks either were reluctant or refused to participate in riot duty stateside. Several times during the Vietnam War regular army units were assigned to riot duty, most notably in April 1968, after the assassination of Dr. Martin Luther King, Jr.[68] Many young blacks in the military were reluctant to turn their weapons on other African Americans and often sympathized with the rioters. Only 14 percent of the black enlisted men in Vietnam surveyed by Wallace Terry said they would follow orders to put down a black ghetto uprising "without reservation." In August 1968, forty-three blacks stationed at Fort Hood, Texas, refused riot duty in Chicago at the Democratic National Convention. Some GIs, like Richard Chase and John Allen, refused to engage even in the twenty-five hours of riot control training, because they felt it was designed ultimately to crush black nationalist groups such as the Nation of Islam and the Black Panthers.[69] Allen, a married father of two and a six-year army veteran, explained that when he "joined the Army I swore to fight and perhaps die to defend the United States from aggression. I would still do this, and although I disagree with our policy in Vietnam, I would not refuse to serve there. But when someone tells me that I have to point as weapon at American Negroes in the streets of an American city, that's where I draw the line." An unnamed black officer commented in *Ebony* that he was

"getting out. We're building to a black and white civil war and black troops
. . . will be used to zap black civilians. I'm getting out."[70]

Peaceful Protest

Many African Americans, however, believed the system could be made to
reach its ideals of nondiscrimination and equal opportunity, and they
sought to change conditions through petition and peaceful protest. Sailors
stationed at the navy's submarine base at Groton, Connecticut, successfully
petitioned their commanding officer for more black-related products at the
post exchange and more black music at the EM and NCO clubs.[71] Minority
cadets at the U.S. Air Force Academy in Colorado also petitioned their
superiors at Wing Staff in 1970. Like many petitions submitted by African
American servicepersons, the cadets' missive was very polite and moderate
in tone. The first line clearly stated that "this paper is *not* a formal protest
of black demands. . . . It makes suggestions for corrections for better relations between blacks and whites here, but it does not *DEMAND* that these
changes be made." The cadets went on to note that "we black men who are
here are trying to prevent unnecessary flare-ups before they have a chance
to happen." Their suggestions were actually quite conservative. The cadets
wanted a black or minority studies room, open to all and, if necessary,
stocked by the cadets themselves. They asked for more equitable enforcement of the rules, noting that whites were allowed to display Confederate
flags in their dormitory windows and on bathrobes but that black cultural
expressions were suppressed; for example, one black cadet was told to
remove a black-painted troll doll from his bookcase because it was "unauthorized." Finally, they simply wanted respect and an end to racist practices. They complained about abusive language and asked that white cadets
and instructors refrain from calling them "boy," "nigger," "snowflake," and
"spook." They also cited an incident where black cadets had been forced to
remain in push-up position for an hour for refusing to sing "Dixie" and
noted that Wing Staff had allowed a rebel flag to be flown and a cross to
be burned at a 1969 rally.[72]

But many African Americans found it difficult to appeal through official
military channels. Those who submitted even moderate requests were often
labeled militants and troublemakers. "If you were black and spoke up, you
were a troublemaker, an instigator, whatever. If you were white, you were
considered an innovator," recalled Allen Thomas, Jr. Instead of encouraging
command to institute reforms, petitioning one's commanding officer often

led to reprisals. Aboard the USS *Sumpter,* marine company commander Captain J. S. Kreuger banned the playing of a black musical group known as the Lost Poets because he believed the band's message was antimilitary and revolutionary. Three black marines, including the ship's disc jockey, Private First Class Alexander Jenkins, attempted to present Kreuger with a petition, signed by sixty-four out of sixty-five blacks aboard ship, protesting the censorship. The officer refused to meet with the three and, after a fight broke out on board the ship, had them arrested and charged with mutiny.[73] At Darmstadt, Germany, the local commander refused to meet with a group of black GIs who wanted to lodge a formal complaint over the arrest of a black after a fight in the EM club. The commander then brought charges against the petitioners and refused to meet with their lawyers until finally ordered to do so by his commanding officer.[74]

At Camp Lejeune in the Fall of 1969, black marines were so concerned that even a "timid, mild-toned missive" might bring reprisals that they petitioned their commanding officers anonymously. A group calling itself the Council of Concerned Marines posted an open letter to base commander Major General Rathvon McClure Tompkins and second marine division commander Major General Michael P. Ryan by slipping one copy under an office door and posting another on a glass display case in Tompkins's headquarters. The letter was hardly inflammatory. The concerned marines simply requested that Tompkins and Ryan investigate charges of discrimination and that a human relations officer be appointed for each battalion, something the Pentagon would do beginning in 1970. To demonstrate their loyalty to the Corps, they signed the letter "Semper Fidelis."[75]

Even black officers, members of the command structure themselves, feared the consequences of going public with their grievances. Testifying before the Congressional Black Caucus's ad hoc hearings into racism in the military in November 1971, seven black officers from Fort Devens, Massachusetts, called for peaceful change through the system. Led by Captain Charles M. Smith, an infantry company commander, the officers told Congress that they were "not revolutionary militants, dissidents or anarchists. . . . However we are concerned black officers that want to see a change in the institutionalized racism that has wrapped itself around the military system. . . . We sit before you today because time is running out." Aware of the dangers attendant on speaking out, Smith asked the Congressional Black Caucus to "monitor the careers of each black officer sitting here today because they will not be worth a plug nickel after this inquiry."[76]

Compounding the problems of institutional racism and command apathy to black cultural needs was the often racist and hostile attitude exhibited by white service personnel. Some of it was unintentional. For most of the young recruits, both black and white, it was the first time in their lives they had really had to interact with members of another race. Shaped by their cultural preconceptions of blacks, many whites behaved in a racist way without realizing that their words or actions were likely to offend African Americans. John "Jackie" Breedlove apparently held his black roommate Tom Cummings in high regard. In a letter to his parents he described Cummings as "colored, and a nice guy. . . . He's twenty-seven and has a wife and two kids." But then Breedlove added, "We give him hell all the time. We tell him if he doesn't shape up, we'll get the Ku Klux Klan after him."[77]

Wallace Terry reported to the Congressional Black Caucus on his 1969 encounter with the chief of staff for the navy in Da Nang, Vietnam:

> He knew I had grown up in the Midwest and he was from Kentucky and he wanted to relax, put me at ease. He said, "You know, son, several years ago when I was boy your age I liked to play basketball. I bet you played some basketball up in Indiana?" He said, "I remember a colored boy, we called him 'Nigger Joe.' Boy, could he play basketball. And do you know if I saw him today I guess I'd just have to call him 'Nigger Joe.'" When I left his office I went to see the leader of the so-called militants at Camp Tien Sha, Ron Washington, a seaman. I said, "Ron, have you met our Chief of Staff." He said, "Yes," and began to smile. I said, "Why are you smiling?" He said, "Did he tell you the story of 'Nigger Joe'?"

Another black soldier in Vietnam simply stated, "Chuck's all right until he gets a beer under his belt, and then it's Nigger this and Nigger that—and besides, to be honest, Chuck ain't too much fun, you dig."[78]

Much of the racism exhibited by whites, however, was both conscious and overt.[79] "Keep those niggers off the [dance] floor," and "Coons please go back to Africa" were common requests in the Camp Lejeune suggestion box.[80] Graffiti such as "Niggers eat shit" and "I'd prefer a gook to a nigger" commonly adorned the walls of bars and latrines throughout Vietnam. At Da Nang whites usually refused to stop and give jeep rides to black soldiers on foot. In Vietnam it was considered a major discourtesy not to stop and give a fellow enlisted man a ride.[81] Blacks were often casually addressed as "spook," "nigger," "boy," and "spear-chucker" by both white enlisted personnel and officers, and some thought it humorous to tell the Saigon bar girls that blacks were "animals" and "had tails."[82]

Everywhere blacks were surrounded by the symbols of racism. James Hawkins remembers finding Klan literature in the guardhouse, a building accessible only to officers and NCOs.[83] In Vietnam, Germany, the United States, and Labrador, Canada, whites often donned real or makeshift Klan robes. On some posts, commanders allowed Klan "Klaverns" to operate openly on base.[84] In May 1969 two white sailors erected and burned a twelve-foot-high cross in front of a predominantly black barracks at Cam Ranh Bay,[85] and in 1970 Army Sergeant Clide Brown found a cross burning outside his tent after he had appeared on the cover of *Time* magazine in conjunction with an article titled "The Negro in Vietnam."[86]

For blacks serving in Vietnam, the most hated and pervasive symbol of racism was the Confederate flag. To African Americans the "Stars and Bars" was not an expression of Southern pride but a despised reminder of slavery and racism. The *Crisis* referred to the Confederate flag as "the tattered banner of that evil and misbegotten system," a "despicable" symbol "of a dead and dishonorable past," adding that "the Stars and Bars and the Swastika are equally the emblem of a false doctrine of racial supremacy."[87] This symbol of racism seemed to be displayed everywhere, in hooches and bars, on jeeps; it even flew below the American flag over some posts in Vietnam. What really angered many blacks was the fact that the flag could be displayed openly but black cultural symbols were suppressed. One black marine in Vietnam was upset because whites could display Confederate flags but he was forced to remove a "Black Is Beautiful" poster from the inside wall of his locker.[88]

When blacks requested that the military ban the display of Confederate flag, their protest often fell on deaf ears. As early as 1966, Phillip Savage, the tristate director of the NAACP in Philadelphia, lodged a formal complaint with Secretary of Defense Robert MacNamara, requesting disciplinary action against military personnel who displayed rebel flags.[89] The Pentagon was willing to ban the flag, but the issue was complicated by the fact that the Stars and Bars was incorporated into many Southern states' flags. Southern legislators successfully argued that the military could not ban the display of state flags, so a compromise was reached in May 1969: Confederate insignias could be displayed only if they were part of a state flag. But to the dismay of black military personnel, the ruling was seldom enforced, especially in Vietnam. Many officers were themselves Southerners and often proudly displayed the flag. In Vietnam on Christmas Day 1965, for example, six whites carrying a rebel flag paraded in front of more than fifteen hundred troops gathered for a Bob Hope USO (United Service Organizations) show. Afterwards, several officers and NCOs posed for pictures under the flag. One black soldier present bitterly remarked that the display made him feel "like an outsider."[90]

Solidarity

Increasingly, many blacks were feeling like outsiders in the military. In response, they sought strength and comfort in racial solidarity. They began to segregate themselves from whites and developed their own black culture within the military. As air force aircraft maintenance specialist Marty Dixon explained, "Blacks . . . became increasingly alienated as we shared our common grievances and saw that the treatment we were receiving was command policy."[91] Official Marine Corps historians Henry I. Shaw and Ralph W. Donnelly found that "more and more, some young black marines tended to draw in upon themselves to develop a brotherhood of racial pride, and to consider white Marines as inherently prejudiced against them."[92]

As the war progressed, so did the trend toward separation, and the military became increasingly polarized along racial lines. At no time, however, was the racial separation complete. There was always some mixing between the races. While on duty, whites and blacks worked side by side with few problems. Captain (later Major) Stewart H. Barnhoft, a white officer who commanded an engineering company at Chu Lai, Vietnam, in 1971, recalled that "the black guys always hung around with the blacks and the whites hung around with the whites," but "on duty everybody tended to work fairly well together."[93] Clinton Hunt particularly remembered solidarity among blacks in his unit but also said that they usually "got along" with most of the whites and had no real problems working with them. Neither did navy machinist mate Alfonza Wright. "We just got along and did our jobs," Wright said, but he added that "most of the white guys were Northerners, you know, from Maine and Massachusetts, so there were very few problems."[94]

In many units, nonracist whites who were "for real" or "real studs" were also considered brothers and included in the black social circle. Marine officer and Vietnam veteran Dwight Rawls explained, "We are not anti-

white and don't bar whites if they dig us." One black specialist four in
Saigon noted the distinction between racist and nonracist whites, claiming,
"I got some white friends who are 'For Real' studs, and hell, they could call
me anything they want, because I know they are for real. I know some
Chucks who I'd most likely punch in the mouth if they said good morning
to me because I know they are some wrong studs."[95] Because of the rigors
of combat, fraternization between whites and blacks was more common in
combat units than in support or rear-echelon units. Captain (later Major)
Eugene White, Jr., stated that "the rapport that . . . developed between . . ."
White and his black staff sergeant "was tremendous" and "just like two
really old friends."[96] Marine sergeant Melvin Murrel Smith, an African
American, predicted in 1968 that "the friendships formed between whites
and Negroes in Vietnam will never die because of what we went through
together."[97]

But most blacks doubted the sincerity of whites who professed friendship toward African Americans, realizing that even the bond forged in
combat in the jungles of Vietnam was likely to be only temporary. One
black army lieutenant colonel observed in 1969 that "the threat of death
changes many things, but comradeship doesn't last after you get [back] . . .
to the village."[98] A black GI who had been seeing off a white departing
Vietnam for the United States told reporter Sol Stern, "We'd been through
a lot together. . . . I wished him the best and I meant it. He said he hoped
he'd see me on the other side and didn't mean it." As a result of such
doubts, most blacks preferred not to socialize with whites; they did not
trust them or feel comfortable around them. Consequently, most of the
self-segregation and separation occurred during off-duty hours. As one
African American stationed in Vietnam explained, "Look, you've proven
your point when you go out and work and soldier with Chuck all day. It's
like you went to the Crusades and now you're back relaxing around the
round table—ain't no need bringing the dragon home with you." Another
simply concluded, "White people are dull, they have no style and they
don't know how to relax." And air force sergeant Jack Smedley, echoing the
sentiments of many black servicemen, said, "A man wants to relax, really
relax, when he's off duty. He doesn't want to listen with half an ear to hear
if some drunken whites are going to call him a nigger."[99]

Blacks who did attempt to patronize white establishments faced verbal
and sometimes physical abuse. Near Camp Humphreys, South Korea, a
club owner and his white GI patrons and backers paid a bounty to Republic
of Korea marines for every African American they beat up in the vicinity,

to discourage blacks from patronizing the bar.[100] In "Saigon, Na Trang, and Ua Nang, and some of the other larger towns, colored persons do not go into white bars except at the risk of being ejected," reported sergeant Donald Duncan. "I have seen more than one incident where a colored newcomer has made a 'mistake' and walked into the wrong bar. If insulting catcalls weren't enough to make him leave, he was thrown out bodily." If black servicemen were escorting white females, the problem was even worse. One reason blacks in Germany avoided the base EM clubs was that every time they brought German women there, some "inebriated white soldiers wanted to fight." At Goose Bay Air Force Base, Labrador, Canada, the base commander even kept a file on white women who dated black servicemen or fraternized with them at the base EM club or local bars, explaining he was "just trying to catch a few prostitutes."[101]

Blacks responded to such treatment by establishing or patronizing "blacks only" bars. This was common both in the United States and in and near overseas defense installations. In Saigon, for example, whites tended to go to the bars and nightclubs along To Do Street and blacks to the establishments along Trinh Minh, located in the Khanh Hoi district. Though the districts were not exclusively white and black, African Americans generally avoided To Do because it was considered more expensive, and country-and-western music was often featured in the nightclubs. One black soldier explained that he preferred Trinh Minh because "I get so tired of the goddamn hillbilly music." In contrast, the "black" bars featured such artists as Aretha Franklin, Wilson Pickett, and the Four Tops. Blacks also had several "soul food" restaurants to choose from in the district. (It is interesting to note that Khanh Hoi had also been a popular recreational area for black Senegalese troops during the French-Indochina War [1946–54]. Half-Vietnamese and Senegalese children and teenagers were common in the district.)[102] In Germany, the Defense Department found that "black men, for so long forced to patronize black only establishments, have come to feel comfortable in them" and by the late 1960s and early 1970s, were "resisting desegregation."[103]

Military officials believed this tendency among blacks toward solidarity and racial separation was a product of civilian society and was brought into the armed forces by young inductees. "Remember they feel they've got where they have only by solidarity," explained marine lieutenant colonel Kenneth Berthoud; "they come in with the idea of brother-above-all." Westmoreland cited "attitudes and beliefs developed before they enter the services,"[104] and the sociologist William Stuart Gould said officials believed "that many of the racial problems encountered in the Army are products of the social conditions in the host society, i.e., the United States."[105] Undoubtedly, African Americans did bring certain preconceptions from civilian life with them into the military. But it was the conditions they found in the armed forces that proved to be the deciding influence in the development of and a catalyst for black solidarity. In fact, many of the symbols of black cultural pride and solidarity did not come from civilian society but originated among blacks in the military—and in particular, among African Americans stationed in Southeast Asia.[106]

In Vietnam many blacks began to make and display black-power flags. Black marines in Da Nang designed one that would become a model for others. The flag had a red background to symbolize the blood shed by African Americans in the war. A black foreground represented black culture. At the center were two spears crossed over a shield and surrounded by a wreath, meaning "violence if necessary" but "peace if possible." Across the flag was a legend in Swahili proclaiming, "My Fear Is for You." Variations of the flag appeared in South Korea and Germany as well as elsewhere in Vietnam.[107]

In Vietnam, especially in combat units, uniform codes were seldom strictly enforced, and both whites and blacks began wearing what were technically unauthorized additions on their clothing. It was common for whites to wear peace symbols and patches displaying Confederate flags or marijuana leaves and to chalk "Peace" and "Fuck the War" across their combat helmets. Blacks had their own set of symbols, and most were expressions of cultural pride and racial solidarity. Some took bootlaces and weaved them into slave bracelets, that they wore on their wrists. Others carried black-power canes, which were usually ebony-colored canes with a clenched fist at the top. Another cultural expression that originated in Vietnam and became popular in the United States was the black-power salute, a clenched fist raised in the air. Between black officers and enlisted personnel, the black-power salute, or "check," was often substituted for the standard military salute.[108]

Perhaps the most important and influential cultural expression to emerge from the war was the dap, the ritualized handshake used by blacks when greeting one another. The term dap was derived from *dep*, a Vietnamese word meaning "beautiful." By most accounts, the handshake originated among black prisoners confined at Long Binh Stockade. Every step in dapping had a specific meaning. Clinching fingers together and then touching the back of the hand meant "My brother, I'm with you," and pounding the heart with a clenched fist symbolized brotherly love and solidarity. Though there were some basic and common gestures, the dap was not standardized and numerous variations appeared, some lasting as long as five minutes. Some additions were more sinister than others. One common addition to the standard handshake was a gesture across the throat, which symbolized cutting the throats of white military police (MPs).[109]

For many, dapping was a meaningful affirmation of cultural solidarity and brotherly love, and in fact, many sympathetic whites dapped with their black comrades in arms. But more often than not, dapping, like certain other black cultural expressions, was a source of friction between blacks and whites. Whites were generally frightened, angered, or just annoyed by expressions of black unity and began to resent African American solidarity and self-segregation. Dapping in chow lines particularly became a source of racial friction. John Ellis, a white captain (later major), was somewhat understanding, noting that the ritualized but often time-consuming hand-shake "was a very meaningful thing to young blacks. It meant a lot to them and sometimes, like in anything like that, what starts out to be meaningful sort of gets made into something sort of ridiculous."[110] But most whites were far less sympathetic and objected to being made to wait for their meals while African Americans ahead of them in line went through lengthy daps. "Well, the favorite time for blacks to do that was in line in the mess hall," explained Captain (later Lieutenant Colonel) Vernon Conner, "and sometimes they would go into a five or ten minute dapping period, and the whites would not be real thrilled about waiting in line while a couple of the bro's went through their dapping procedures."[111] The Department of Defense's Task Force on the Administration of Military Justice noted that "dapping has become a source of considerable friction both between the black serviceman and his white counterparts and between him and the military system. It seems to provoke a reaction of white anger out of proportion to its own importance."[112]

Many whites did react to dapping and other expressions of black cultural solidarity with anger and hostility. Some whites developed a power salute or "white-power check" of their own. Others mocked African Americans or ridiculed them when they dapped. Often this disparagement was the reason for fights between blacks and whites. In Japan in 1971, marine private Raymond Burns fought and killed Lance Corporal Thomas L. Bertler after Bertler had taunted him about dapping.[113]

Many commanding officers reacted by banning dapping. In 1973 the navy banned dapping and black-power salutes during working hours.[114] The Marine Corps did not ban them directly, but in September 1969, marine commandant General Leonard F. Chapman issued a directive head-lined "Racial Relations and Instances of Racial Violence within the Marine Corps;" that narrowly circumscribed the situations when such gestures would be permissible. Chapman ordered that "no actions, signs, symbols, gestures, and words which are contrary to tradition will be permitted during formations, or when rendering military courtesies to colors, the National Anthem, or individuals."[115]

Though dapping usually was not banned at the highest levels of military authority, except in the navy late in the war, it was often prohibited by base and company commanders. Commanders almost always cited the fact that it caused considerable delays in mess-hall lines and racial friction with whites as their reasons for banning it. Captain George L. Youngblood, a white officer stationed at Camp Holloway, Vietnam, explained, "There's a time and a place for everything. . . . When there are jobs to be done you shouldn't waste time doing the dap. . . . It should be put aside during duty hours." Many black officers agreed and did not view policies that banned dapping and black-power salutes as discriminatory. Captain Alfred Thomas, a black helicopter pilot, supported such policies "simply because blacks were spending too much time dapping and they were holding up the chow lines."[116]

But prohibiting dapping and other black greetings was only one part of a military-wide campaign to eliminate the symbols of black pride and unity and to destroy African American solidarity within the armed forces. Blacks were given Article 15s or in some cases were court-martialed for uniform violations involving black cultural symbols or for dapping. Similar violations by whites were usually overlooked, but the punishments meted out to African Americans for such infractions were often severe. Marine Private First Class Victor Lucky was court-martialed and sentenced to six weeks of solitary confinement in 1972 for dapping in the mess hall at Camp Schwab, Okinawa. "In order to promote racial harmony," Lucky's battalion commander had banned "all gestures that have been used to express particular ethnic groups' pride, unity and identification."[117]

Some commanders made a deliberate attempt to identify and eliminate individuals or groups of blacks when they considered to be the "trouble-makers" who promoted African American unity and separation. Captain (later Major) Eugene J. White, Jr., resented the fact that, on returning to base camp after a three- or four-day mission, "the blacks would all get together on one side of the perimeter it seemed like and they would be shucking and jiving with their big broboxes, the big tape decks that they carried to the field." White attempted to break up these "cliques" by assigning new African Americans in his company to a platoon in which he had "identified a very stable black soldier," who would act as a mentor and a buffer between the new arrival and the "massive amount of peer pressure" he was likely to receive from the more militant blacks in the unit.[118] First Lieutenant (later Major) Donald Dean recalled a black first sergeant in his company at Da Nang in 1971 who "had a little clique of blacks that hung around with him and he caused a bit of separation." Dean "initiated a program through the command structure against him," and he was eventually "caught and convicted . . . and later run out."[119] Raymond Wells said that in his army company in Vietnam in 1970–71, "the brothers would be separated from the Caucasian," but in general, they had few problems with the "rabbits," or whites. This began to change, Wells claimed, when "troublemakers," or "house niggers," were deliberately planted in the unit to disrupt black solidarity "and to cause trouble, an excuse to get rid of the ones you need to get rid of." "Man, when I just got here [Vietnam]," Private First Class Charles Allen related, his white superior officers warned him "not to participate with too many blacks . . . but man, I couldn't dig the rabbit. . . . I want to be with my brothers."[120]

Some commanders went so far as to break up groups of African Americans who bunked together in predominantly or exclusively black barracks, or "hooches." In Vietnam, particularly at the more remote firebases, it had become something of an enlisted man's prerogative to choose his hooch-mates on a voluntary basis, but many officers balked at all-white or all-black living arrangements. Lieutenant (later Major) William C. Long recalled a "tendency at first . . . for the blacks to stay together" when allowed to choose a barracks. Long finally "broke up the cliques and re-assigned different bunk-mates."[121] Captain (later Lieutenant Colonel) Vernon L. Conner also found when he "took over the battery [that] they had black barracks and white barracks." Like many other officers he halted the practice. Conner remembered that it was part of the "polarization of blacks against whites" in the unit; "I made them stop that, but you couldn't stop them from socializing with the people that they wanted to."[122]

But some commanders did try to prevent blacks even from socializing together, and on many bases, both stateside and at overseas installations, military police were under orders to break up groups of African Americans. One black sailor complained that "whenever we get together, they go out of their way to break it up. . . . Whenever four, five brothers would get together they'll come up to the group and say 'break it up.' "[123] Former army staff sergeant Emmett Doe added, "Whenever blacks seem to unite, whites panic."[124]

The efforts by white authorities proved counterproductive. Instead of breaking black solidarity, they encouraged many African Americans to increase their self-segregation from whites and to pressure the less militant to do the same. Sergeant Pinkie Hauser, one of the relatively few women to serve in Vietnam, recalled being admonished by more radical blacks for having white friends. "Even the girls," she remembered, "would look at me like to say what are you hanging around with honkies for?" Not only were whites no longer welcome; they were dehumanized. To counter many of the pejoratives used by whites to describe blacks, African Americans in the military developed their own slang terms for whites, such as "Chucks," "honkies," "Caucasians," "beasts," "dudes," "pigs," "foreigners," and "rabbits." Signs reading "No Rabbits Allowed" and "Black Only" appeared over hooches and bars, and more African Americans began openly to display the trappings of black militancy.[125] Some even joined self-defense organizations, such as the Blackstone Rangers and the Mau Mau in the army and the Ju Ju in the Marine Corps. "De Mau Mau," or Black Mau Maus, were formed, according to one spokesperson, because black GIs in Vietnam "suffering from racism . . . found it necessary to unite against the oppression" of whites.[126] In Vietnam the Ju Ju wore black shirts and black gloves into combat "as symbols of their black pride and of their inability to accept the status quo." Even at stateside bases black service personnel organized into protective groups. In late summer of 1972, African American service personnel in the San Diego area formed the Black Servicemen's Caucus, to "combat racism in the military while trying to develop ties with the black community."[127]

African Americans viewed their increasing solidarity and self-segregation as a defense mechanism against racism, but whites increasingly saw such behavior as hateful and hostile. One white Green Beret stated that "blacks pretty much stuck to themselves and hated everyone else." One general in Germany was informed that he was a "pig" and that all whites were pigs. Lieutenant Charles Anderson claimed that most of the black prisoners at the Da Nang stockade were hard-core militants and "thoroughly full of hate for all whiteys."[128] In 1972 the Department of Defense's Task Force on the Administration of Military Justice saw "evidence of blacks separating themselves from their non-black comrades in hostile ways, going beyond affirming their racial and cultural solidarity." [129]

For many blacks, the situation had gone beyond peaceful but separate coexistence in the military. Bobby Seale, chairman of the Black Panther Party, stated in 1969 that it "will take more than soul music on the EM club juke box and Afro haircuts to satisfy the legitimate demands" of black service personnel. [130] Many now thought in terms of open warfare between whites and blacks. John R. White, an African American serving in Vietnam in 1969, summed up the feelings of many blacks when he said, "No more talk . . . we just kill them off or they kill us off. That's just how bad it is here." [131]

Given the feelings of racial hostility shared by many blacks and whites in the military and the tensions that developed in many units, it is not surprising that by 1968 the friction generated by racism, misunderstanding, and the command structure's indifference to the growing problem resulted in an unprecedented wave of racial violence in the armed forces. This violence occurred in every branch of the services and virtually everywhere the United States maintained defense installations. The interracial warfare was particularly bad, however, in Germany, the United States, South Korea, and Vietnam, and it led military authorities to question seriously whether the command structure could prevent the disintegration of the U.S. Armed Forces.

5

"Going to Mess up Some Beasts Tonight"
The Outbreak of Racial Violence in the Armed Forces

Rumble at Camp Lejeune

On the night of 20 July 1969, the First Battalion, Sixth Marines, at Camp Lejeune, North Carolina, threw themselves a "going away" party at the base service club, before departing the next day to join the Sixth Fleet at Rota, Spain. The party was attended by about one hundred black and seventy-five white marines, and through the course of the evening, several minor flare-ups and scuffles took place between the two racial groups. Tensions were already running high when the most serious of the incidents occurred: a black marine attempted to cut in on a white sailor dancing with a black Wave, and a fight ensued. Order was restored, and many of the partygoers left to return to their barracks.

Shortly before eleven 11 P.M., an "extremely bloody" white marine burst back into the club and announced that he had just been beaten by several black marines. Within the next half hour another fifteen injured whites staggered into the club, many of them hurt in a brawl that was taking place in front of the building between about thirty blacks and Hispanics yelling "White beasts" and "We are going to mess up some beasts tonight" and a lesser number of whites. By the time the fighting was over, dozens of men had been injured: two white marines were hospitalized with knife wounds, and another was in serious condition with severe head injuries. And a white corporal, Edward Bankston, lay dead from a fractured skull. The twenty-year-old from Picayune, Mississippi, had not participated in the brawl and was apparently an innocent victim of the fighting.

After the violence, forty-four men were arrested and charged, but charges against twenty-four of the marines were later dropped. All of the remaining defendants, with the exception of two Puerto Ricans, were African Americans. Eventually, five were acquitted; thirteen were convicted of rioting, disobedience, or assault; and one deserted before his case came to trial. The remaining black defendant was convicted of involuntary manslaughter and sentenced to nine years of hard labor.[1]

The incident at Camp Lejeune sent shock waves through the military establishment and brought renewed promises by Pentagon officials to fight racism and provide equal opportunity, regardless of race, for all American military personnel. The command structure, as evidenced by the series of courts-martial after the fight, also intensified efforts to identify and eliminate perceived troublemakers and militants from the ranks. But the disturbing fact about the "rumble" at Camp Lejeune was that it was not an isolated incident, and it was not totally unexpected. In fact, in many respects, the conditions at Camp Lejeune that led to violence were typical of the racial climate that existed throughout the military establishment.

By 1968, all of the elements needed to trigger racial violence in the armed forces were present. A distinct and, in some cases, nearly complete racial polarization existed at most defense installations. African Americans felt like outsiders in a white-dominated institution and, largely in response to personal and institutional racism, had developed a black subculture, based on racial pride and solidarity, within the ranks. Most simply distrusted whites and did not feel comfortable around them; but for some, this black subculture became a vehicle for venting their hatred and frustration with white society.

Many whites were also quite willing to engage in racial warfare. Southerners in particular were likely to provoke fights with blacks, especially if they believed the African Americans were getting too "uppity" or were infringing on traditionally white prerogatives. It was "the Southern guys" who started most of the fights in E-4 Clinton H. Hunt's unit in Vietnam in 1968–69.[2] Allen Thomas, Jr., was informed quite bluntly by a young white trooper from Louisiana that the latter "wasn't going to take orders from a nigger." The trooper "turned out to be a pretty good kid," remembers Thomas, "after he spent thirty days in the stockade." James Hawkins, who was born and raised in Kentucky, questioned, "How could it, the army, be anything but racist with 99.99 percent of the NCOs Southerners?"[3] Many whites also blamed Southerners for starting much of the trouble. One white sailor from Iowa remarked in 1968 that "the white boys from Louisiana, Texas, and Alabama grew up with this all their lives . . . they push it."[4]

Reverse Discrimination

It was not just Southerners who provoked interracial confrontations. A majority of whites who did not consider themselves to be racists still held subtle but important notions of black inferiority and deference to whites. It shocked and offended them when blacks acted aggressively, and they resented the outward manifestations of cultural pride and solidarity. Some became openly racist in response. One white Green Beret claimed that he was not prejudiced when he entered the army but "became a bigot" after being "accosted" by African Americans on a military bus. Others complained about "reverse racism" and charged that African Americans gave fellow blacks preferential treatment whenever possible. One twenty-one-year-old white marine stationed at Camp Lejeune bitterly complained:

> Within the Negro community here . . . there exists no rank structure . . . that is to say, a private and a sergeant consider themselves equal. They are "brothers." I went to get my leave papers from a Negro sergeant and was kept waiting with no recognition for about forty-five minutes. A Negro private walked in and said, "Hey brother, how about my leave?" The sergeant answered immediately, "You got leave? Come, let's see if I can get you a ninety-six hour pass. . . ." I'd been on guard duty all week and was entitled to a ninety-six, but I only got a seventy-two. This little private experience shows me how much the Negroes have solidified.[5]

Captain (later Major) Michael Colacicco, who removed a white platoon leader because of racism, also had a black sergeant transferred out of his company because of racial discrimination. "It was obvious," Colacicco stated, "that he wasn't recommending soldiers for promotion to Sp. 4 [specialist four] unless they were black."[6] Whites in Lieutenant (later Major) Richard Anshus's infantry company originally thought it "was the greatest thing going, got rid of all the blacks there for awhile," when Anshus sent his black troopers to Chu Lai for a USO show featuring Miss Black America; but "as it turned out, they were back there about eight days. Other whites thought they were being discriminated against because they were white and the blacks got to get out of the fire fight because they got to go back to the floor show." Ironically, the then-lieutenant mollified the discontented whites by asking them, "Would you rather be black and go back there or would rather be white and be out here?"[7]

Whites also charged that the command structure had given in to pressure from black activists and organizations and now extended preferential treatment to minority service personnel. One naval officer, writing under the pseudonym "Lt. John Paul Jones," sarcastically wrote in the *National Review*, "Some whites agree that the system of naval discipline does, in fact, discriminate with respect to blacks—in favor of them, not against them. These whites feel that infractions of discipline which might bring them before the captain are tolerated when the perpetrators are black; that commanders are reluctant to impose discipline when charges of discrimination might make waves."[8] In 1969 whites claimed that a new Marine Corps directive requiring at least one black or Puerto Rican on a court-martial panel if a minority serviceperson was involved, constituted "preferential treatment."[9] Representative Dan Daniel (D-Virginia) and several members of his Subcommittee on Recruiting and Retention of the House Armed Services Committee expressed opposition in 1971 to a new Department of Defense policy that would give preference to minorities volunteering for the reserves and the National Guard, claiming this was a form of reverse discrimination.[10]

There were, of course, incidents where African Americans did engage in forms of reverse racism, but for the most part, such charges were groundless. The Department of Defense's Task Force on the Administration of Military Justice labeled claims of reverse discrimination "unfounded in most cases." Often it was simply a case of whites failing to understand the problems blacks faced in the military. As black marine corporal Gregory Cogg saw it, "the problem is in white over-reaction. They're trying to label our legitimate efforts reverse racism."[11]

Real or imagined, the complaints of reverse discrimination provoked a white backlash, and the perception was one of many factors that contributed to a climate of racial hostility.

The King Assassination

Another factor that increased racial antagonism was the callous behavior displayed by many white servicepersons when Dr. Martin Luther King, Jr., was assassinated on 4 April 1968. Many openly celebrated the murder. John

Brackett recalled the "overt joy expressed by some of my white colleagues that this 'troublemaker' had been eliminated."[12] At Cam Ranh Bay, whites hoisted a Confederate flag above the Naval Headquarters Building after hearing the news.[13]

Some whites were sympathetic. Brackett was grateful he had a "couple of good friends who were white and not racist, and that helped."[14] A white airman first class from Mississippi named Logan Hill, said, "I talked to some people who thought it was a pretty good thing," but "speaking for myself, I'm appalled." Some whites were relatively apathetic, like the white MP who stated, "We feel sorry they got King. . . . He's a martyr now, and his people will probably follow the Rap Browns and Stokely Carmichaels," then added, "We have 300 Americans dying here each week. . . . King was one man. What about the people out here who are dying?"[15]

For blacks, however, King's death changed everything. Clinton Hunt spoke for most black military personnel when he expressed his admiration for Rev. King, and most felt bitter and disillusioned when he was killed. Describing the reaction of African Americans in Vietnam to the murder, Private Morocco Coleman wrote that "almost everywhere here you can see the unity which exists among the Negro soldiers. After the assassination of Dr. M. L. King you could also feel the malcontent."[16] "Some of the younger guys were angry and just wanted to hurt someone," related Allen Thomas, Jr., "and there were some fistfights between whites and blacks, but most of the men were simply in shock. Several hundred men just sat down in a field, drank, smoked pot, but mostly just talked." Serious violence was avoided because the black NCOs convinced the officers to "back off" for a few days and let the men work through their anger and frustration. "The unit was in stand-down anyway, and the last thing you wanted to do was set them off, you know, seasoned veterans with guns," Thomas said. James Hawkins agreed that "Dr. King's death changed things, it . . . made a lot of people angry—angry people with weapons."[17]

At Mannheim Stockade in Germany, a fight broke out between blacks and whites when a "white prisoner opened up his damned trap and made a racial remark" after King's assassination, according to USAREUR provost marshal Brigadier General Harley Moore. "He got decked by a Negro and the thing spread. This boy was a real jewel. What an idiotic thing to say, especially in a time of tension like that."[18] But blacks remembered such remarks. As a result, the gulf between the races widened, and many African Americans rejected King's emphasis on nonviolence in favor of retaliation and retribution.

The Causes of Racial Violence

Some of the influences on the growth of racial conflict were arguably beyond the control of local and base commanders. To begin with, the military was undergoing a very rapid expansion by 1968, as it sought to raise troop levels in Vietnam to a half a million men by the end of the year in addition to maintaining the United States' other defense commitments around the world. Since the primary vehicle employed to meet these manpower requirements was the draft, it many enlisted men were unwilling inductees.

The military's personnel policies regarding service in Vietnam also complicated the problem. On the experiences of the two world wars and the Korean conflict, it was decided very early to limit enlisted personnel's service in Vietnam to one-year tours of duty.[19] After initial deployment, entire units were seldom rotated in or out of the country; rather, new troops were constantly fed in to replace those killed, wounded, or whose term had expired. This policy further disrupted the stability and cohesion of companies and made it difficult for men to bond together and trust one another. They were essentially strangers, thrown together into a situation few of them wanted to be in, in the first place.[20]

The rapid turnover in personnel was matched by an even more rapid transition of officers. This was especially true with regard to Vietnam. The armed forces wanted officers with a wide range of experience in both command and administrative positions. The war offered the opportunity to expose as many officers as possible to combat command situations; to facilitate this exposure, combat commands were usually limited to six- to eight-month tours. Again, this affected unit cohesion and stability. It was difficult for an officer to deal effectively with growing racial problems in his command, because by the time he fully understood the situation, knew the men involved, and possibly solved the problem, he was gone. Also, in the combat units, the enlisted men more often than not were dealing with inexperienced and immature officers, not much older or wiser than the recruits they commanded.[21]

All of these factors meant that defense installations—whether Camp Lejeune in the United States or the sprawling compound at Long Binh in Vietnam—were overcrowded, with a large percentage of the military population composed of transients or men on temporary assignment. There was little familiarity or trust between blacks and whites or between officers and enlisted personnel.[22]

The fight at Camp Lejeune offers a good example of the problems facing the armed forces, because most of the elements that contributed to racial violence were present at the marine base. It was a large installation, with more than forty thousand marines stationed there. Many had just returned from overseas service, and many, like the First Battalion, Sixth Marines, were scheduled to begin overseas tours. As at Camp Lejeune, the typical fight between whites and blacks occurred during off-duty hours, on or near a large defense installation, and was likely to begin in the base service club or a nearby drinking establishment.[23] Colacicco had no problems in his engineering company in Vietnam as long as they were out in the field, but when they were back at their base camp at Bien Hoa, they often had fights at the local service club.[24] Captain (Later Lieutenant Colonel) Charles Shrader recalled that the EM club at Long Binh in 1968 was "a never ending source of problems," because most racial problems in his transportation company "usually centered on this club."[25] In May 1968 the enlisted-men's club at Qui Nhon, Vietnam, was closed after a "racial melee," as was the club at the Naval Medical Center in Bethesda, Maryland, in March 1971.[26]

The fights often started over what type of music would be played at the clubs. At Tien Sha Naval Base near Da Nang, officials were forced to close the local service clubs and restrict access to the recreational facility at nearby China Beach in both 1966 and 1968, after repeated fights over whether country-and-western or soul music would be featured at the clubs.[27] In 1970 a black airman was knifed during a fight over music on the club jukebox at Goose Bay Air Force Base, Labrador, Canada; thirteen whites were injured in the fight and five black airmen were arrested. At Darmstadt, Germany, in 1972, whites taunted blacks with racial slurs and by playing loud country-and-western music on their tape recorders. When African Americans retaliated by playing soul music on the jukebox, a major gang fight ensued.[28]

The use of alcohol and racial slurs, or "trigger words," also contributed to the violence at the EM and NCO clubs. At Tien Sha, seaman Robert Riley got into a fight after a white sailor referred to Riley and a friend as "just plain old niggers." Later, at China Beach, a situation involving whites throwing rocks at blacks and calling them "black motherfuckers" escalated to the point where both sides were facing each other with loaded weapons. After naval officials convinced both sides to stand down, Base Commander Linus Wensman banned beer and liquor sales at all nearby service clubs.[29]

The service clubs may have been the most typical location for racial violence, but fights were likely to occur whenever large groups of off-duty blacks and whites congregated, especially if one side or the other had been drinking. On the night of 30 July 1969, fifteen white marines stationed at Millington Naval Air Station near Memphis, Tennessee, armed themselves with billy clubs and went looking for blacks after an "informant" told them that "the colored people were coming to take over the barracks." A fight with a group of African Americans returning from a drinking session quickly developed when one of the whites yelled, "Here come those drunken niggers now." The fight lasted over fifteen minutes and even drifted from the barracks into a nearby bar, but there were no serious injuries. However, four black marines were charged with rioting and conspiracy.[30] A fistfight between a white and a black stationed at the Second Army Division Headquarters at Tongduckon, South Korea, in conjunction with African Americans displaying a black-power flag over a local barracks, sparked a racial gang war that wrecked a local "white" bar.[31]

Because the underlying factors truly responsible for the violence were so intense and widespread, almost anything could trigger a racial gang fight, and one could break out virtually anywhere service personnel were stationed.[32] In January 1971 thirty-five to forty African Americans at a base in Germany confronted their company commander, Captain Richard Johnston, demanding an investigation into the death of an eighteen-year-old black private, Marvin H. Powell. Authorities claimed Powell accidentally fell down a flight of steps, but the blacks believed he had been pushed. When Johnston delayed meeting the men, a "general disturbance" broke out. Johnston was struck with "flying objects" and a white private suffered a punctured lung and a broken rib.[33] At Fort McClellan, Alabama, on 15 November 1971, a march and meeting to protest discrimination and racial policies on base turned violent, and a white civilian employee was beaten by some protesters for refusing to open the restrooms before the regularly scheduled time of 10 A.M.[34]

A race riot occurred at Machinato, Okinawa, on 24 September 1972, after MPs attempted to arrest an African American GI suspected of involvement in a theft and assault.[35] John Brackett recalled another big fight on Okinawa that started over a group of whites taunting and provoking another white who was drinking and socializing with a group of African Americans.[36] A major race riot occurred at the naval installation at Cam Ranh Bay, Vietnam, in 1969, resulting in injury to two white colonels.[37] Stateside, a gang fight took place involving more than two hundred blacks and whites at Fort Bragg, North Carolina, and seventeen marines were injured during a rumble among newly returned Vietnam veterans at Kaneohe Marine Corps Air Station, Oahu, Hawaii.[38]

Racial Warfare and Military Stockades

Second only to the service clubs as a likely location for racial violence were the military brigs and stockades. As in the base installations, large groups of blacks and whites were concentrated together in these locations, with little to occupy their time. Many of the prisoners had, in fact, been incarcerated because of their involvement in militant activity or racially motivated fights. In a November 1968 letter to his parents in the United States, executive officer for the navy's Da Nang Brig, marine lieutenant Charles Anderson, remarked, "Our brig population is getting back up around two hundred and fifty so we'll probably have some trouble again. Got twenty-two in last night, colored, for staging a race protest-riot in Da Nang." Anderson added that there "have been several race incidents over here this year but you may not have heard back there."[39] The brig also held "hard-core riot leaders" awaiting trial after a racial disturbance in the Philippines.[40]

Two of the earliest large-scale racial confrontations of the Vietnam era actually occurred at military stockades in Vietnam; both began in August 1968. The first was at Da Nang Brig. On 15 August, a group of mostly black prisoners fought white prisoners and guards and took control of the main compound. They held the compound for twenty hours before brig commander Lieutenant Colonel Joseph Gambardella and Lieutenant Anderson could restore order. A renewed outbreak of racial violence on 18 August was quelled with the use of tear gas.[41] Anderson described the aftermath as "only a few injuries but a big mess to clean up. They burned down our cell block so we've got the hard ones in the sentry dog cages."[42]

Eleven days later, on 29 August, a more serious riot erupted at the army's sprawling Long Binh Stockade. The riot at the stockade—"Long Binh Jail," or "LBJ," as everyone referred to it, a pun on then-President Lyndon B. Johnson's initials—began with a fight among a "relatively small number of blacks and whites" in the medium-security section.[43] Groups of MPs and prison guards who rushed in to stop the fighting were quickly overwhelmed by black prisoners yelling, "Kill the Chucks." Keys taken from the military police allowed the rebellious African Americans to free those in the maximum-security blocks.[44] Afterward, a number of buildings, including the administration building, were set on fire and burned to the ground. Reinforcements of military police arrived about an hour after the riot began and, backed by machine gunners in the guard towers, ordered the prisoners to "cease and desist." Though many of the rebels obeyed the order, about 250 prisoners, the majority of them black, shouted obscenities and refused to surrender. After dousing the rioters with tear gas, MPs fixed bayonets and advanced into the compound. The prisoners fought back with clubs, rocks, and metal rods but were soon overpowered by the MPs. Seventy blacks and seventeen police were wounded and a white prisoner, Private Edward O. Haskett, was killed, beaten to death with a shovel by black prisoners.[45]

Stockade officials assumed the rioting was over and made the mistake of sorting the prisoners into two groups, the "cooperatives" and the ones who had resisted, the "uncooperatives." There were about 220 prisoners in the latter group, and with the exception of three Puerto Ricans, the uncooperatives were African Americans. They were then herded into an enclosed section of the stockade. But once inside, the uncooperatives quickly seized control of the compound. Many shed their uniforms in favor of African-style dashikis made from army blankets. One white officer reported that the prisoners were "running around naked or wearing bits of clothing as loin cloths. . . . Others were beating out jungle sounds on oil drums."

Instead of pushing the issue, base officials decided to wait and allow the prisoners to surrender at their own pace. Cases of canned field rations (C rations) were thrown over the fence into the compound each day, and "scores of Army psychologists and stockade officials" were allowed in to question the men about their grievances. The prisoners complained about bad food and not enough mail, and in particular, they claimed the guards were racists and treated black prisoners with brutality. White prisoners, they argued, received preferential treatment. But "most of them," according to one military psychologist, "just wanted out of the Army and out of Vietnam" and, "rightly or wrongly, felt they faced the same kind of prejudice that they had in the ghettos of the U.S." After three weeks the rebellion collapsed, and only thirteen prisoners continued to defy prison authorities.[46]

Some brig or stockade riots were directed not at white prisoners but at white authority. A brig riot aimed at prison officials erupted at the Norfolk Naval Brig in Virginia on 26 November 1972. What began as a fight between a white and a black inmate escalated into a violent confrontation between

African American prisoners and white guards. Blacks armed with baseball bats beat "some particularly racists guards," but in general, white prisoners were not assaulted. One black inmate reassured frightened white inmates, telling them, "Don't worry, this isn't against whites. We're just fed up with this discrimination. . . . We're not taking it anymore." An official inquiry into the riot exonerated the MPs and blamed the prisoners for the violence. Sixteen blacks were charged with assault and rioting, and all but one were given additional time at hard labor, forfeiture of monthly pay, and bad conduct discharges.[47] The sentence handed down to inmate Bruce Taylor, was typical. Taylor was found guilty of rioting, two counts of assault, and two counts of threatening to injure the brig's marine guards and was given two months in confinement and a bad conduct discharge on completion of his jail term.

Racism at Sea

The navy had its share of racial problems at its shore installations and of racially motivated fights between individuals or very small groups, but it was not until the early 1970s that the service experienced large-scale racial violence on its ships at sea. The reasons had more to do with luck than with planning or foresight. Throughout much of the Vietnam War era, the navy was not as heavily involved in the war as the other services. Navy pilots flew countless missions over both North and South Vietnam, and navy boats patrolled the numerous meandering rivers and deltas of Southeast Asia, but the war was primarily a ground campaign, and this initially placed the emphasis on the army and the Marine Corps.

By 1972, however, the United States was de-escalating its direct involvement in Vietnam. As part of President Richard Nixon's program of the "Vietnamization" of the war effort, Americans were turning much of the responsibility for ground combat operations over to the Army of the Republic of Vietnam. The United States still pledged to provide air support for the South Vietnamese, but as more American airbases in the country were deactivated or turned over to the ARVN, this support role fell increasingly to the navy, which could station carriers off the Vietnamese coast. As the navy stepped up its involvement in the conflict, the general American involvement was decreasing, and morale on board ship was affected. The average sailor was working eighteen-hour days, fighting a war virtually everyone had already conceded as lost.[48]

Also, as the war progressed, the percentage of African Americans serving in the navy increased. Of all the armed services, the navy had the most "lily-white" tradition, and at the start of American involvement in Vietnam, blacks made up less than 4 percent of the ranks. Alfonzo Wright recalled being one of only seven African Americans in a crew of more than two hundred on the *Hartley* in the early 1960s. By 1968, however, the number of blacks enlisted in the navy had risen to more than 6 percent, and in 1972, more than 12 percent of the recruits were black. But African Americans still constituted only a fraction of the officer and senior NCO populations; they received a disproportionately high number of Captain's Masts and courts-martial; and most were assigned to the nontechnical military occupational specialties.[49]

Racism was widespread, and this was recognized by the new chief of naval operations, Admiral Elmo R. Zumwalt, Jr., when he assumed his post in June 1970. Zumwalt launched a series of reforms aimed at relieving racial tension and providing equal opportunity for minorities. His attempts, however, prompted a white backlash throughout the navy. Black expectations of racial reform gave way to frustration and bitterness, and Zumwalt's slogan to attract minorities to the navy, "You can be Black and Navy too," had an increasingly hollow ring to it for many African Americans. Far from lessening racial tensions, Zumwalt's reform program added to them.[50]

In 1972 these underlying tensions erupted into racial warfare on board several ships. On 11 and 12 October 1972, violence and rioting occurred on the aircraft carrier *Kitty Hawk* as it steamed from the Philippines to its duty station in the Gulf of Tonkin. Forty whites and six blacks were injured, and twenty-six black sailors were arrested and charged. A few days later, a confrontation on board the oiler *Hassayampa* sent four whites to the hospital and eleven blacks to the brig. During the first two weeks in November, the carrier *Constellation* was the scene of several racial fights and confrontations between black seamen and the white command structure. When it docked at San Diego on 9 November, 120 African American sailors left the ship to protest discrimination, and all were charged with absent-without-leave offenses and fined. Racial violence also broke out on other naval vessels in 1972-73, most notably on the carrier *Intrepid* and on the *Inchon* and the *Sumpter.*[51]

In many respects, the incidents on the *Kitty Hawk* and on the *Constellation* were quite similar. On both carriers, blacks made up less than 10 percent of the crew and had but token representation among the ship's officer complement. Out of a crew of 4,135 men and 348 officers on the

Kitty Hawk, for example, only 297 men and 5 officers were black. Morale was poor on both ships because of long working days, antiwar sentiment, and continual racial friction among crew members. On the *Kitty Hawk,* this friction had included a fight between white and black crew members at an enlisted-men's club at Subic Bay in the Philippines on 10 October.

In the case of both ships, violence erupted on board after the commanding officer attempted to initiate disciplinary action against one or more African Americans. On 11 October, a black seaman was questioned by an investigative officer on the *Kitty Hawk* with regard to the fight at the Subic Bay shore facility. The African American had been accompanied by nine other black sailors, who demanded the captain address their grievances. After a hostile meeting with the investigating officer, the black crewman was informed of his rights but released. Shortly afterward, two white cooks were attacked by a group of African Americans apparently including the suspect. On the *Constellation,* violence broke out after an acrimonious meeting between the ship's executive officer and a representative party of African American sailors. Again, the meeting had proved fruitless, and afterward, a white cook was attacked and suffered a fractured jaw.[52] Captain J. D. Ward of the *Constellation* identified sixteen blacks as "agitators" and initiated discharge procedures against six of them the next day. Rumors spread through the *Constellation* that 250 blacks would be eliminated from the ship's complement and given undesirable discharges. Violence followed; Ward reacted quickly to quell the disturbance but was eventually forced to leave twenty black crewmen on the shore.

On both ships, gangs of five to twenty-five blacks roamed the vessels attacking whites. On the *Kitty Hawk,* a large group of black sailors nearly engaged in an armed brawl with a marine detachment reaction team dispatched by the captain to quell the disturbances. Confusion reigned, and false reports circulated the ship that the captain had been either killed or injured by blacks on the hangar deck. The crisis was diffused largely by the ship's African American executive officer, Ben Cloud. Cloud separated the two factions and, by about 2:30 A.M., managed to end the fighting on board ship.

On both the *Constellation* and the *Kitty Hawk,* only black crewmen were charged and prosecuted for the violence, a typical pattern after many of the racial fights in the military. Only blacks were punished for the stockade riots at Da Nang, Long Binh, and Norfolk, and though whites were at least equally responsible for the rumbles at Millington Naval Air Station, Goose

Bay Air Force Base, Tien Sha, and Okinawa, as well as most of the other confrontations, no whites were ever punished.[53]

Black on White, White on Black

While large-scale confrontations of the type on the *Kitty Hawk* or at Camp Lejeune generated the greatest publicity, most of the racial violence in the armed forces involved only a few participants on each side. Often it consisted of one or two whites or blacks being accosted by a slightly larger number of assailants of the opposite race. The attacks almost always occurred at night and usually at a secluded location on one of the large defense installations. Most attacks were basically muggings, and many of the victims were beaten, then robbed.

The perception held by whites throughout the military was that blacks were responsible for most of the gang fights and the low-intensity racial warfare. One white marine in Germany was quoted as stating, "The statistical trend is obvious, it's blacks assaulting whites and the blacks are in groups."[54] A white soldier agreed, claiming "head-hunting" gangs of blacks made it unsafe for whites to enter the barracks alone at night. "I'm much more afraid of getting mugged on the post than I am of getting attacked by the Russians," another soldier added. Kelly Hill, one of the barracks areas at Fort Benning, Georgia, was the scene of so many black-on-white attacks that a white enlisted man bitterly remarked, "Kelly Hill may belong to the commander in the daytime, but it belongs to the blacks after dark."[55]

In Vietnam Captain Shrader's unit had several "random attacks" on white soldiers, including "one white soldier beaten senseless and in the hospital" and "another one knifed and damned near dead" during one particular incident.[56] At Da Nang such assaults were so frequent that, according to Captain (later Major) Bruce Cary, "we had some real problems . . . they had attacked a white officer at night and we had to have people traveling in groups of two or three within the group area at night."[57] Captain (later Major) Thomas Cecil recalled one incident at Cam Ranh Bay during his 1970–71 tour of duty in Vietnam, where a "racial problem finally culminated in a group of blacks going up to the enlisted men's club one night . . . and I think all they wanted to do was choke a few people up because they came up to the club, and they threw four or five smoke grenades inside. . . . Unfortunately, they were white phosphorous and they ended up burning a whole bunch of people, some civilians, some girls were in there and one of the troops ... died." A black soldier from Cecil's company was then charged with murder in connection with the incident.[58] In Bien Hoa and Dong Tom, Wallace Terry reported, "roving gangs" of black troopers "waylaid unsuspecting whites," and at Chu Lai, white officers were severely beaten after refusing to give jeep rides to black marines.[59]

White officers were frequently the target of black violence, and in Vietnam in particular, where weapons were plentiful and soldiers commonly went armed, those attacks often were in the form of "fraggings." Fragging was the deliberate attempt by enlisted personnel to kill a superior officer, and the practice derived its name from the fact that soldiers favored the use of fragmentation grenades to accomplish their purpose. In Vietnam grenades were plentiful and left no incriminating evidence, such as fingerprints, and unlike bullets, they could not be traced through ballistics tests. The most common method of fragging involved wiring several grenades to the door of an officer's hooch or the officer's latrine. The culprit or culprits did not have to be in the vicinity when the grendaes exploded, and because nearly all combat soldiers knew how to construct such booby traps—or "rat traps," as they were called—the list of suspects was endless. Captain (later Major) Richard Barnes in 1971 assumed command of a field artillery company in Vietnam in which there had been attempted fragging on both the previous commanding officer and the white first sergeant.[60] Captain (later Major) Henry Parker was informed that his predecessor had been fragged, and there was at least one attempt on his life.[61] Lieutenant Charles Anderson wrote to his parents in disgust about the "black trash" who killed two of his fellow officers,[62] and Captain (later Major) Thomas Peoples recalled a "racially motivated attempt in the company next door."[63]

Captain (later Lieutenant Colonel) Vernon Conner related an attempt on his life at Long Binh in 1970. By spring the company was "relatively inactive ... as a result, there was a considerable amount of drinking and too much spare time. I had a conflict about a week before with some whites and some blacks and I stopped in a hootch with a front door and a back door." Luckily, instead of going through the front entrance as usual, Conner entered through the rear door. He quickly discovered the front had been booby-trapped, a "rat trap with a live grenade in it."[64] Captain (later Major) Richard Bevington had so little trust in his own men that he slept with a loaded .45 under his pillow.[65] Captain Cecil was so worried about attacks on his life that during his last month in Vietnam he slept in the military intelligence (MI) bunker, and only his battalion commander knew where he was at night.[66]

Bevington and Cecil were not overreacting, and many officers took precautions against what was often a real and tangible danger. By May 1971 the *Pittsburgh Courier* could report with accuracy that many white officers were "cowed" by threats of fragging.[67] The Department of Defense began to keep track of fragging incidents in 1969, and the numbers confirmed the serious nature of the problem. There were 126 reported cases in 1969 and 271 in 1970. The worst year was 1971 with 333 incidents. Between 1969 and 1972 the department documented a total of 788 fraggings or attempted fraggings. A congressional investigation arrived at an even higher figure, reporting a total of 1,016 incidents during the same period.[68]

Again, more often than not it was an African American that was usually charged and convicted for a fragging. In a well publicized case, Melvin X. Smith was found guilty of murder and sentenced to life in prison in 1971 for shooting two whites in Vietnam;[69] similarly, the same year the army developed a ballistics test of dubious accuracy for hand grenades in its successful attempt to convict Billy Dean Smith of a fragging that occurred in South Vietnam.[70] But the charge that blacks were largely responsible for the fraggings was grossly inaccurate, as was the belief that blacks were to blame for much of the racial violence, whether the large-scale confrontations or the more individual attacks that were endemic in the military.

To begin with, not all fraggings were racially motivated. In hearings on "Attempts to Subvert the United States Armed Forces," former chief of personnel and administration for Military Assistance Command, Vietnam (MACV), Brigadier General Lawrence Greene, discounted any racial motivation or any serious underlying causes for the fraggings. Indeed, Greene dismissed the problem as "not serious" and told the congressional committee that fraggings could be attributed to "personality" and "personal factors," such as bad news from home or a "buddy getting killed," bringing out "latent characteristics."[71] Greene was, of course, wrong. Fragging was a serious concern, and racism, not "personality" or "latent characteristics," was often the reason; but there were other causes.

Drugs and drug abuse, particularly the use of heroin, were major problems in the military, especially in Vietnam, and officers who sought to eliminate drug users and drug dealers from their units often were the targets of fraggings. Many believed that the real cause of the fraggings was the tremendous availability of drugs; and most of the abusers were white.[72] Still, ironically, it was the use of drugs in some units, especially the use of marijuana, that bridged the gap between the races. In many companies there was no group solidarity based primarily on race; rather, the units divided according to choice of recreational drugs. Generally, whites and blacks who used marijuana—"heads"—fraternized together and fought the "juicers," whose primary recreational drug was alcohol. Almost all the juicers were white, career officers or NCOs, Southern and rural and favored country-and-western music over soul or rock. Even though the attempt on his life was triggered by a racial incident, Conner believed that both blacks and whites in his company were involved, and he suspected his attempts to curb drug use among his men were the real provocation for the attack.[73] The fragging of a white in Raymond Wells's company was listed officially as a racial incident, but everyone in the unit knew "it was just one of those things" over a drug deal that had gone sour. No one in the unit saw it as racially motivated.[74]

Soldiers of both races also fragged officers for what the soldiers believed to be faulty or callous combat command decisions that had resulted in excessive or unnecessary casualties. Zealous young officers who rejected the advice of older or more experienced combat veterans and ordered their men into ambushes or meaningless firefights were favorite targets. Entire companies might be involved, and "bounties" of anywhere from fifty to one thousand dollars might be placed on the head of the intended victim. After the costly and largely futile assault on "Hamburger Hill" in the A Shau Valley in 1969, many of the soldiers involved publicly offered a ten-thousand-dollar reward for the fragging of the officer who had ordered the attacks, Lieutenant Colonel Weldon Honeycutt. Despite several attempts on his life, Honeycutt survived his tour of duty and returned safely to the United States.[75]

The same problems the command structure had in determining whether a fragging was racially motivated or due to another cause also applied to many of the smaller-scale racial confrontations. Often a fight or an argument between a white and a black had nothing to do with race but might be considered a racial incident. While serving aboard the USS *Hartley,* navy machinist mate Alfonza Wright got into a fight with a "big, burly Italian named Bruno," who responded to Wright's order to "get to work," with a "Look nigger, . . . ," but Wright contended that the fight was over "Bruno's" refusal to work and not the racial slur. Corporal Dale Reich got into a fight with a black cook in a beer line, but this confrontation also had nothing to do with race. Reich's sense of "fair play" had been offended when the cook cut in front of him in line; the corporal didn't realize at the time that the cook had been given permission to do this because he had just completed his work shift.[76] Clinton Hunt said many of the confrontations in his unit

Allen Thomas, Jr., and Ray Smith, sitting on top of a bunker at Dakto, Vietnam, 1967.
Photo courtesy of Allen Thomas, Jr.

Allen Thomas, Jr., at Dakto in November 1967, during his second tour of duty in Vietnam. Photo courtesy of Allen Thomas, Jr.

A young Alfonzo Wright at Guantánamo Bay, Cuba, while serving with the pre-Vietnam U.S. Navy. Photo courtesy of Alfonzo Wright.

Sergeant Alfonzo Wright shortly before retiring from the army in 1993. Photo courtesy of Alfonzo Wright.

African Americans often found it easier to cut each other's hair than to trust military barbers, many of whom were not trained to cut black hair correctly. Photo courtesy of the U.S. Army Military History Institute.

In Vietnam, African Americans gained overdue recognition as good soldiers and the equals of their white comrades on the battlefield. Here, a young black trooper confidently mans an M60 machine gun. Photo courtesy of the U.S. Army Military History Institute.

Soldiers in Vietnam combat units often displayed a cohesion and camaraderie between the races that was missing from support units or among those stationed stateside. Here, an African American stands guard over a wounded white comrade. Photo courtesy of the U.S. Army Military History Institute.

Black soldiers often wove "slave bracelets" out of bootlaces and wore them as a sign of racial solidarity and pride. Note the slave bracelet on the man in the center. Photo courtesy of the U.S. Army Military History Institute.

African Americans won their share of recognition and awards in Vietnam. Here, air force general Moore presents the Air Medal to Specialist Six Williams. Photo courtesy of the U.S. Army Military History Institute.

Colonel Frederic Davison (left), the first African American to command an army battalion in Vietnam, confers with other officers. Photo courtesy of the U.S. Army Military History Institute.

Soldiers of all races decorated their helmets with slogans, and those of African Americans often carried a statement of black power or black pride. This one, covered with names, reads, "We Enjoy Being Black." Photo courtesy of the U.S. Army Military History Institute.

African Americans often volunteered for the more elite units and the more dangerous assignments, as did this "lurp," or long-range reconnaissance specialist, on patrol in Vietnam in 1967. Photo courtesy of the U.S. Army Military History Institute.

African Americans often complained about the lack of black entertainers for the troops in Vietnam. Here, Ms. Black America is welcomed by GIs in February 1971. Note the "black power" salutes in the background. Photo courtesy of the U.S. Army Military History Institute.

Air force general Daniel "Chappie" James shortly before his retirement and early death in 1978. Photo courtesy of the U.S. Army Military History Institute.

were just "fights between individuals" and nothing more.[77] James Hawkins's fight with a white sergeant was over the sergeant's dog.[78] Captain (later Major) Michael Colacicco found that a lot of the superficially racial problems in his company were "just misunderstanding." One fight involved "a black guy and a white guy" who were actually "very good friends."[79]

The same tendency to view all trouble between blacks and whites as racially motivated contributed to the false belief that most of the violence was initiated by blacks against whites. Numbers can be distorted and inaccurate, and there were several reasons why the statistics appeared to support the conclusion that African Americans were usually at fault.

To begin with, whites were far more likely than blacks to report racial assaults. The command structure was overwhelmingly white, often racist, and usually apathetic to blacks' concerns. This was particularly true with regard to the military police and the shore patrol. With the exception of those in the air force, the vast majority of military police were white. Captain (later Major) O. J. Golphenee described his police battalion at Long Binh in 1970 as an elite unit composed of "ninety-five percent Caucasian males," and Golphenee's command was typical of MP detachments in its racial composition.[80] One black soldier in Germany explained that "a white guy, if some brothers jump on him, now he is going to report it because all his life he has been used to running to the authorities—to the police. If a brother goes to the police, he knows he isn't going to do anything for you noway. So what's the use of going to him? The brothers don't even bother with the police." Instead, blacks were likely to try to solve the problem without recourse to the authorities. "You got to consider something about those crime statistics," the soldier added. "The brothers got a lot of pride in a lot of things, see. If I went outside and three white guys jumped on me, I'm not going up there and tell the desk sergeant. I'm going home and get some brothers together and come back." A white marine private stationed at Camp Lejeune agreed that blacks were far more likely to retaliate to white violence through collective action than to report an incident to the command structure. "The reason you people are so tight," he told a black reporter, "is because of needs in the past. We [whites] don't have this, we can act as individuals."[81]

Many cases of black-on-white violence were in retaliation for incidents initiated by whites. At Tan Son Nhut Air Base near Saigon, a white described as a "race baiter and a bully," was shot and wounded by a black whom he had been stalking and taunting with shouts of "I'm going to kill you, nigger."[82] Captain Cecil described an endless cycle of "small gang wars going back and forth between companies. Blacks against whites, whites would attack blacks, Hispanics would attack blacks, and it was a constant give and take which just went on."[83]

Despite the reluctance of African Americans to report racial assaults to military authorities, there is plenty of evidence that these attacks occurred; and blacks often were willing to talk to civilians about them. John Brackett, for example, recalled witnessing a Blackstone Ranger's being attacked by three whites outside a service club at Quang Tri in Vietnam,[84] and at Lai Khe two of John Williams's friends were assaulted by whites, and "one of them was almost killed by those dogs"; as usual, "they got full of their liquor and decided they would relieve their pressure by beating up the brothers."[85] In June 1968 three black GIs, James E. Bowen, Menriew Moore, and Elijah Witherspoon, were stabbed to death in Knielingen, West Germany, by two whites from Alabama who had spent the evening drinking in an all-white bar with fellow Southerners.[86] Reporter Wallace Terry, as well as the Reverend Jesse Jackson, the Congressional Black Caucus, and the NAACP, documented cases of racial violence aimed at blacks and instances in which whites were at least equally culpable to blacks in instigating a fight.[87]

But white critics who sought to target blacks as responsible for racial hostilities usually ignored the evidence. Representative Floyd Hicks (D-Washington), who chaired the House committee investigating the *Kitty Hawk* and *Constellation* incidents, dismissed the rioters as "a very few men most of whom were of below average mental capacity . . . and all of whom were black." "Lt. John Paul Jones," who declined to sign his real name to an article in the *National Review*, casually dismissed black complaints of institutional and personal racism in the navy and blamed navy "permissiveness" and black militants for causing racial violence. And Colonel Robert D. Heinl, Jr., whose publications reflected the views of most white career military personnel, detailed numerous examples of black-on-white violence in an article for the *Armed Forces Journal* but conveniently neglected to mention even one instance of whites attacking blacks.[88]

The reality was that it was just as likely for a white to start trouble as for a black, and that by 1969 racial violence was one of the most critical problems facing the military. Westmoreland claimed in 1969 that racial confrontations had reached a "serious stage" in the army, and it was the same for all the services.[89] At Camp Lejeune in 1968, for example, more than 160 racial assaults were recorded, and a biracial committee of seven officers charged with investigating racial tension at the post warned that "an explosive situation of major proportions has been created and continues to be aggravated." As one white marine at Lejeune remarked, "Violence is our only meeting ground now."[90]

Solidarity in Combat

As serious and widespread as the problem of racial violence was, it was not everywhere; many units had few racial problems. This was particularly true for active combat units in Vietnam. As late as 1970, the *Baltimore Afro-American* could confidently report that there was a "total absence of racial unrest" at the frontline firebases.[91] There was, of course, some racial friction in the frontline companies, but it resulted in very little overt violence. Survival in combat usually depends on teamwork and cooperation, and this forced blacks and whites in combat units to develop the cohesion often lacking in the support units. Marine Corps historians Henry Shaw and Ralph Donnelly admitted that "there were racial incidents and confrontations in rear areas in Vietnam," but they stressed that "these disruptions did not extend to the sectors of fighting where the color of a person's skin was of no import to his role as a combat Marine."[92] A survey of 126 black and 359 white returning Vietnam veterans, conducted in the late 1960s by sociologists Byron G. Fiman, Jonathan F. Borus, and M. Duncan Stanton found that "black-white relations were reported to be better in Vietnam than in the United States, especially among soldiers who served in actual combat."[93] And in August 1968 veteran reporter Thomas Johnson wrote that "as it happens in any situation of great stress, racial differences between blacks and whites have disappeared on the fighting fronts. At the front, the main thing is to stay alive and you do this most often by depending on the man next to you."[94]

Combat and the threat of death are great equalizers, and both white and black veterans who served in line companies have claimed there was a solidarity and camaraderie between the races. Doris "Lucki" Allen described a "togetherness that I think you can only get in times of peril," and Major William Riederer, who commanded two different infantry companies in Vietnam in 1969, recalled, "I never really felt there was any tension. . . . We pretty much operated on everybody pull their own and everybody was liable to go out and get shot and everybody would go out and get shot at."[95] A black paratrooper from the 173d Airborne Brigade reflected, "When you drink out of the same canteen and eat off the same spoon, you get real tight together."[96] Henry Dority recalled it was "stick together or die together."[97] Cecil F. Davis had some problems in a Signal Corps company he commanded, but in the infantry company he led in Vietnam, he had "absolutely nothing, we were all in there together."[98] James Hawkins agreed: "In the jungle, you don't think in terms of black and white . . . it doesn't matter, it can't matter. . . . Out in the jungle thirty, forty days at a time, we just thought of each other, together."[99]

Other factors, in addition to the demands of combat operations, helped keep racial friction and hostility to a minimum. Some of the companies engaged in direct action against the enemy, such as long-range reconnaissance and air cavalry units, were considered elite formations, and the men in these commands tended to be highly trained and motivated volunteers. They generally had a high degree of unit cohesion and a clear and commonly shared sense of mission. Richard H. Torovsky, Jr., who captained an air assault company that specialized in counterguerrilla operations in 1970–71, was proud of the state of race relations in his command: "I want to comment specifically on drug abuse and racial strife, mainly from the fact that I don't think they were in my unit." Torovsky added that the vast majority of his men were excellent soldiers; "sleeping together, fighting together, being dirty together, and them playing together," he saw "very little problem with the soldiers . . . getting along."[100] Major Patrick Carder claimed:

> My company didn't have too much of it [racial problems] because . . . we were . . . what could have been considered a rather elite company. All the personnel in the company were Airborne. They were all parachute riggers. Because the requirements for parachute rigger school required individuals to have a pretty high I.Q. just to get in, the people were fairly smart and didn't get into the racial problems. They tended to join together regardless of race, color, or creed.[101]

Max V. Terrian, a first lieutenant (later Major) in a reconnaissance and surveillance company, also cited his unit's elite status as the major reason that they "didn't have any racial strife problems," claiming, "Morale was good, everyone was hand-picked, and they knew they were hand-picked."[102]

Throughout the armed forces, racial problems generally occurred during off-duty hours, and companies engaged in active operations had a lot of work and very little spare time. James Hawkins, recalling the boredom and tedium of combat operations, said it was "just get up in the morning and hump [march], just shoot and get shot at, and hump."[103] Remembering his tour as a Lieutenant in Vietnam, Richard Anshus admitted, "We'd rather be out in the field. We had fewer personnel problems."[104] Because Captain (later Major) Robert Arnold's frontline ordnance company had a "good work schedule" and "the troops kept busy," there was little opportunity for racial friction to develop.[105] Bruce Cary said the "tensions did not build up" in his transportation company "because my unit was working, the guys were kept extremely busy for twelve hours a day and we were pretty tired at night and have a couple of beers and go to bed."[106]

Finally, most enlisted men and officers realized that in a combat unit, where everyone was extremely well armed, it was simply too dangerous to allow racial friction to escalate into racial violence. Raymond Wells could not identify with Angela Davis, Huey Newton, and many of the other radical leaders who preached armed rebellion against whites, because these people were "not dealing with my situation; I was already armed," but so were the whites, he explained.[107] One black army soldier serving in the Ninth Division summed it up simply and eloquently: "You know when I am out in the bush carrying a grenade launcher, no white man is going to call me nigger."[108]

The Importance of Leadership

Like the active combat units, many of the support units serving in Vietnam also experienced very few racial problems. Again, there tended to be less racial friction in those formations that had a clearly defined mission, lots of work, good morale, and a more elite status than the average company. Captain (later Major) Steven Townsend, for example, had no major racial problems in his communications company; his men, who were mostly "technician types," had good morale despite working long hours.[109] But there was one major difference between these and the combat units: in support units, much more than in combat units, the quality of leadership was often an important influence in determining the level of racial friction.

Unit cohesion was virtually forced on troops in combat because of the battle conditions, but in support units, where there was no immediate threat or common enemy to unite the men, a strong, fair and decisive commanding officer, assisted by competent NCOs was a necessity in preventing racial violence. Many officers found they could reduce racial tension and keep it to a minimum just by listening to their men and taking their complaints seriously. Robert Arnold took command of a company with "some serious racial problems" but greatly reduced tensions by "getting in and talking with my people and establishing some working coun-sels."[110] Richard Barnes had some racial tension in the field artillery com-pany he captained, but "when we did, we would get the principals out and discuss it. It was out in the open and not festering underneath. . . . My approach was to get them together, the two individuals who were fighting . . . have them talk through their problem. If they wanted to go slug it out, we would work something out. But if they articulated it, we were really able to diffuse it."[111] Michael Colacicco also had rap sessions with his men and "race relations councils" to diffuse tensions in his company, but like most officers, with mixed degrees of success: "We had these rap sessions once a month, we would pull everybody in and we talked about race. That's invitation to a riot because the tensions were there. It was supposed to be cathartic, everybody talk out their problems and then I'd end up having a fight on my hands." Despite his genuine attempts to ease racial tensions, conditions in his unit became so bad that at one point he had to "walk out in the middle of the company street," where there were, "a hundred guys on one side of the street and a hundred guys on the other side of the street and they were getting ready to square off," to stop a racially motivated gang fight among his troopers.[112]

Good communication between officers and men was an important factor in diffusing racial tensions, but as Colacicco's experience demon-strates, it was not a guarantee of success. In addition to the ability to talk with his men, a commanding officer needed fair and competent noncommissioned officers. Without a loyal and effective chain of com-mand, it was difficult for any commanding officer to ensure fair and equal treatment for the personnel under his authority. Colacicco's policies were undercut by the fact that he did not have enough officers and NCOs in his company, and many of those he did have were racists. Donald Dean had a racial problem in his quartermaster unit, "instigated" by his racist first sergeant,[113] and Major James Love described his first sergeant as a "worth-less alcoholic."[114] Captain (later Major) Richard Bevington also attempted to deal with racial problems through better communication with his sol-diers but often found his efforts undercut by his company NCOs. He considered them "generally no help," white or black. One of his African American sergeants was ridiculed and nicknamed "Oreo" by the men, and his white NCOs were afraid to go into the enlisted-men's section at night.[115]

Conversely, units with strong officer and NCO leadership throughout the chain of command tended to have fewer racial problems than did units with poor leadership. Private Henry Dority could not recall any serious racial conflict in his company and said that most of his NCOs were black and "cool," as were some of the white sergeants.[116] Lieutenant Colonel Joseph DeFrancisco experienced "almost no racial strife" in his field artillery battery, in part because of a "very strong chain of command,"[117] and Bruce Cary also had very few problems because of "real strong" and competent sergeants and squad leaders in his company.[118]

Many officers, in fact, considered racial hostility to be nothing less than a leadership problem, and those men who were considered strong but fair commanders did seem to experience fewer problems than those who questioned their own abilities. Captain (later Major) John Ellis claimed, "I don't think there was a [racial] problem, so much as a leadership problem,"[119] and Major Henry Koren, Jr., felt he was "very fortunate in taking over both" his company commands "from strong commanders" who had established good race relations in both units.[120]

A creative approach to race relations also helped. Major Michael Yap was able to alleviate racial friction in his artillery battery by exploiting his Japanese ancestry. Yap explained to his men that as an Asian, he was "right in the middle, and if you want to talk minorities, I'm a minorities minority. I think from that standpoint, both sides looked to me at the middle and I really did not have a problem."[121] The appropriately named Captain (later Major) James Love cured both the racial tension and a troubling epidemic of venereal disease in his unit by establishing a "whorehouse" for his men, after the local EM and NCO clubs had been closed due to repeated racial clashes. "It may or may not have been legal," Love admits, but it helped to solve both problems.[122]

Good leadership abilities and a bit of ingenuity helped Thomas Peoples diffuse a potentially disastrous situation at Cam Ranh Bay in 1969–70. Peoples was given command of an ordnance company composed largely of misfits, troublemakers, and military offenders. "My biggest problem was the quality of troops I got," Peoples remembered. "My first fifty men came out of Long Binh jail in leg irons, they were survivors of the Cam Ranh race riot in 1969." Peoples proceeded to create a chain of command by making several of the men acting buck sergeants; he instituted strict but fair discipline and made sure everyone knew the rules. He explained the company's mission to his men—retrieving damaged battlefield equipment—and helped generate a sense of esprit de corps in the company, which the troops soon nicknamed the "Peoples Army." Peoples did have some racial friction in the unit but solved the problem by lining up "all the white guys on one side and all of the blacks on the other and told them to have at it," while Peoples and his first sergeant watched. His men were too embarrassed to fight, and "that was the end of racial trouble in the company."

About a month later, Captain Peoples's policies helped prevent a racial gang fight in a neighboring company from spreading to his command. When the fight developed in the adjacent unit, Peoples's troopers "fell out with their beer and sodas, and set on the side of the hill and watched it, not a single one of my men became involved in the action over there. They were not at all disposed to join in the general anarchy." At the end of his tour, Peoples was most proud of the fact that all fifty of his original recruits from Long Binh jail remained out of the stockade and honorably completed their tours in Vietnam. All of them returned home with a rank of E-4 or above.[123]

Peoples, Yap, Arnold, and Love all demonstrated that a good officer could deal effectively with racial problems in his command; but they were exceptions. Most officers simply did not have the training, experience, or temperament to deal with interracial friction, and instead of alleviating the tension, they often made it worse. Cecil admitted that "anarchy reigned" in his company and that "it was certainly ... much worse in May of 71 when I left than it was in May of 70 when I got there."[124] Another officer also confessed that racial conditions had deteriorated under his command but was more concerned with the potential negative effect this would have on his efficiency report than with his inability to deal with the problem.[125]

It was usually up to the company grade officers—junior lieutenants, first lieutenants, and captains—to cope with racial problems in their units. But these officers were young, sometimes not much older than the men they led, and in many cases, their tour in Vietnam was their first command experience. The vast majority were white, and until they joined the armed forces, they'd had little interaction with African Americans or their culture. Eugene White, Jr., was only twenty-one years old when he first went to Vietnam in March 1970; within a few months, he became a company commander. For White, the problem was that "not only was I in a combat environment having to do with these military things, but I was trying to learn about people ... I had no experience, up to that point in my life, of even trying to relate to. Because being from a military family and middle class background, I didn't associate with lower class blacks."[126] Gary Tucker admitted, "I didn't really understand it. ... I was only twenty-four or twenty-five years old. I wasn't raised around blacks so all this was new to me."[127] Thomas Cecil had been in the army only two years when he assumed command of his ordnance company at Cam Ranh Bay; he had "thought I knew everything there was to know about people," only to admit later that he just "wasn't prepared to handle" racial problems.[128]

In addition to being young and inexperienced, many officers were simply incompetent. The expansion of the armed forces during the Vietnam War era meant the military needed to increase greatly the size of its officer corps, and this was accomplished by reducing the standards for officer candidate school. The most striking example of the products this policy is Lieutenant William Calley, whose unit was responsible for the massacre of Vietnamese at My Lai. There were thousands of officers who, like Calley, might not have been awarded commissions had the standards not been lowered.

But even those officers who were competent and hardworking were facing a difficult task—one not of their making, and one they had not been adequately prepared to handle. In 1971 the Department of Defense established the Defense Race Relations Institute, and within a year, more than seven hundred instructors had been trained to conduct a mandatory eighteen-hour course on race relations for officers and NCOs.[129] But many officers, especially before 1971, never received any training in race relations. James Hollis, who commanded an armored company in 1968, said the chain of command was not even aware of racial problems, much less trained to deal with them.[130] Major Clay Melton served in Vietnam in 1971–72, after race relations courses had been instituted, but could not recall racial problems "ever being addressed at all, nothing,"[131] and Thomas Cecil admitted he "was just totally untrained to handle racial problems," adding, "I don't think anybody around senior to me was in much better shape."[132]

Other officers doubted the effectiveness of race relations training. Field artillery captain Richard Barnes claimed he was aware of what he "was getting into because I had seen a film and had been subjected to considerable training on this in our basic course" but credited his "training with the Boy Scouts as I was growing up" with putting him "in much better stead" to handle racial problems.[133] Peoples believed his background, not his military training, allowed him to deal effectively with his African American troops. "I was from the city of Cleveland," the major explained; "I was raised on the street, and I know how to operate on the street, and I operated with those guys."[134]

Black Officers and Leadership

Another problem, in addition to the officers' lack of training and experience, was the racial makeup of the officer corps. There were too few black officers in command assignments, and especially in senior decision-making positions, to have much impact on military race relations. A certain distance and distrust usually existed between officers and men anyway, but the issue of race widened the gap between white officers and black enlisted personnel to a gulf. Most African Americans believed that the presence of more black officers would alleviate some of this distrust, help guarantee more equal treatment for blacks, and reduce racism between black and white. Captain Charles Smith told the Congressional Black Caucus that if "black officers in the military had the proper backing, eighty percent of the racism in the military would not exist at the troop level." In an October 1972 interview, Major Edward L. Green, the first black marine assigned to the faculty of the U.S. Naval Academy at Annapolis, Maryland, stressed the importance of recruiting more African American officers. Green stated it was of "paramount importance to correct the under-representation of blacks in the officer structure of the services. Until we achieve an adequate black officer distribution throughout the command and policy making levels, the basic fairness of the entire institution will remain in doubt." The NAACP came to the same conclusion, finding in one study that "among the recommendations of Negro enlisted men for improving race conditions in the military, the need for more black officers was high on the list. In other words, Negro servicemen strongly urged that one method of overcoming race discrimination in the Army would be by placing black officers in command positions where white junior officers would be accountable to them." [135]

The need for more black officers may have been apparent, but during the Vietnam War era, the percentage of African Americans in the officer corps would not rise significantly. In 1962 blacks constituted slightly less than 2 percent of the officer corps in all the armed services; ten years later, they still accounted for only 2.3 percent. [136] Throughout the war years the percentage of African American officers remained close to the 1968 total of 2 percent, when out of more than 400,000 officers in the military, only 8,325 were black. [137] The army had the highest percentage of black officers, but its percentages also barely changed during the war years: in 1962 there were 3,150 black army officers, or 3.2 percent of all army officers; a decade later there were 4,788 black officers, but this was out of an officer corps that numbered more than 150,000 men and women, meaning African Americans still made up less than 4 percent of the total.[138]

Though African Americans accounted for less than 4 percent of the officer corps in the army, this percentage compared quite favorably to those in the other services. Before 1973, in no other branch of the armed forces did African Americans account for even 2 percent of the officers. There were only thirty-two black officers in the Marine Corps in 1962, barely 0.21 percent of the total.[139] By 1967 there were 155 African American officers in the Corps, but this was out of a total of 23,000 marine officers. By 1972 the number of black marine officers had nearly doubled, reaching 285, but this was still only 1.5 percent of the total. Only after direct American involvement in the war ended did blacks account for slightly above 2 percent of all officers in the Corps. By 1973 there were 378 black officers, including 11 women, accounting for 2.03 percent of the total.[140]

The numbers for the air force were not much different. In 1962 the 1,300 black air force officers represented only 1.24 percent of that service's officer corps; by 1972 the 2,124 blacks holding commissioned rank still were only 1.7 percent of the total. In contrast, blacks made up 12.6 percent of the air force's enlisted personnel, slightly below the 13 percent average of black enlisted personnel in the entire armed forces.

The navy had the lowest percentage of black officers of any of the services throughout the war years. In 1962 the 174 African Americans holding navy commissions accounted for a mere 0.24 percent of the total. Ten years later the number had more than tripled, reaching 660, but this was in an officer corps that numbered more than 76,000 men and women, which meant blacks constituted only 0.9 percent of the total.[141]

The shortage of black officers was even more pronounced in senior command and staff positions. As late as 1968, only 2 out of the 1,342 admirals and generals in the armed forces were black, and out of 8,335 active-duty black officers only 2,524 were field grade, holding the rank of major or above, and only 65 held the rank of colonel or above. But the gains made by African Americans at the field grade level were appreciably better than their achievements at the company grade level.[142]

With regard to blacks holding senior rank, the army again had the best record in the armed forces. In 1962 there were no black generals in the army, the first—and to that date, the only—black general in the history of the army, Brigadier General Benjamin O. Davis, Sr., having retired in 1954. The highest-ranking African Americans in the army at the time were six colonels, followed by 117 lieutenant colonels and 424 majors.[143] It was not until 1968, fourteen years after Davis retired, that one of the more promising of the then forty-two black colonels, Frederic Ellis Davison, was promoted to flag rank.[144] By 1972 there were seven black brigadier generals and two major-generals, including Davison; there were also ninety-three black colonels, and more important, twenty black senior officers had been chosen to attend the elite senior service schools, where officers were trained for the more important command and staff positions.[145]

The air force's 1962 record was comparable to the army's, in terms of the numbers of majors, lieutenant colonels, and colonels, but unlike the army, the air force did have a black general, Major General Benjamin O. Davis, Jr.[146] But Davis would remain the only black air force general until January 1970, when Colonel Daniel "Chappie" James was promoted to brigadier general. This increase in the number of black air force generals was only temporary. Davis, who had been promoted to lieutenant general, the highest rank attained by an African American at that time, retired on 1 February 1970, leaving James as the only black flag officer in the air force.[147]

In both the navy and marines, there were virtually no black senior officers until late in the war. In 1962 the three highest-ranking African Americans in the navy had obtained only the rank of commander.[148] As late as 1970, the navy had no black admirals and only three captains, and of these three only one, Samuel L. Gravely, Jr., was a line officer. One captain, Paul S. Green, was a doctor; the third, the highest-ranking black in the navy, Captain Thomas D. Parham, was a chaplain, and he had been appointed to that rank only in 1966.[149] Gravely finally became the first African American to hold flag rank in the navy when he was promoted to rear admiral in May 1971, but he would remain the only senior black line officer for the duration of the war.[150]

There would be no black Marine Corps generals during the Vietnam War. In 1962 seven captains were the highest-ranking blacks in the Corps, and as late as 1970, three lieutenant colonels, including Frank E. Petersen, Jr., and Kenneth H. Berthoud, Jr., held that distinction. There were no black female officers holding field grade commissions in the marines. As late as 1973, the highest-ranking African American woman officer in the Corps was Captain Gloria Smith.

The lack of black officers during the Vietnam War could be traced at least in part to America's segregated educational system. The same substandard education that worked to keep black enlisted personnel out of the more advanced and lucrative technical fields in the military also disqualified many African Americans who aspired to officer candidate school (OCS). A college education was usually a prerequisite to OCS, but few blacks could meet this requirement. During the war, only about 5 percent of the adult African American male population held college degrees.

But education was only one factor. Another was the ambivalence of the armed services toward increasing the number of black officer candidates. Though the potential manpower pool was admittedly small, the military displayed little interest in finding and recruiting qualified African Americans. In May 1967, after pressure from the assistant secretary of defense for manpower, the Marine Corps did name Lieutenant Colonel Kenneth H. Berthoud, Jr., the special adviser for minority officer procurement to the deputy chief of staff for manpower and charged him to double the number of black officers in the Corps. Using a variety of tactics, including sending qualified enlisted men to OCS, heavily using the media, and increasing the visibility of African American marines in the black community, Berthoud succeeded. But the goal set by the Corps was a modest one, and there were still fewer than three hundred black marine officers by the end of 1970.[151] The navy, for its part, by and large neglected to tap a potentially rich source of officer candidates: the black universities. Only in 1968, at Prairie View A. & M. in Texas, was the first naval Reserve Officers' Training Corps (ROTC) unit established at a predominantly black college. The value of this move was underscored by the fact the program attracted twenty-four candidates its first year.[152] In comparison, the army, which had the highest percentage of black officers in the military, had fourteen ROTC units operating on black campuses in 1970 and nineteen by 1972.[153]

The military's apathy toward recruiting African Americans was most apparent at the three service academies. Throughout the Vietnam War, blacks were chronically underrepresented among the cadet populations at Annapolis, West Point, and the Air Force Academy, and this despite the 1962 announcement by military officials of a new program to increase the number of black cadets and midshipmen. In 1968, at the height of American involvement in Vietnam, there were only seventeen black cadets at West Point and only ninety-seven African Americans out of ninety-eight hundred underclassmen at all three service academies. One black critic remarked that the numbers were "hardly evidence of a successful six-year campaign" to recruit more African American cadets.[154]

The problem was not that blacks were failing to take advantage of the opportunity to attend the academies; those who were appointed graduated at the same rates as did white cadets. The problem was that so few were being chosen to attend. Between 1969 and 1972, 18,782 whites but only 105 blacks graduated from the three institutions.[155] The situation did begin to change somewhat toward the end of the war. In 1971 fifty-three African Americans attended West Point, and in 1972 there were forty-five blacks in the first-year class at Annapolis (for a total of 150 black midshipmen at the academy) and twenty-five enrolled at the Air Force Academy.[156]

As bad as the numbers were for the service academies during the Vietnam War era, they were actually an improvement over previous years. When Benjamin O. Davis, Jr., graduated from West Point in June 1936, for instance, he became only the fourth African American to do so and the first since Charles Young in 1889. Annapolis did not graduate a black midshipman until 1949. The fact that before 1950, very few African Americans had graduated from the service academies or from other officer training courses contributed to the lack of black senior officers in the 1960s and early 1970s. Seniority was a very important criterion in achieving flag rank, and most officers promoted to brigadier general or rear admiral had at least twenty-five years of service behind them. Few blacks could claim that distinction.[157] African Americans were not even allowed to enlist in the Marine Corps until June 1942, and the navy began to accept black officer candidates only in January 1944. In the army and its Air Corps there were far more black officers—more than 7,768 by August 1945—but all but eight were company grade, and few would remain in the military. The importance of seniority should not be underestimated. Benjamin O. Davis, Jr., made brigadier in 1954 after only eighteen years of service, but he had served in both the Second World War and Korea, and promotions generally come faster during wartime. It also helped that he was a West Point graduate and the son of a general. Gravely had been one of the first fifty African Americans commissioned in the navy in 1945, and it took him slightly over twenty-six years to reach rear admiral.[158]

Serving a requisite number of years, however, was no guarantee of promotion to flag rank. Appointments to brigadier general or rear admiral were relatively few, and there was fierce competition. Only a tiny fraction of the eligible colonels in the army, air force, and marines and captains in the navy ever made the jump to a Silver Star. In 1967, for example, only twenty-three out of more than forty-two hundred eligible colonels in the army were promoted to brigadier general, and in 1971, Gravely was one of only forty-nine captains, out of more than two thousand in the navy, promoted to rear admiral.[159]

In addition to the normally rigorous selection process, black officers seeking promotion had to contend with racism and with an institutional reluctance in the armed forces to place African Americans in important staff and command positions. Until the late 1960s, for example, few blacks were chosen to attend the prestigious senior command schools. It was at institutions such as the Army War College or the Naval War College that promising officers on "fast-track" career paths were groomed for senior leadership positions. By 1968 only seven African Americans had attended any of the six advanced military schools, but the impact on their careers is apparent. Benjamin O. Davis, Jr., was the first. In 1949 he attended the newly established Air War College, and he retired a lieutenant general, the highest-ranking black officer to that date. Major General Frederic Davison graduated from the Army War College in 1962, and Gravely, the navy's first black admiral, attended the Naval War College from 1964 to 1965.[160]

A stint in a combat unit facilitated promotion, but blacks were often frustrated in their attempts to secure a combat command in Vietnam, or an equally important equivalent. A few were successful. Davison became the first black to lead an active combat brigade when he assumed command of the 199th Light Infantry Brigade in Vietnam in 1968.[161] The same year, the first black aviator in the Marine Corps, Lieutenant Colonel Frank E. Petersen, Jr., became the first African American to command either a navy or Marine Corps fighter squadron.[162] Also in 1968, in the air force, Vietnam veteran Colonel James E. P. Randall was in charge of flight-testing advanced fighter aircraft at Nellis Air Force Base near Las Vegas, Nevada,[163] and Lieutenant General Davis commanded the Thirteenth Air Force at Clark Air Force Base in the Philippines.[164] In 1972, "Chappie" James was named deputy assistant secretary of defense for public affairs, making him the second highest ranking black at the Pentagon.[165]

But more often than not, black officers found themselves assigned to insignificant duties or administrative assignments. In many cases they were not even adequately trained. One black officer, a "Captain Burns" who was wounded in Vietnam, found himself assigned to post headquarters at Fort Devens, Massachusetts, as a "snow removal" officer. Burns, who had been hospitalized for six months and was awarded the Silver Star for his service, bitterly remarked that the black officer was routinely assigned "these menial jobs except when he is in combat." He noted that a white officer in a new assignment was counseled "constantly, every time he makes a mistake, no matter how menial it may be . . . told what he has done wrong and what not to do. Whereas a black officer, he makes a mistake, nothing is said to him about it until efficiency report time comes around."

"Super-Soldiers"

To compensate for "dead-end" assignments and the slow promotion rate, black officers were often forced to become, in the words of one critic, "super-soldiers." They had to be more intelligent, more motivated, more patriotic, and more aggressive than white officers to get the same consideration for promotion.[166] Many did excel. When Davison was promoted to brigadier general, his superior, General Creighton Abrams, remarked, "No man has worked harder or deserves promotion more than General Davison." Still, Davison literally had to fight to get command of the 199th Light Infantry Brigade.[167] Lieutenant Colonel Petersen distinguished himself in this way as commander of Fighter Attack Squadron VMFA-314 in Vietnam, and his unit was awarded the Marine Corps's Hanson Award for the best fighter squadron in 1968.[168]

In spite of the obstacles, most black officers and senior NCOs were extremely patriotic and sincerely grateful to both the nation and the armed forces for giving them the chance to succeed. Their loyalty to the military was reinforced by the knowledge that civilian society would not have given them the same opportunity. Benjamin O. Davis, Jr., admitted to some discrimination in the armed forces but stated that the military was far less racist than any other institution in America, and he held himself and his father up as proof that blacks could succeed in the military.[169] When he was promoted to brigadier general, Frederic Davison praised the army for making "unbelievable progress against prejudice,"[170] and Daniel "Chappie" James, who made lieutenant general before his early death in 1978, commented, "It is strange not to be patriotic in a country that has afforded me as many opportunities as mine has."[171]

Their patriotism and loyalty to the system may have aided black officers in their quest for success and promotion, but they also alienated these officers from black enlisted personnel and greatly limited their ability to fight racism in the armed forces. Like their white contemporaries, black military career personnel tended to be conservative, and they viewed African Americans who accused the services of racism as militants and troublemakers. Samuel Gravely dismissed the black sailors responsible for the disturbances on the *Kitty Hawk* as "a bunch of youngsters who were going to do what they did regardless" of any racial reforms in the navy,[172] and

Davison told the *Pittsburgh Courier* he was against militants whether they were black or white, right-wing or left-wing.[173] At best, senior black officers were considered "neutral" on the issue of civil rights. Throughout his tremendously successful career, Lieutenant General Davis was never viewed by fellow blacks as a "racial reformer," though he often worked quietly and "behind the scenes" to aid black officers and enlisted personnel. Davis had few black friends and was rarely honored by black organizations. One writer in *Ebony* stated that "because of the general's neutral position on civil rights and his noninvolvement policy, his tremendous Air Force record has had little impact" on race relations.[174]

A sizable number of African Americans in the armed forces held a far more critical view of black career officers and NCOs. Cornelius Cooper, a 1969 West Point graduate and former army lieutenant, admitted that "if his uniform is always clean and pressed, if he is tougher than his contemporaries, if he can wheel and deal, if he is loyal to his immediate chain of command," a black officer could succeed in the military—but only at a price. Cooper said that even though "black officers, black NCOs end up becoming super soldiers . . . they are the most militaristic acting individuals in the Army. Many times they are more racist than their white counterparts."[175] Sergeant Milton White, founder of the Malcolm X Association in the air force, characterized Chappie James as "the only song and dance general in the history of the Armed Forces" and condemned the general for "being the first to be used to make speeches in repudiation of his own race in its revolutionary struggle" and for insinuating "that being an Uncle Tom is all right as long as he can share the company of such as Roy Wilkins."[176]

The distrust that black enlisted personnel displayed toward senior black officers was also directed at company grade officers and senior NCOs. Allen Thomas, Jr., claimed that many of the black NCOs were tougher on African Americans than the white NCOs. James Hawkins claimed that the black NCOs and officers in the army had to be "whiter than white" and displayed a "house nigger mentality." Their primary loyalty was to their careers and the military, not to their fellow blacks.[177] The senior NCO appointed as mediator to handle racial complaints after the fights at Tien Sha Naval Base was viewed as an "Uncle Tom" by blacks at that installation,[178] and another African American serving in Vietnam explained, "I had a black platoon leader—excuse me, I had a colored platoon leader— and everyone around him was white . . . so he was not about to help me."[179] In his final report to Congress as the army's chief of staff, Westmoreland admitted that "many young black soldiers" regarded black career military personnel "with the same distrust they had for white officers and soldiers."[180]

Despite these negative perceptions held by African American enlisted men, a greater number of black officers, especially in command positions, would have had a positive impact in addressing racial violence in the armed forces. It is also clear that most white officers would have been more successful in handling this problem had they been more experienced and received more or better training in race relations. But as important an officer's role was in controlling racial violence in his unit, his influence was ultimately limited. A good officer could improve race relations in his unit, and an incompetent or racist officer could make racial friction worse. But the factors that led to racial violence between blacks and whites were endemic in the armed forces and usually beyond the effective control of junior officers. Rather, it was the failure of senior military officials to take seriously the issues of personal and institutional racism and to deal effectively with them that led to the unprecedented outbreak of racial violence in the armed forces that began in 1968.

The Military Response

It is not that military officials were unaware of the problems. In August 1968, nearly a year before the deadly racial gang fight at Camp Lejeune, Marine Corps headquarters began tracking incidents "which might be considered as being basically racial" and delineated the factors that led to the violence. They realized that the violence was widespread; that it often occurred during off-duty hours, in service clubs or nearby drinking establishments; and that alcohol and racial slurs often "triggered" the confrontations. Much of this was confirmed in an April 1969 report prepared by a seven-officer team for the commanding officer of the Second Marine Division at Camp Lejeune, Major General Michael P. Ryan. The candid and explicit report detailed many of the racial problems facing the Corps. The officers claimed that "bigotry and prejudice were practiced in the corps. and by white businessmen in the adjacent community," and that "seniors placed obstructions in the way of young Marines seeking to grapple with the race problem." Specifically, the officers attributed the racial violence to a failure in leadership at both the junior and the senior level, stating that most officers and NCOs were "unenthusiastic" about enforcing existing Marine Corps directives concerning discrimination and equal opportunity policies. The report ended with the warning that "an explosive situation of major proportions has been created and continues to be aggravated."[181]

The House Armed Services Committee, after investigating the racial violence at Lejeune, came to similar conclusions. In its report, released in mid-December 1969, the committee found that a "deterioration of discipline" that took place at Lejeune had been caused by a "shortage of mature leadership," the result of rapid turnover of officers and NCOs, and that the "racial differences and misunderstandings . . . can be attributed in large measure to lack of effective communication at the junior levels of command as well as vertically between the young Marine and his commander." The committee did note, however, that "insufficient" precautions had been taken by the chain of command, "despite some warning of impending trouble." The committee concluded that "the same conditions that led to racial strife at Lejeune were also the root causes of similar disturbances at other bases."[182]

In the army, a report prepared for General William Westmoreland by a black staff officer, Lieutenant Colonel James S. White, in the summer of 1969 detailed many of the same problems, listing lack of effective leadership, racial polarization among enlisted personnel, and institutional racism as contributing to an "alarming" situation.[183] And in mid-September of the same year, a racially mixed fifteen-member human relations team headed by Deputy Assistant Secretary of Defense for Equal Opportunity Frank Render II, the highest-ranking African American at the Pentagon, repeated many of the criticisms found in the earlier studies, as did an air force study released in July 1971.[184]

But military officials were slow to respond to the crisis, despite the mounting evidence of racial unrest detailed in the reports and the warnings that more violence was likely. It is true that they had other, equally serious concerns competing for their time and energies. The war in Vietnam had become a quagmire, with no honorable solution in sight; morale was at an all-time low and substance abuse at an all-time high in the services. But it is also true that most whites simply did not care if the military discriminated against African Americans and they casually dismissed legitimate black concerns as nothing more than the complaints of a few militants and agitators. The military was also reluctant to admit its problems and tarnish its erstwhile favorable image with regard to race relations. As long as the problems were considered to be manageable and did not attract much attention outside the armed forces, military officials chose to limit their response. The Camp Lejeune report, for example, was never acted on because "it was considered too open and shocking," according to one officer on the human relations committee. For his work in uncovering and revealing racism and racial violence in the armed forces, Deputy Assistant Secretary of Defense Render was forced out of his post at the Pentagon.[185]

But military officials would be forced to react to racism and racial violence. The violence and frustration among African American personnel was threatening to disrupt the ability of the armed forces to perform its various missions efficiently, and just as important, it was beginning to attract interest from outside the military. As racial turmoil within the services began to make headlines, various interest groups and organizations, both inside and outside the armed forces, began to concern themselves with military racism. Some, such as the NAACP and the Congressional Black Caucus, did so out of genuine concern for black service personnel. Radical organizations, such as the Students for a Democratic Society and the Vietnam Veterans Against the War/Winter Soldier Organization, became involved because they viewed racism as yet another manifestation of America's corrupt political, economic, and social institutions. Other elements, such as the government of the Democratic Republic of (North) Vietnam, tried to use the issue of racism in the American armed forces for their own purposes. Even within the military, multiracial organizations such as the American Servicemen's Union (ASU) and the Movement for a Democratic Military (MDM) made racism one of their primary concerns and helped publicize the issue.

The military would react to correct its impaired efficiency and to counter its critics by finally taking vigorous action against institutional racism and racial violence within the ranks. It would be a twofold approach. First, the armed forces would institute much-needed reforms, aimed at eliminating any vestige of institutional racism and addressing the cultural needs of African American service personnel. But military officials would remain firmly convinced that many of the problems were caused by radicals and militants, and in addition to its legitimate reform efforts, the armed forces would also begin a ruthless campaign to eliminate militants and radical influences from the services.

6

"We Have a Problem"

The Military Response to Racial Violence and Radicalism

Military Reforms

As the 1960s came to a close and a new decade dawned, military officials were reluctantly forced to concede that they had not fully eliminated institutional racism from the armed forces, and that racial violence was now a crisis of the highest priority. After a two-week fact-finding tour of marine commands in Southeast Asia and the Pacific in the fall of 1969 by marine commandant General Leonard Chapman, the Corps senior officer admitted that "there is no question about it . . . we've got a problem. We thought we had eliminated discrimination in the Marine Corps and we are still determined to do so. It is apparent . . . that we've not been as successful as we thought."[1] The chief of naval operations, Admiral Elmo R. Zumwalt, Jr., was just as forthright as Chapman when he told reporters in 1972 that in previous years, "the Navy has made unacceptable progress in the equal opportunity area."[2] That same year, army chief of staff William C. Westmoreland described what he called a "regression in the excellent progress that had been made in racial harmony within the Army," explaining that the services had failed to keep pace with changes in civilian society.[3]

Determined to keep pace with advances in civil rights in the civilian sector, and anxious to restore their once-favorable image in this area, military officials launched ambitious reform programs in the late 1960s and early 1970s, aimed at accomplishing four separate but interrelated goals. First, they wanted to better enforce existing directives on discrimination and equal opportunity. Second, the military sought to eradicate all vestiges of institutional racism, particularly in the areas of testing, promotion, and the administration of military justice. Third, officials wanted to suppress and eradicate the racial violence that now seemed endemic in the armed forces.

But as much as officials saw the need for constructive reforms, the chain of command was equally convinced that many of their racial problems were caused by small numbers of influential radicals and dissidents. Hence, the fourth goal of military officials was to identify and eliminate African Americans whom command they considered to be militants and troublemakers.

In instituting racial reforms during the Vietnam War era, the one thing military officials did not have to ban was overt and officially sanctioned discrimination. Technically, racial discrimination as an institutionally sanctioned policy had been strictly outlawed in the armed forces since President Harry Truman's historic 1948 executive order, mandating "equality of treatment" for all service personnel regardless of race, color, religion, or national origin.[4] On the eve of direct American involvement in Vietnam, in July 1963, this commitment to equal opportunity was reiterated in a directive issued by Secretary of Defense Robert MacNamara. MacNamara called for all the services to follow Department of Defense guidelines concerning equal treatment and opportunity, and he stressed the need to eliminate the remaining vestiges of institutional racism in the armed forces and to combat the overt racial discrimination being practiced off base. The "MacNamara doctrine," as it was soon called, established the Department of Defense's racial policies for the next decade.[5]

With equal opportunity already established as official Department of Defense policy, most of the reforms instituted during the war years were aimed at eliminating specific areas and instances of racial discrimination. For instance, the military enacted numerous reforms in the administration of military justice. By 1972 all Article 15s given to personnel in the lowest four pay grades had to be published; personnel were to be fully informed of their rights, including the right to appeal or to demand a court-martial; and limits were placed on the use of pretrial confinement. Overcrowding was eased at most military prisons. The population at the Camp Pendleton Brig had been reduced from a high of more than one thousand prisoners in 1968 to fewer than five hundred in 1971. The population at Long Binh Stockade dropped from 739 to between 400 and 500 in the same period.

Trained penologists were assigned as prison wardens. At Long Binh, for example, the commanding officer in 1971, Lieutenant Colonel Paul Grossheim, held master's degrees in penology and criminology. Abusive guards were removed. According to Captain Sam Saxton, the assistant warden at Camp Pendleton, "When we see a guard go sour . . . he's out of here in seventy-two hours."[6]

Other measures sought to correct inequities in testing, placement, and promotion. The culturally neutral Army Classification Battery was introduced to replace the Eurocentric AFQT, and in 1970 army commanders were instructed to include "minority group representation" on all promotion boards.[7] In December 1970 affirmative action was extended to the armed forces. The army's affirmative action plan, implemented in 1972, contained 138 recommended changes and reforms designed to address the underrepresentation of African Americans in most military occupational specialties.[8] In addition, a goal of 15 percent minority representation in future officer candidate school classes and greater black participation in the senior command schools was set. Better attempts were made to stock post exchanges with black-oriented products, and post libraries began to carry works by black authors and on subjects of interest to African Americans.

To help ensure compliance with the reforms, more black officers were given assignments relating to military race relations. Air force brigadier general Daniel "Chappie" James, Jr., was named deputy assistant secretary of defense for public affairs in 1972, and Major General Frederic E. Davison was appointed chief of staff for enlisted personnel for the Seventh Army in Europe. Captain Curtis Smothers was made general counsel in the Pentagon and became the chief assistant to Don Miller, a black civilian who had recently been named deputy assistant secretary of defense for equal opportunity, replacing Frank Render II.[9]

Two of the most important innovations developed by military authorities in the late 1960s and early 1970s were the creation of race relations classes and programs and the training and placement of equal opportunity officers. By 1972 all four branches of the service and the Department of Defense would establish race relations institutes or councils, most would do so beginning in 1969. In April 1969, Secretary of Defense Melvin R. Laird established the Domestic Action Council and charged it with developing major race relations programs for implementation throughout the armed forces.[10] Two years later, this movement led to the establishment of the Defense Department's Defense Race Relations Institute at Patrick Air

Force Base, Florida. The main duties of the institute were to monitor race relations in the armed forces; to formulate programs aimed at easing racial tensions and ensuring equal opportunity; and to train officers and NCOs to conduct a new mandatory eighteen-hour race relations course. In 1972, its first full year of operation, the institute trained more than seven hundred equal opportunity officers, who were then assigned to various defense installations. In addition to their teaching duties, equal opportunity officers were to monitor compliance of Defense Department equal opportunity directives, investigate charges of racism and discrimination, and help promote good relations between the races.[11]

Both the army and Marine Corps also initiated servicewide race relations programs in 1969. At marine headquarters, an equal opportunity office was established to formulate new plans and programs, and the post of special assistant to the commandant for minority affairs was created and led by the senior black officer in the Corps, Lieutenant Colonel Frank E. Petersen, Jr. Three years later, on 1 July 1972, the Marine Corps Human Relations Institute was formally established at the Marine Corps Recruiting Depot in San Diego, California. Like the Pentagon's Race Relations Institute, the purpose of the Corps's new institute was to train instructors in teaching human relations programs and to "evaluate the effectiveness of the program at all organizational levels." Eventually, every marine, regardless of rank, would receive twenty hours of race relations courses and seminars developed by the institute.[12]

In the army, both Westmoreland and Secretary of the Army Stanley Resor made race relations a top priority in 1969. Resor made the need for improved race relations the dominant theme of his speech at the annual meeting of the Association of the United States Army, and in October, Westmoreland reiterated the army's "continued commitment to equal opportunity and treatment" in a new directive to all field commanders. The next month, Westmoreland ordered the Continental Army Command to develop a mandatory race relations course, initially for all junior, warrant, and noncommissioned officers but eventually extended to all enlisted personnel as part of their basic training. In 1970 the Department of the Army sponsored a series of seminars, at every major army installation in the continental United States, aimed at developing answers to the racial problems then plaguing the service. One of the results of the "frank discussion" at the seminars was the founding, in November 1971, of the Department of the Army Race Relations and Equal Opportunity Committee, staffed by general officers and charged with developing and administering servicewide equal opportunity and affirmative action programs.[13]

The air force and navy also developed race relations and equal opportunity programs, but in neither service were the programs as comprehensive or established as early as they were in the army and Marine Corps. The air force began in 1969 to assign at least one equal opportunity employment officer to each air force installation.[14] In 1971 the air force's then-established mandatory race relations course was expanded from four to nine hours and became part of both basic and OCS training, and a "human relations" institute was established as Lackland Air Force Base.[15]

Serious racial reform in the navy dated from Zumwalt's appointment as chief of naval operations in November 1970. Zumwalt, like Resor and Westmoreland in the army, made race relations and equal opportunity top priorities in the navy. Between 1970 and 1972, the navy began more than two hundred race-related programs and expanded and reconfirmed its commitment to existing ones. An African American, Lieutenant Commander William S. Norman, was named minority affairs assistant to Zumwalt and given the authority to investigate racially based complaints and to correct legitimate grievances. In June 1971 the navy established the Human Resource Project Office to oversee its new Race Relations Education Program. The program was designed to eliminate "racism from the United States Navy" and, in particular, to train race relations officers to conduct racial awareness and equal opportunity classes and seminars. A steady stream of navy operational directives—or "Z-Grams," as they were called—concerning race relations continued to flow from Zumwalt's office, and in November 1972, after the incidents on board the *Constellation* and the *Kitty Hawk,* the navy inaugurated "phase one" of a new race relations program. At the heart of the program was the training and assignment of race relations education specialists (RRES) who were to conduct classes and monitor navy equal opportunity and race relations programs throughout the service.[16]

In all the services, the equal opportunity or race relations officers commonly worked in conjunction with local race relations committees and coordinating groups, which existed on most defense installations. These committees usually emerged because of initiatives taken by local base commanders, and their creation often predated the establishment of formal, servicewide programs of a similar nature and mission.

The main task of the local base committees and coordinating groups was to ease racial tension and violence by improving communication between the command structure and African American and white service personnel. The committees proved to be one of the more successful innovations developed to ease racial problems and correct injustices. The Defense Department's Task Force on the Administration of Military Justice praised both local committees and servicewide equal opportunity programs as "an important key to reducing racial discrimination, or the perception thereof," throughout the armed forces.[17] Race relations coordinating groups started by Major General Orwin C. Talbot at Fort Benning, Georgia, were credited with diffusing racial tensions at that installation, and a racial relations committee established by Major General John C. Bennett, commanding officer of the Fourth Mechanized Division at Fort Carson, Colorado, "kept Carson cool for over a year" after racial unrest at that facility in 1970.

At Camp Lejeune, the scene of some of the worst racial violence in the armed forces, conditions began to improve after a series of reforms instituted by Second Marine Division commander Major General Patrick Ryan. On 27 June 1969, Ryan issued Division Order 5390.2, "Fostering Unit Pride and Esprit Within the 2nd Marine Division, FMF," in which he stressed the importance of communication between officer and enlisted personnel; detailed most of the causes of racial friction at the base; and outlined procedures by which complaints of discrimination could be handled. Ryan also introduced race relations committees and other reforms at the marine facility, and by 1971, one critic claimed that Ryan "appears to have turned off the race war that two years ago was clawing at the vitals of his division."[18]

In Vietnam, race relations committees also proved valuable in easing racial tensions. By November 1970 nearly 190 committees had been established by commanding officers in I-Corps, the northernmost section of the Republic of Vietnam. At Tien Sha, the local committee helped diffuse much of the racial tension that had rocked the facility. Often trouble could be avoided simply through better communication between blacks and whites and more flexibility and understanding on the part of both African Americans and the command structure. At Chu Lai, marine corporal Joseph Harris, the local race relations coordinator and a black militant, suggested to base officials that the installation commemorate the anniversary of Dr. Martin Luther King's assassination. The marine command responded to Harris's request by organizing a picnic and supplying food and soft drinks. What in the past what might have erupted into a violent demonstration was instead turned into a friendly outing.[19]

By 1972 military officials were optimistic that race relations programs, seminars, and officers had enabled the armed forces both to reduce the level of racial violence in the ranks and to address the grievances of black service personnel. The new Marine Corps commandant, General Robert E. Cushman, praised marine efforts to eliminate racial discrimination and prejudice in a 6 June 1972 letter to all general and commanding officers. Cushman wrote with pride that "our Corps is in the front line of the nation's effort to improve the areas of understanding and cooperation among all Americans. I view our human relations efforts as major steps in helping the Corps to attain that environment of equal opportunity, understanding, brotherhood, and professionalism so vital to our future effectiveness."[20]

That summer Chappie James, in his role as deputy assistant secretary of defense for public affairs, praised Secretary of Defense Melvin Laird's "real moral commitment to solving the problem" of racism and claimed "we have not solved it fully yet, but we are getting there." James stated that institutional racism had all but been eliminated from the services, but he admitted that a problem remained because "there are still individual practicing bigots in the services." He assured his audience that "if we catch any practicing bigot, he is dead, professionally in this service. We do not have any place for a commander who cannot be concerned about racism and have a commitment against it. Mr. Laird has stated there will be no more of that. And if we find them out, they will not command a latrine detail in this service anymore, anywhere, I can promise you. That is going to help solve it."[21]

Problems of Implementation

James was probably being a bit generous in his glowing assessment of the military's race relations and equal opportunity programs, but he was essentially correct. By late 1972, in all fairness, the armed forces had made tremendous progress in admitting to and attempting to eliminate institutional racism in the services. And as the general pointed out, the major problem was not in the substance of the reforms but in their implementation.

Where James erred was in his estimation that only a few "practicing bigots" remained to impede progress. As was the case with earlier reforms, the measures undertaken by authorities in the late 1960s and early 1970s were less than successful because there existed within the officer corps a widespread ambivalence toward racial reform. Throughout the chain of command, there was a failure of leadership to implement and enforce existing racial reforms and equal opportunity policies. Central to the success of most of the programs, for example, was the local equal opportunity officer. In most instances, however, the officer assigned these duties was not very enthusiastic or competent. The air force's human relations team, investigating racism in that service, in 1971 found "an enthusiastic, knowledgeable, communicative, imaginative and concerned individual that was the EO [equal opportunity] officer" at only three of the fifteen bases it visited.[22]

In addition, base commanders were often unenthusiastic about implementing new reforms. Curtis Smothers told Pentagon officials that he doubted local commanders in Europe would comply with new off-base housing regulations in 1971, because they had failed to enforce a similar directive in 1969. In 1972, Zumwalt issued several Z-Grams ordering local commanders to strictly enforce the navy's equal opportunity and racial awareness programs, warning them that a "response which lacks commitment from the heart is obstructionist."[23]

But even when a local base commander or equal opportunity (EO) officer attempted to enforce policy, he seldom received much support or direction from the senior command structure. The commanders and EO officers often discovered that military reforms were more form than substance. In the summer of 1970, Lieutenant Joseph H. Hall was assigned to organize an "equal opportunity seminar" at Fort Monmouth, New Jersey, and to write a report summarizing the results. Hall dutifully wrote and submitted his report to the chain of command, but as he remembered, "the response was unfortunately familiar—none." Eventually, a report summarizing the findings of all the seminars conducted at defense installations was sent back to Fort Monmouth by Army Material Command, but no recommendations were ever acted on and nothing was ever accomplished. The net result of the seminar program, according to Hall, was that it "produced one unhappy black Lieutenant-Colonel . . . and one interested Lieutenant."[24]

Hall's experience was typical of that of many officers involved in equal opportunity or race relations programs. The Task Force on the Administration of Military Justice found "a gap between verbal commitment" to equal opportunity programs and "physical support in terms of money, manpower and good management" for these measures.[25] In September 1970, Deputy Assistant Secretary of Defense for Equal Opportunity Frank Render II came to a similar conclusion. In his report for Secretary of Defense Laird concerning racial conditions at American defense installations in Europe, Render castigated the chain of command for its failure to enforce the military's equal opportunity policies and considered "failure in too many instances of command leadership to exercise its authority and responsibility" to be the primary cause of poor race relations in the armed forces. In 1972, Admiral Zumwalt publicly complained that his attempts at racial reform in the navy were being undercut by senior officers who paid only "lip service" to his orders, rather than actually enforcing compliance in their commands.[26]

Outside Radicalism and Civilian Influences

But apathy and racism were only two of the obstacles to implementing racial reform in the armed forces. An equally important and formidable obstruction was the widespread belief among civilian and military officials that the military's racial problems, particularly the confrontations between black service personnel and the command structure and between black and white service personnel in general, were not really the fault of the armed forces. Instead, officials claimed that the racial problems facing the military were caused primarily by radical changes in civilian society, such as a growing militancy among young African Americans, and that the services were relatively powerless to contain these influences or keep them out of the ranks. "Given the ... description of the effects of ghetto life on the black soldier," wrote sociologist William Stuart Gould, "it is clear that many of the racial problems encountered in the Army are products of the host society, i.e. the United States."[27]

The belief that the military's racial problems were largely the result of outside radicalism and civilian influences was commonly held throughout the chain of command. Marine colonel Robert D. Heinl, Jr., for example, claimed that "sedition—coupled with disaffection within the ranks, and externally fomented with an audacity and intensity previously inconceivable—infests the Armed Services," and air force major George M. Boyd stated in 1970 that "as a direct result of the national urban crisis the military is faced with the problems of racial conflict."[28] Senior officials such as Gravely, James, and Deputy Assistant Secretary of Defense L.

Howard Bennett came to the same conclusion.[29] In 1970, Bennett, while admitting that "there are problems within the military that we must tackle," nevertheless blamed external influences for the severity of the racial problem in the services. "There is a new dimension to the recent troubles. They represent a spillover from the problems of the civilian community." Fellow Pentagon official Assistant Secretary of Defense Roger T. Kelley reflected the same viewpoint, stating, "I think we have to admit that some of the same racial tensions that explode in the civilian sector also explode in the military."[30] Even William Westmoreland, who was usually more candid than other senior officials in admitting the military's racial shortcomings, blamed certain "attitudes and beliefs developed" by African Americans during "the racial unrest which marked American society in the 1960's" for many of the problems in the army.[31]

The belief that the military's racial crisis was a "spillover" from American civilian society also found a receptive audience in Congress. The House Armed Services Committee, in its investigation into the racially motivated gang fight at Camp Lejeune, concluded that "the racial problem at Camp Lejeune is a reflection of the nation's racial problem."[32]

Undoubtedly, many of the racial problems that faced the armed forces did have their genesis in civilian society. The Civil Rights movement had galvanized African Americans into taking action against prejudice and unequal treatment, and black nationalist groups such as the Nation of Islam and the Black Panthers had helped instill in young blacks both a new sense of racial pride and a sensitivity toward racial injustice. Many African Americans were more militant. A Harris poll conducted in March 1970 for *Time* magazine found that 9 percent of black Americans, or roughly two million, considered themselves to be "revolutionaries," and 25 percent said they admired the Black Panthers "a great deal." Nearly a third of those surveyed thought that African Americans would probably have to resort to violence to win civil rights. A poll of black Americans living in New York, San Francisco, Detroit, Baltimore, and Birmingham, Alabama, conducted for an ABC TV documentary on the Black Panthers in April 1970, also reflected a growing militancy among blacks. Sixty-two percent said they admired the work of the Panthers, and the party was ranked third, behind the NAACP and the Southern Christian Leadership Conference (SCLC), among the organizations who had done the most for blacks since 1968. But both the NAACP and SCLC were also viewed as being in decline, and the Panthers were considered to be the best hope for future advances by African Americans.[33]

Consequently, many of the African Americans in the armed services after 1968 were more militant; they expressed admiration for black radicals such as Malcolm X and Eldridge Cleaver and were influenced by their works and writings. James Hawkins liked the Panthers and Malcolm X because they "showed white America the other side of the coin . . . the threat of violence and they know it's going to be carried out . . . shoot a few people, and whites would listen."[34] Ronald Washington, a militant leader at Tien Sha Naval Base, stated that he, like many other black veterans, planned to join the Black Panthers after his discharge from the navy. More than 70 percent of the blacks interviewed by Wallace Terry in Vietnam in 1970 expressed admiration for Malcolm X, and one-third said they would join the Panthers or a similar black organization when they returned home to the United States. "The Black Panthers gives the Beast something to fear like we feared the Ku Klux Klan all our lives," stated seaman Milton Banion; and another black sailor added that of course, "I'd join em, and I'd help them kill all those honky muther fuckers [sic] because do unto him before he do unto you."[35] Henry Dority recalled that radical literature sent by friends and family to African Americans serving in Vietnam definitely "made them more militant,"[36] and activists Milton White, Joseph Miles, and Andrew Pulley often used the recordings and writings of Malcolm X in meetings and in "rap" or discussion sessions with their fellow blacks.[37]

Military Radicals

By the late 1960s, some of the militants were using the informal rap sessions as a catalyst for establishing black nationalist and leftist organizations within the armed forces, such as the American Servicemen's Union, the Black Berets, and the Movement for a Democratic Military. These groups were part of a larger dissident movement building within the military, the GI movement, which saw a proliferation of radical Marxist and antiwar organizations in the services. Collectively, all the radical groups were dubbed RITA—an acronym for "Resistance in the Army"—by military officials. The Pentagon estimated that by 1971 there were, in addition to known civilian radicals, at least fourteen military dissident organizations—including two made up exclusively of officers—and six or more veterans groups attempting to subvert the armed forces and the war effort in Vietnam.[38]

The individual black organizations within RITA varied in size and importance. Some were small, like the People's Justice Committee, and operated only at a single installation—in this case, Fort Hood, Texas.[39] Others, like the Malcolm X Society, shunned direct revolutionary action in favor of intellectual study and dialogue.[40] Virtually all were short-lived and quickly collapsed due to internal dissension, lack of interest, or lack of operating funds or, more often, because the group's original leadership cadre soon found themselves transferred to other posts or forced out of the military entirely.

Three of the largely black organizations in the services—the MDM, GIs United Against the War, and the ASU—were large and highly organized. Their influence extended throughout the military. The American Servicemen's Union was probably the biggest of the three and one of the largest dissident groups in RITA. In 1970 the ASU claimed more than ten thousand members and boasted active chapters at more than one hundred stateside and sixty overseas bases, as well as on fifty navy vessels. The ASU was relatively well funded and even operated its own radical newspaper, *The Bond,* for service personnel.[41]

What the black organizations, large or small, had in common was that they were usually modeled on civilian black nationalist and leftist organizations, such as the Black Panther Party, or they were named in honor of Malcolm X and reflected his philosophy. Malcolm X was the inspiration for one of the first African American organizations established in the military, GIs United Against the War, founded by Joseph Miles at Fort Jackson, South Carolina, in January 1969 and at Fort Bragg the following April. Andrew Pulley, one of the leaders of GIs United, recalled that "it started when Joe Miles suggested to some of us in the barracks . . . that we listen to some Malcolm X tapes. It started as all black and Puerto Rican just listening to the tapes and talking about it later."[42] In March 1970 two black air force sergeants, Milton White and Mayanard Jordan III, organized the Malcolm X Society at Vandenberg Air Force Base, California, and named it in honor of the slain activist because blacks on base "wanted a militant organization of persons interested in promoting awareness." Of all of America's black leaders, according to White, "Malcolm X was the most appropriate symbol . . . of the continuing struggle for change" within the armed services.[43]

Other organizations, such as the leftist American Servicemen's Union, established by army private Andrew Stapp in December 1967,[44] and the Movement for a Democratic Military, started for black marines at Camp Pendleton in November 1969,[45] looked to the Black Panther Party (BPP) for guidance and inspiration and considered the Panthers close allies in the common struggle against white oppression. Bob Wilkinson of the Socialist Workers Party, for example, stated that the "Movement for a Democratic Military . . . identifies with the Panthers and has a vague 'anti-imperialists' program,"[46] and the Maoist Revolutionary Union, dedicated to "overthrowing the state" from within the military, announced their "support of the Black Panther Party."[47] The military radicals and the Panthers shared similar political and cultural ideologies, which could best be described as a synthesis of black nationalism and Marxism. They believed that African Americans were being systematically exploited by a capitalist power structure, particularly in Vietnam, where the military was using blacks as cannon fodder to prosecute a colonial war of aggression against the Vietnamese people. To protect themselves, these movements maintained, blacks must seize control of their own future, politically, economically, and culturally, and prepare for what might easily become an armed struggle, a war of black liberation fought on America's streets.

Where the Panthers and all the military radical movements differed from the pure black-cultural nationalists, such as Maulana Karenga's California-based US movement, was in their emphasis on class over race. Cultural nationalists were radical Afrocentrists who viewed all whites as exploiters and inherently racist, and they claimed it was impossible for a black to be an enemy of African American people. The leftist nationalists defined their movement as one of a repressed class that was predominantly black but also included poor whites against a power structure that was predominantly white but included some token black accommodationists. Finally, the Panthers and the military radicals emphasized the need for blacks to take direct and immediate action against oppression, and they ridiculed the cultural nationalists as passive and idealistic, more interested in talking than in acting to solve the problems facing African Americans.[48]

Ironically, one area in which the cultural nationalists and the leftist nationalists seemed to agree was in their treatment of women; virtually all of the organizations were pervaded with a patronizing sexism. Women were usually consigned to subordinate roles within the black radical movements and with few notable exceptions, such as Kathleen Cleaver and Elaine Brown in the Black Panther Party, were not generally in positions of power or decision making. In a 1969 editorial titled "The Role of a Revolutionary Woman," June Culberson of the Los Angeles chapter of the Black Panthers complained that "many sisters have not been allowed to participate in the many facets of the Revolution" and bluntly warned the party's male leadership that "it will be the direct fault of the brothers when the sisters become conditioned to the easy life and pampering . . . and they will be unable to adjust to the hard life of fighting." Elaine Brown, who would become the only female chairperson of the Black Panther Party, castigated Karenga's US movement for its demeaning and sexist treatment of women, an opinion she would eventually extend to most other black radical organizations—including the Panthers.

Many black men, no matter how politically radical or fervent in their opposition to racism, were very sexist, and they brought their chauvinism with them into the military, where it was further magnified by conditions there. Women constituted only a tiny fraction of the active-duty personnel, making them often unwanted intruders in a male-dominated world. Added to this was their inferior status in the services, being restricted from many of the more glamorous and powerful military occupational specialties such as fighter pilot and combat specialist. Consequently, while African American servicewomen did participate in the demonstrations and movements— they were well represented in the MDM, for instance, and led demonstrations at Fort McClellan—they were not involved in any great numbers or in any visible leadership capacity.

Another similarity between the cultural nationalists and leftist nationalists was that neither permitted members to join the armed forces, either voluntarily or involuntarily. Yet despite this self-imposed restriction, there were some Panthers in the ranks of the military. It was against party rules for a current member to join the armed forces, but in practice, the rule was usually interpreted to allow blacks already in the services to join the Panthers, and members who could not successfully fight the draft to remain in the party. As a result, party members were active in recruiting and organizing in Vietnam and Germany, and some North American bases, such as Camp Lejeune and Goose Bay Air Force Base, may have had regular party chapters.[49] But as a rule, the party frowned on its members serving as tools of the oppressors, and the Panthers preferred to remain largely an organization of civilians. Though they did urge veterans to join after leaving the service, as their skills were sorely needed in defense of the black community, the BPP's actual numbers within the military remained small.

Instead of organizing directly within the ranks, the Black Panthers were content to work in conjunction with the military radicals, and there was a great deal of interaction and cooperation between the two groups of leftist nationalists. The ASU's Andrew Stapp, for instance, was a featured speaker at the Black Panthers Party's Conference for a United Front against Fascism in July 1969. In turn, Panthers were frequently the guest speakers at the MDM coffeehouse in Seaside, California, near Fort Ord; Robert John Bryan, who managed the house, was a member of both the BPP and the MDM.[50] The Panthers helped sponsor antiwar rallies, such as the one in Philadelphia in January 1970 that featured speeches by Panther Reggie Schell, Andrew Pulley of GIs United, and various Socialist Worker Party representatives,[51] or the demonstration staged by several groups, including the Panthers, on 15 May 1971 at the main gates at Fort Campbell, Kentucky.[52] The Panthers also used the party newspaper to praise the work of black military radicals, such as ASU organizer Henry Mills and a white associate, John Lewis, at Fort Dix, New Jersey,[53] and GIs United's José Rudder, Joe Cole, and Andrew Pulley at Fort Jackson.[54] In a general appeal to all black GIs, BPP Communications Director Kathleen Cleaver wrote in the 14 December 1970 issue of the *Black Panther*:

> Right inside of the U.S. imperialist beast's Army, you are strategically placed to begin the process of destroying him from within. . . . You don't have to wait . . . to begin to fight. . . . Sabotage from within until you get into a position to destroy from without! We need you, your military skills, your military equipment and your courage for our own struggle.

In return, the military radicals expressed solidarity with the goals and concerns of the Black Panthers and acknowledged their contribution to the struggle for black liberation. Number 9 on the Movement for a Democratic Military's "Statement of Principles" was a general call to "free all political prisoners," but only Panthers Eldridge Cleaver and Huey Newton were mentioned by name. And in a January 1969 interview with the *Workers World*, Andrew Stapp announced that the ASU was "building an Army within an Army . . . and along with the Panthers and others we're going to make that revolution."[55]

The Panthers may have been one of the civilian radical organizations with the most influence on the black liberation movement within the services, but as Stapp acknowledged, there were others. Some of these were black nationalist groups, such as Maulana Karenga's US movement. But most often, the "others" Stapp referred to were predominantly white civilian Marxist and antiwar organizations, such as the Trotskyite Socialist Workers Party, the Young Socialist Alliance, the Progressive Labor Party, the Students for a Democratic Society, the Vietnam Veterans Against the War/Winter Soldier Organization, and, on rare occasions, the Communist Party, U.S.A.

Allies and Exploiters

By the late 1960s, racial discontent and violence in the armed forces had attracted the attention of numerous U.S. domestic interest groups, as well as the government of the Democratic Republic of Vietnam. Some groups, such as the Southern Christian Leadership Conference (SCLC), the NAACP, and the Congressional Black Caucus, worked primarily through the system and sought to use their power and influence to improve conditions for black military personnel. The more radical organizations, which had traditionally opposed and worked outside the American power structure, displayed, at times, a genuine concern for the plight of the black serviceperson, but they also saw an opportunity to exploit the issue of racism to further their own agendas; for both reasons these groups began to extend their influence within RITA.

Cooperation and interaction between the largely white Marxist and radical antiwar organizations and the black military radicals were very close, and at times the relationship was similar to that of the military radicals and the Panthers, in that the military and civilian radicals shared common philosophies, goals, and usually membership rolls. For instance, the black organizations in the armed services quite naturally listed racism and the war in Vietnam as their two main grievances against the military. The four stated goals of GIs United included a complete "end to racism" and a total withdrawal of American forces from Vietnam. The American Servicemen's Union also called for an end to the war, as well as "an end to racial discrimination in job training, assignments and promotions,"[56] and the MDM demanded that the command structure "end all racism everywhere and bring to trial all officers and senior enlisted men who foment and exploit racial tensions."[57]

White radicals issued similar statements and called for black service personnel to join them in a united front against military racism. The Pacific Counseling Service (PCS), a coalition of radical groups that began operating near Fort Ord in May 1969, announced that because of the "pervasive racism . . . much of the concern of the PCS is directed toward . . . the non-white soldier."[58] The Vietnam Veterans Against the War/ Winter Soldier Organization (VVAW/WSO) referred to racism as the primary problem in the military and claimed that "the struggles of minority GIs provides the focus for current work around the GI movement."[59] In a joint statement with another veterans antiwar group, the Flower of the Dragon, the VVAW/WSO invited black GIs to join their white brothers in the antiwar movement, in the hope "that we can begin to struggle as one people against our common oppressor."[60] "What the GIs Think," a flier distributed by the Progressive Labor Party, urged black and white service personnel to unite in the "common struggle" and touted party success in fighting military racism.

Radical entertainers such as Jane Fonda and Donald Sutherland, whose fund-raising appearances often helped enrich the radical organizations' coffers, also made racism one of their major concerns. In the early 1970s the two entertainers organized and headlined a traveling variety show called "Free the Army" (FTA) that performed near defense installations and for predominantly enlisted audiences. The FTA performers lampooned a variety of topics for their GI audiences, including the officer corps— always a favorite for enlisted personnel—and the war in Vietnam; but army intelligence estimated that "eighty percent of the show's content" had themes concerning "white racism" and "racial agitation." Fonda, who was then married to SDS leader Tom Hayden, liked to style herself as both a leader and a spokesperson for the white radical movement and expressed what was often a very militant solidarity with black military radicals. At a "Peace and Justice" festival held at Exposition Park in Los Angeles on 2 May 1971, Fonda told the audience that even though "the guys are made to turn their guns in at night, . . . still any blatantly racist officer can expect a hand grenade might roll under his tent flap some night when he's turned in."

In addition to warm expressions of solidarity, the black military radicals and the civilian Marxist organizations shared more concrete links. Many of the African Americans involved in the GI movement were also members of leftist groups and parties. This was particularly true with regard to the leadership cadres of the black military organizations. Joseph Miles and Joseph Cole, two key leaders of GIs United, were members of the Socialist Workers Party (SWP) when they entered the service. Miles was also a member of the Young Socialist Alliance (YSA), the youth arm of the SWP, and after leaving the service became the SWP's congressional candidate in a Boston district. Andrew Pulley joined the SWP while still in the service, and fellow GIs United activist Eugene "José" Rudder was a former member of both the Student Nonviolent Coordinating Committee and the Communist Party, U.S.A. (CPUSA) before joining the YSA in the army. Andrew Stapp of the ASU was also an important figure in the Committee for GI Rights, a Communist front organization.

Like Stapp, many of the black radicals had close ties to one of the three major Communist parties operating in the United States: the CPUSA, the SWP, and the Progressive Labor Party (PLP). MDM's Robert Mandel, who started a coffeehouse near Fort Campbell and then a MDM-type organization on the post itself, was a member of the revolutionary Weathermen and probably of the CPUSA, in which his father had long been an active member.[61] Many of the radical white GIs also had communist affiliations. At Fort Knox, Kentucky, two of the editors of a base underground newspaper, *EM-16*, Private Mack Smith and his wife, Sallie, were Communists and active members of the Progressive Labor Party;[62] so was Dennis Davis, who edited the *Last Harass*, the alternative, radical paper for GIs at Fort Gordon, Georgia.[63]

The fact that many of the radicals also belonged to Marxist parties naturally led many government officials and some members of the Left to charge that the black military organizations were creations of the Marxists and were largely controlled by the parent organizations. To a limited degree, the charge was accurate. Stapp admitted he had joined the army "specifically to organize resistance against U.S. imperialism."[64] Three civilian activists, Kenneth Cloke, Kent Leroy Hudson, and Hideko Patricia Sumi, were instrumental in the formation of the MDM, despite the fact the MDM billed itself as an organization "started by black Marines" for black marines.[65] Al Greengold of the SWP went so far as to characterize the MDM as being "made up of elements from the SDS," claiming that "like the ASU," the MDM was "begun by civilians" and is still "controlled by civilians."[66] The House Committee on Internal Security, in its report on attempts to subvert the armed forces, concluded that "the Socialist Workers Party helped organize GIs United Against the War in Vietnam at Fort Jackson, South Carolina."[67]

Civilian Marxist organizations were certainly instrumental in the creation of many of the radical black military groups and would continue to exert a great deal of influence over them throughout their existence. But the MDM, the ASU, and GIs United were not under the control of civilian Marxists, and their members were not unwitting dupes of a Communist conspiracy. A natural affinity existed between radical African Americans and the predominantly white Marxist organizations, because the leftists had traditionally welcomed black members and had long championed their fight against racism and discrimination.[68] Whereas the Democratic or Republican parties had generally treated African Americans and their concerns shabbily, blacks had wielded real power and influence in the CPUSA, PLP, and SWP, so it was not surprising that when black party members decided to organize African American service personnel, they would use the civilian groups as organizational models and look to them for guidance and inspiration, in much the same way that they looked to the Black Panther Party. They were all involved in the same class struggle anyway, and every organization, whether the ASU or the SWP, was just a vehicle for organizing the masses and promoting the movement for people's liberation. Thus many of the radicals belonged to several organizations, and new fronts and coalitions were formed and dissolved according to the needs of the time or in order to capitalize on a particular opportunity.

The relationship between the military and civilian radicals is best characterized as symbiotic, as an alliance of mutual interests, and not as the relationship of a puppet to a puppeteer. Hence there was a tremendous degree of cooperation and interaction between the civilian and military radicals in attempting to politicize service personnel, in staging demonstrations and rallies, and in publishing underground newspapers and operating coffeehouses near military installations.

The Instruments of Radicalism

The coffeehouses in particular were popular locations for meeting, planning, and organizing. Many were operated by the United States Servicemen's Fund, a front organization sponsored at various times by the Pacific Counseling Service, the MDM, the Black Panthers, and the SWP, among others.[69] There was usually at least one coffeehouse near every major defense installation, and their names often reflected some aspect of military life. The Oleo Strut, one of the more famous coffeehouses, was named after a part on a Huey helicopter and was located in Killeen, Texas, near Fort Hood. The Green Machine coffeehouse attracted marines from Camp Pendleton, and the Home Front was just outside Fort Carson, Colorado. Most of the coffeehouses were near army and marine bases, but the Liberty Hall in Philadelphia was geared toward navy personnel, and air force enlisted personnel frequented such establishments as the Covered Wagon near Mountain Home Air Force Base, Iowa, a popular meeting place for the VVAW/WSO, and Off the Runway, a coffeehouse located in Holyoke, Massachusetts, and staffed in part by airmen from Westover Air Force Base.

The coffeehouses provided inexpensive refreshments and entertainment for their military clientele, and occasionally there might even be a live band or a comedy show in the evening. But the main functions of the coffeehouse were to promote the revolutionary education of the enlisted masses, provide a forum for radical speakers, and serve as a meeting place for dissident organizations. The MDM was initially organized at the Green Machine, for example, and the all-black, People's Justice Committee for Fort Hood was founded at the Oleo Strut. GIs United, the ASU, and the MDM regularly held their meetings and planning sessions at coffeehouses. Consequently, most houses were more likely to sponsor "political education classes" than concerts, and even when entertainment was provided, it usually contained a political or cultural message.[70]

The movies shown at the coffeehouses are a good example. Most were distributed by the U.S. Servicemen's Fund and generally had antiwar or antiracist themes, such as *Inside Vietnam* and *No Vietnamese Ever Called Me Nigger*. Others dealt with domestic unrest and carried such titles as *Yippies, Hey Stop That!* and *The Streets Belong to the People* or were documentaries on leading black nationalists, profiling Huey Newton, Malcolm X, and Bobby Seale, among others.

The reading material available at the coffeehouses was similar in content to the movies. One could usually find copies of the *Black Panther* or *The Bond*, as well as works by Malcolm X, Eldridge Cleaver, Tom Hayden, and other leading radicals. At many of the houses one could also peruse the works of V. I. Lenin, Mao Tse-tung, and Ho Chi Minh, or perhaps an edition of the local underground newspaper, over a cup of coffee or tea. Many of the alternative newspapers were written and published out of the local coffeehouses.[71]

The term *underground* newspapers was, of course, a misnomer, because even though the content was radical and often "subversive" by military standards, there was nothing illegal about their publication. But they were underground publications of a sort, because base commanders usually barred their sale or distribution on base. In September 1969, for example, authorities at Fort Bragg banned the distribution of the local GI paper, *Bragg Briefs*, on post.[72] Defying the ban could be costly for a military activist. That September, Rudder and Coles were court-martialed for distributing the banned newspaper *Short-Times* at Fort Jackson,[73] and just two months earlier, Private Kenneth C. Cross had been sentenced by special court-martial to three months at hard labor in the stockade, reduction in rank by one grade, and forfeiture of two-thirds of his pay (equivalent to seventy-three dollars a month) for six months for distributing copies of *Short Times* at Fort Jackson without permission.[74]

Many of the dissidents did seek official permission to distribute their publications on base. GIs United, for example, sought permission on three separate occasions to distribute *Bragg Briefs*. Between 1970 and 1972, nearly fifty groups sought permission to distribute newspapers on various bases, but since authorities almost always considered the editorial content of the papers detrimental to "good morale" and the "best interests of the military," permission was usually denied, and only nineteen of the fifty applications were eventually approved.[75] Occasionally, the radicals would even threaten to take the military to court over the right to distribute an underground publication on the grounds that prohibiting distribution was a violation of their First Amendment rights. GIs United made such a threat after officials turned down their request for permission to distribute *Bragg Briefs* at Fort Bragg.[76] Though they could freely distribute their newspapers to service personnel off base, it was important for the radicals to be able to dispense their product openly on base, not only because it gave their movement a certain credibility among the enlisted personnel but also because it was on base that their target audience was concentrated.[77]

Military authorities estimated that between 1967 and 1972, at least 245 underground newspapers aimed at a military audience were published by radical and antiwar organizations.[78] Some, like *The Bond* and *Camp News*, survived for years, virtually becoming counterculture institutions, and boasted respectable nationwide circulations. In 1969, for example, the ASU claimed a press run of nearly twenty-five thousand copies a month for *The Bond*.[79] But most of the papers lasted for only a few issues, and in any given year, there were only about forty to fifty in circulation at any one time. The number of underground newspapers peaked at about sixty-five in May 1970, according to Brigadier General S.L.A. Marshall, a special aide to Westmoreland, but by August 1970 there were only thirty still known to be in publication.

A few of the GI newspapers, such as the *Black Voice* at Fort McClellan, were operated by black nationalists and targeted a black audience; most, however, even the papers published by the ASU and GIs United, aimed at a wider GI audience. But they all devoted a lot of their attention to the issues of racism in the military and to ending American involvement in Vietnam, and like the coffeehouses, they carried names that reflected some aspect of the military experience. *Travisty* was published by airmen stationed at Travis Air Force Base, California, and soldiers at Fort Hood read the *Fatigue Press*.[80] Some of the larger bases had more than one paper in circulation; soldiers at Fort Knox, Kentucky, could choose from three underground papers—the *EM-16*; *Fun, Travel, and Adventure (FTA)*; and *In Formation*.[81] Alternative newspapers were also available to Americans at overseas bases and were usually published locally. There were two newspapers published on Okinawa, the *Omega Press* and *Right to Revolution*, and two more, *Fall in at Ease* and *Semper FI*, were available in nearby Japan; and personnel stationed in Europe could read *Act*, published out of Paris, France.[82]

In addition to operating the coffeehouses and the underground newspapers, the radical coalitions claimed responsibility for much of the organized dissent in the armed forces against the war and military racism, two issues that were inseparable to the militants. Stapp claimed that the ASU played "a meaningful role at both Long Binh and Da Nang where the men revolted and fought the brass over abominable stockade conditions and racist terror unleashed on the prisoners."[83] Both the ASU and GIs United were heavily involved in the antiwar movement. Terry Klug of the ASU helped organize resistance at Fort Dix, New Jersey,[84] and fellow ASU member Kenneth Dupre went AWOL rather than serve in Vietnam.[85] On 20 March 1969, GIs United staged a large antiwar rally at Fort Jackson, and the organization often cosponsored other demonstrations with groups such as the VVAW or the Panthers. Similar rallies staged by the ASU, mostly near Fort Jackson, typically attracted sixty to eighty spectators.[86] Large demonstrations protesting racism and discrimination were organized at Fort McClellan[87] and at Fort Hood,[88] and nearly five hundred black enlisted men attended a Malcolm X rally at Youngsen Military Reservation in South Korea on 19 May 1971.[89]

The Movement for a Democratic Military was also involved in demonstrations and protests, staging two major ones in 1970 alone, at Fort Ord, California. The MDM and the Black Berets rallied first on Armed Forces Day, which they celebrated as Armed "Farces" Day, and again on the Fourth of July. But the MDM and its splinter groups, the Black Berets and the Peoples Army Defense Council, also acquired the reputation as some of the more revolutionary and violent groups among the black leftist nationalists. The MDM and Black Beret members stole weapons from the military and stockpiled them for use in the coming revolution, and military authorities suspected they were responsible for a wave of terrorist bombings and arson cases, such as the burning of two mess halls at Fort Ord on 12 August 1970 and incidents at other installations where these groups had active chapters.[90]

Special Treatment

The cooperation between the military radicals and the civilian Marxist and antiwar organizations concerned authorities, but they were even more alarmed about the apparent connection between the radicals and foreign Communist states, particularly the USSR, the People's Republic of China, and the Democratic Republic of Vietnam. The Communists did offer some aid and encouragement to the black militants. Black enlisted personnel, such as Jay Wright and Terry Whitmore, who deserted from Southeast Asia with the aid of the Pacific Counseling Service or Bahrein, its sister agency in Japan, routinely surfaced in Moscow for a press conference on their way to Sweden, for example.[91]

Communist news services followed the activities of black radicals, glorified them in news stories and radio broadcasts as heroes of the people, and provided them with an international forum. Patrick Graves, a white lieutenant stationed at Canh Tinh, Vietnam, confided bitterly in his diary:

> I listened to Radio Peking and the distorted news this morning. I wish it were possible for that certain group at home in the United States that is responsible for our many domestic troubles, for them to hear the use made of it in the Communist news. The only news that is broadcast concerns our racial troubles and the few, very few who protest openly our involvement in Vietnam.[92]

The radicals responded with declarations of solidarity with the Communist states. Andrew Stapp was a featured speaker at the Sixth Congress of the League of Socialist Working Youth in North Korea on 21 June 1971, where he praised the Democratic People's Republic of (North) Korea's President Kim Il Sung, condemned American imperialism, and promised the delegates that in the United States, "the class struggle of the progressive people and soldiers against racism and Wall Street's war policy is gaining momentum daily."[93] The *Black Panther* routinely ran editorials expressing solidarity with the worldwide people's liberation movement in general and the Vietcong in particular. The paper often ran cartoons depicting solidarity between black GIs and the Communist forces; one, for instance, showed a black soldier dapping with a member of the Vietcong.[94] In the 4 January 1969 issue of the party paper, the Panthers congratulated the National Liberation Front on the ninth anniversary of its struggle "to free South Vietnam from the dictatorship of the U.S. puppet regime," noting with satisfaction that the Vietcong "have not only matched every increase in U.S. strength, but have defeated each successive U.S. plan for victory."[95] Another issue referred to "the gallant and heroic people of Vietnam who are waging such an unyielding fight against the American Imperialists."[96] The *Black Liberator,* a black nationalist publication of the Black Liberation Alliance in Chicago, declared the Alliance's "solidarity with the Vietnamese people" on the cover of the November 1969 issue.[97]

Much of the radicals' praise was directed toward the president of North Vietnam, Ho Chi Minh. On the occasion of Ho's seventy-ninth birthday, on 19 May 1969, the *Black Panther* ran a profile on the aged leader, referring to Ho as "one of the greatest Marxist-Leninists of all times" and adding that "the Black Panther Party and the revolutionary peoples of racist America wish Ho Chi Minh a very happy birthday and many returns of the day. Having faced the same enemy for four hundred years, we the Black Panther Party want him to know that we stand in complete solidarity with the revolutionary people of Vietnam. We will fight imperialism with proletarian internationalism."[98] When Ho died four months later, the Panthers expressed their condolences "to the courageous Vietnamese people" and lauded his contribution to the world socialist struggle.[99]

The Democratic Republic of Vietnam (DRV) responded very favorably to these statements of solidarity; and quite naturally, it was the DRV that made the most serious attempt, among the socialist states, to ingratiate itself with the black radical movement and to exploit racial unrest in the American armed forces. The DRV and the Vietcong routinely expressed their solidarity with the black radicals, pointing out that Ho had long been interested in the plight of black Americans, ever since he had visited Harlem as a young man. In April 1968, North Vietnamese premier Pham Van Dong sent Hanoi's condolences to the SCLC over Dr. King's assassination, stating that the Vietnamese people shared with "our Afro-American brothers this deep grief" over King's death.[100] In August 1969 the *Black Panther* printed an "appeal of President Ho Chi Minh" calling for solidarity between African Americans and the Vietnamese.[101]

Leading black activists and radicals were invited to North Vietnam. Civil rights activist Diane Nash Bevel spent eleven days in North Vietnam in December 1966, as a guest of the Women's Union of the DRV,[102] and the Reverend Phillip Lawson, associated with the Kansas City, Missouri, Black Panther Party and an organizer of the New Mobilization Committee to End the War in Vietnam, also visited Hanoi, in September 1970.[103]

The treatment accorded Diane Nash Bevel and her three female traveling companions was typical of how Hanoi used these visits to express solidarity with the radicals but also to exploit them for propaganda purposes. Shortly after arriving in North Vietnam, for example, the American women were shown a movie about the life of Ho Chi Minh. "Uncle Ho," they were told, "had visited Harlem in his youth and observed and resented the exploitation of Negroes in the United States," as did most of his comrades in the Democratic Republic of Vietnam. After these expressions of sympathy and solidarity the women next were shown evidence of American atrocities caused by the air war against North Vietnam, including bombed-out Catholic churches, residential houses, and hospitals. At one hospital Dr. Fat, their guide, expressed the belief that the United States "has deliberately and systematically attacked medical institutions" as part of a vicious campaign to colonize the Vietnamese people. Upon request, Bevel and her party were then allowed to meet with two of the American pilots partially responsible for these "war crimes," who were then being held as prisoners of war (POWs) by the North Vietnamese. Bevel claimed that despite their "savage" crimes against the people, the pilots were generally "well-treated and in good health," and they gave her letters from other POWs to take back home to the United States.

The highlight of the trip was a personal audience with the venerable and aged leader of North Vietnam, Ho Chi Minh. Like most of the leaders of the DRV, Ho made a clear distinction between the actions of the American government and the goodness of the American people, expressing his liking of Americans in general and his solidarity with the oppressed in particular. Ho also expressed his personal regrets to Bevel that so many young Americans were being forced to come to Vietnam to die, adding, "If they come to teach or to help us build we would welcome them, but they come to our country to kill us, so we have no other choice but to kill them."

While in Vietnam, black activists would often be asked to make a statement on the war or to broadcast an appeal to African Americans serving in Vietnam over Radio Hanoi or its clandestine sister station in South Vietnam, Liberation Radio. Bevel appealed to her "black brothers" fighting in South Vietnam, telling them that "the Vietnam War is a colonialist war. If you fight in it, you are fighting Asian brothers who are determined to prevent their country from becoming owned and managed by racist-capitalist white men."[104]

Bevel was just one of many black activists willing to make a broadcast or appeal on behalf of African American and Vietnamese solidarity. Black

Panther Party minister of information Eldridge Cleaver, then a refugee in Algeria, made two broadcasts over Radio Hanoi, on 24 and 27 August 1970, aimed at black servicemen in Vietnam. Cleaver said he welcomed "this opportunity to proclaim to the entire world the absolute, unequivocal and enthusiastic support and solidarity of black people of the U.S. for our Vietnamese comrades." The Reverend Phillip Lawson made a similar broadcast to U.S. troops on 20 September 1970. In addition to the black activists, the North Vietnamese for years used black military deserters in their propaganda campaign over the airwaves. As early as July 1965, Radio Hanoi began to broadcast tapes made in Beijing, China, by a black Korean War deserter named Clarence Adams. This practice would continue throughout the war. As late as April 1972, U.S. army intelligence recorded broadcasts over Radio Hanoi and Liberation Radio by "a black serviceman who self-admittedly is a defector to the Vietcong" and noted similar broadcasts by two others.[105]

The most popular tactic used by the DRV and the Vietcong was to promote the belief that African Americans were not the enemy of the Vietnamese and that the socialist forces would accord blacks "special treatment" as revolutionary comrades. Special treatment took many forms, but it was designed to reinforce the notion that there were differences between white GIs and black GIs, and that "liberation" forces would favor the African Americans. In January 1966 the Vietcong released two black Special Forces Sergeants, George E. Smith and Claude McClure, as a goodwill gesture,[106] and in November 1969 the Democratic Republic of Vietnam offered to release some American prisoners of war if, in exchange, the U.S. government would drop all pending felony charges against Huey Newton and Bobby Seale.[107]

In the field in Vietnam special treatment usually meant that People's Army of Vietnam (PAVN) and Vietcong forces would refrain from shooting at blacks during an ambush or firefight or that they would not take African Americans prisoner. Stories attesting to such special treatment for blacks were widely circulated and were sometimes true.[108] Raymond Wells was caught by the Vietcong after he mistakenly missed curfew and was stranded in a Saigon suburb that was controlled by the insurgents at night. Wells feared for his life and for that of his Cambodian girlfriend, but the Vietcong just confiscated his drugs and, to his relief, told them both they were free to go.[109] In 1971, Private Tommy Gladney and another black soldier were trapped in a Montagnard village by the Vietcong; but instead of taking them prisoner, the Communist guerrillas shared their supper with them. After smoking some marijuana with the two African Americans, the Vietnamese departed back into the jungle.[110] Corporal Terry Whitmore was in a marine unit ambushed near Con Tien and recalled that the Vietcong allowed him to pass first safely through an ambush but then shot all of the whites, including a wounded lieutenant whom Whitmore was attempting to carry to safety.[111] Even Bronze Star recipient Sergeant Arthur Westbrook claimed that "the enemy would rather kill a white soldier than a black one."[112]

Many African Americans heard or related such stories. A Vietcong propaganda flier that was circulated in Vietnam opened with "Everyone's heard stories of black GIs being let through ambushes" and went on to assure readers that "if you go AWOL because you don't want to fight or because you can't put up with the Army racism . . . the NLF will get you out of the country."[113]

For the Vietcong and the PAVN, to attempt to create dissension in the American ranks was a sound military tactic, but their "special treatment" of African Americans was more often than not just a propaganda ploy. North Vietnam freed very few prisoners, black or white, during the course of the war. Smith and McClure may have been released, but they spent nearly two years in a POW camp first.[114] Despite Whitmore's assertion that the Vietcong had shown him preferential treatment, after the insurgents had killed all the whites, they shot and severely wounded the African American corporal as well.[115] Often the reason an African American was not shot at during a firefight was because the individual was on point, ten to twenty meters ahead of the rest of the unit, and it was standard practice in staging an ambush to allow the point man to go by first and to concentrate fire on the main body of troops. Few blacks believed the stories anyway. James Hawkins stated emphatically that there was "no special treatment" for blacks—"They shot at everyone . . . and the blacks shot back"[116]—and the more than five thousand African Americans killed in action attest all too grimly to the fact that blacks were considered legitimate targets by the Communist forces.

"The Enemy among Us"

The activities of the radical organizations and their seemingly close connection to the very groups the United States was currently fighting in Vietnam convinced government officials that they were correct in assuming that many of the Military's racial problems were the result of civilian and organized subversive influences. Representative Richard H. Ichord of Missouri, a member of the House Committee on Internal Security, warned that the issue of racism was being "highly exploited" by radical groups "seeking to subvert the military." Various witnesses before Ichord's committee, including representatives from army intelligence and the attorney general's office, identified the Black Panthers, the ASU, GIs United, the MDM, the SWP, the YSA, the Revolutionary Union, and the U.S. Servicemen's Fund as being "groups within the GI movement" that "have revolutionary Marxists in leadership positions" and seek to undermine the armed services.[117] The House Armed Services Committee decided that the fight at Camp Lejeune was "generated in part by a few militant blacks who fanned the flames of racism."[118] Bahrein and the Pacific Counseling Service were blamed for racial violence on American bases in Japan, and authorities considered the Progressive Labor Party's plans for starting "rebellions within the Army" to be typical of all of the leftist and antiwar organizations.

The Black Panthers had the distinction of being singled out most often by authorities as a leading catalyst of racial unrest and violence in the services. Roland A. Morrow, director of the Department of Defense's Investigative Program, considered the Panthers to be the most influential of all the black leftist nationalist groups within RITA, and the House Committee on Internal Security concluded that "the Black Panther Party, through its deliberately inflammatory rhetoric and through the actual arming and military training of its members, has contributed to an increase in acts of violence and constitutes a threat to the internal security of the United States."[119]

At the company level, many officers also thought that much of the racial unrest in their units was the result of a determined few, organized dissidents who were out to create racial unrest and disrupt cohesion. Donald Dean blamed many of the racial problems in the unit he commanded on a black NCO who was a "troublemaker,"[120] and Charles Shrader claimed that a "professional hard-core agitator" stirred up trouble in his company.[121] Captain Richard Bevington was convinced that racial violence in his command was caused by "a handful" of black militants,[122] as was John Ellis, who characterized his company's racial unrest as the result of a "highly motivated subculture—black power types."[123]

The belief that the racial unrest and violence plaguing the armed forces were the result of the activities of a few organized militants and dissident groups, exploiting tensions and factors that originated in civilian society, was attractive to those who supported and trusted the armed forces for several reasons. It meant that their much-beloved institutions were really not at fault, as critics of the armed forces were wont to charge. It also diminished the argument that the military needed to be aggressive in implementing fundamental racial reforms, something that many military supporters, both in and out of uniform, considered a waste of time and energy.

Some even argued that the reforms themselves were at least partially responsible for the racial violence and unrest, because they eroded discipline and morale, especially among white enlisted personnel, and contributed to a climate of "permissiveness" that allowed black militants to recruit freely and to spread their subversive gospel throughout the ranks. Representative John M. Ashbrook (R-Ohio) complained that "of course, racism has two sides, one side which is obvious or at least appears to be obvious; in some cases there does not seem to be the same treatment of black militants as there would be of white militants. . . . In talking to military personnel, there is a feeling that sometimes the black agitator is given more leeway than the white agitator in the same circumstance."[124] In 1969 the House Armed Services Committee cited "too much permissiveness" as one of the causes of the rumble at Camp Lejeune, and three years later, in 1972, the committee again cited permissiveness as a primary cause for the black uprisings on the *Constellation* and the *Kitty Hawk;* "concern over racial problems," concluded the committee, "seemed more important than the question of good order and discipline."[125]

While most enlisted personnel applauded Admiral Zumwalt's racial reforms and his attempts to ease "Mickey Mouse" regulations regarding hair length and uniform code violations, many of his senior and junior officers balked at implementing the reforms and publicly stated that they hurt discipline and contributed to a climate of permissiveness. "Lt. John Paul Jones," who was representative of this feeling throughout the military, argued that "such panaceas as appointing 'minority affairs advisors' to all ships will do little to help," because "the problem is more personal and cultural than it is organizational." Instead of more reforms, Jones argued that "a revival of firm discipline would create an atmosphere in which radicals and dissidents of all colors would find it almost impossible to employ their tactics; it would rob them of their freedom to operate, and thereby discredit them and their ideologies."[126]

More traditional discipline was needed, argued military supporters such as Ichord, Heinl, and Jones, and not more reforms that helped protect and "coddle" the dissidents. These supporters feared that the armed forces were being deliberately and systematically undermined by militants, and while they admitted that some internal reform was probably justified, they contended that the services needed to purge themselves of the radical elements if racial unrest was ever going to be eliminated from the ranks. Those who viewed the military's racial problems in this light constituted a powerful lobby within both the government and the armed services, and even those who truly believed reforms were necessary admitted that the radicals and outside, civilian influences contributed to and exploited the problem. As a result, military officials continued to seek meaningful internal reform, but they also instituted programs designed to identify and eliminate from the services personnel who were considered militant or subversive.

In attempting to suppress radical activity, the military authorities encountered several problems. The first was in determining exactly which organizations were actually subversive and posed a threat to the security of the United States and which ones were simply a nuisance. The attorney general's office provided some assistance; since the 1950s the Justice Department had published a list of organizations considered to be revolutionary in nature and dedicated to the violent overthrow of the government of the United States. By the early 1970s there were eighteen such organizations on the attorney general's list, including the Black Panther Party, the Nation of Islam, the W. E. B. DuBois Clubs of America, and the Republic of New Africa. Communist organizations such as the CPUSA, the SWP, and the YSA also made the list, as did the Students for a Democratic Society and white supremacist organizations such as the Ku Klux Klan. But the list was not updated very often and focused primarily on civilian groups, so it did not include relatively new organizations such as GIs United or the MDM, the very ones causing most of the concern for military authorities. Identifying subversive organizations operative in the armed forces was further complicated by the fact that new fronts, coalitions, splinter groups, and factions were constantly developing, and it was difficult to keep track of all of them or even to determine their leadership cadres or their relative influence in the GI movement.

Simply identifying which organizations were officially subversive was of only limited value, because membership in a group on the attorney general's list did not in itself constitute grounds for dismissal from the armed services. Admitted radicals could sometimes be discharged or prevented from enlisting on the basis of their membership in an officially designated subversive organization, but the process was cumbersome and open to challenge in federal courts.

As a result, the services just tried to keep track of the admitted radicals in the services and prohibited them from any military occupational specialties that required a security clearance. This process was known as "flagging" and was permissible under Article 604-10 of the Uniform Code of Military Justice, and it included all individuals affiliated with an organization "which has adopted, or shows, a policy of advocating or approving the commission of acts of force or violence to deny other persons their rights under The Constitution of the United States by unconstitutional means." But even this was of only limited value. In May 1971, when radical activity was at its height in the services, only fifteen enlisted men were flagged in the army and only twenty in the navy. When asked by the House Committee on Internal Security just how many Black Panthers were in the armed forces, Roland Morrow, the director of the DOD investigative program office, replied that the military did not know and was not attempting to find out how many Panthers were in the services.[127]

The military's internal apparatus for identifying and flagging subversives was the Military Personnel Security Program, established by Department of Defense Directive 5210.9 on 19 June 1956. In addition to allowing officials to track military radicals, the directive established "commonsense guidelines" for determining whether a particular organization should or should not be considered subversive. But the 1956 directive was rather vague, and on 12 September 1969, Secretary of Defense Melvin Laird issued new directive 1325.6, titled "Guidelines for Handling Dissident and Protest Activities among Members of the Armed Forces." Laird informed commanders that "the service member's right of expression should be preserved to the maximum extent possible," but this was to be "consistent with good order and discipline and the national security." The secretary warned that "no Commander should be indifferent to conduct which, if allowed to proceed unchecked, would destroy the effectiveness of his unit," and to this end he empowered the command structure to take action against subversive activities. Commanders were now authorized to impound printed materials considered detrimental to the best interests of the military; to discipline personnel working on an underground newspaper, "if such a publication contains language the utterance of which is punishable under federal law"; and to place off-limits coffeehouses and other establishments that promoted activities likely to have "a significant adverse effect on members' health, morale, or welfare." Members of the armed forces were also now "prohibited from participating in off-post demonstrations when they are on duty, or in a foreign country, or when their activities constitute a breach of law and order, or when violence is likely to result."[128]

Activist Milton White stated that there were three basic types of black organizations operating within the armed forces. The first type consisted only of fraternal societies; they stressed solidarity but did not have a political agenda. The second type he identified as "action structured educational and cultural organizations," such as his own Malcolm X Society, which "purported to lawfully but militantly promote an awareness and understanding of Black America." The first two groups were essentially cultural nationalist in their outlook and approach and shied away from any overt, direct action against the military establishment. The third type involved "purely revolutionary organizations like MDM," essentially leftist nationalists who did seek to subvert the armed forces and government of the United States.[129]

Most officials in the command structure, however, were not aware of— or chose not to make—any distinction between a fraternal or intellectual black organization and one that was revolutionary in nature. Even though Laird stressed the importance of preserving the rights of military personnel as much as possible, and he relied on "the calm and prudent judgment of the responsible Commander" to differentiate between lawful protest and subversion, few bothered to observe the distinction.[130] Most in the command structure considered any display of black pride or unity to be inherently dangerous and used their newfound powers to suppress virtually all black-oriented activity in the military, regardless of whether it advocated outright revolution or just a more militant type of black pride. As White ruefully but correctly observed, "Justify and Jeffersonize all day, but the white man . . . was not about to permit the Malcolmization of niggers."[131]

So even organizations like the Malcolm X Society that did not have an active revolutionary agenda became legitimate targets in the minds of military officials, and in many cases, so did African Americans and black organizations that worked within the established power structure. The NAACP, for example, was heavily involved in both publicizing and seeking to rectify institutional and personal racism in the armed forces. Its legal department had come to the defense of black service personnel on numerous occasions. At Goose Bay Air Force Base, Labrador, an investigation pursued by NAACP general counsel Nathaniel Jones led to the dismissal of all court-martial offenses against five black airmen who had been charged

in connection with a racial brawl at that installation; Jones's efforts eventually succeeded in getting the base commander, Colonel Benton Fielder,
transferred. At Millington Naval Air Station in Tennessee and at Fort Knox,
Kentucky, the NAACP also successfully defended blacks accused of rioting
and assault, and it assisted in the defense of Airman August Doyle at
Cannon Air Force Base, Colorado, and of the "Darmstadt Fotry-three"
protesters in Germany.[132] In January 1971, Jones led an NAACP investigative
team to Germany to study the administration of military justice, and the
team submitted its formal report on the topic to Melvin Laird in May
1971. Both Laird and Westmoreland seemed to appreciate the civil rights
organization's efforts, and many of the military's subsequent reforms were
based at least partially on the NAACP's recommendations.[133] But throughout the chain of command, most officials resented any interference from
outside groups, and many refused to cooperate with the NAACP or openly
obstructed its investigations.

Another group many officers and civilian military supporters considered
potentially subversive was the Congressional Black Caucus in the House of
Representatives. There were thirteen African Americans in Congress in
1971, and as a group, they were highly critical of military policy and
military command's insistence that the service's racial problems were
caused primarily by civilian or radical influences. The caucus refused "to
accept the often advanced premise that racism in the military is merely a
microcosm of the racism which prevails within the larger society" and
warned military officials that "this kind of assumption only prolongs the
time before real action is taken to combat the problem."[134]

But it was two relatively recent newcomers, Representative Shirley Chisolm (D-New York) and Representative Ronald Dellums (D-California),
who really raised the ire of military officials. In her maiden speech in
Congress in 1969, Brooklyn Democrat Chisolm attacked the Pentagon for
its lavish defense spending and quickly established a reputation as a champion of blacks against the military justice system.[135] In June 1971, Chisolm
first sheltered and then aided in the legal defense of two black GIs, Bernard
Tucker and Nathanial Holms, who had fled West Germany after their
conviction in courts-martial of raping a girl at Bad Kreuznach.[136] Two
years later, the congresswoman announced her support for the sixteen
Norfolk sailors accused of participating in the brig riot of 26 November
1972. Chisolm had nothing but "total disgust with the Department of [the]
Navy" in its handling of the cases and pledged to pursue the matter "to the
fullest extent possible." To this end, she dispatched two aides to interview

the "Camp Allen Brothers," as they were known in the radical press, and called for a Defense Department or congressional investigation into the causes of the Brig riot.[137]

To many of the military's apologists, Dellums was even worse than Chisolm. Many heartily agreed with Vice President Spiro Agnew's assessment of the freshman congressman from Berkeley as "a radical extremist" intent on "bringing the walls down."[138] All were appalled when Dellums denounced the war in Vietnam, stating, "They say the war is not a black issue—but we're dying there." The thirty-five-year-old former marine urged both blacks and whites to resist induction and declared that "black people have a right to stand up and oppose the absurdity of sending our eighteen and nineteen year-olds there to be killed. . . . This country shackles black soldiers and sends them to Vietnam to fight and die."[139]

On 15 November 1971, members of the Congressional Black Caucus visited ten defense installations in the United States to gather information prior to three days of hearings on the issue of military racism. Some commanders cooperated fully with the visiting congresspersons, but many did so only reluctantly, and a few openly challenged the caucus's findings.[140] During Representative Parren J. Mitchell's (D-Maryland) visit to Fort Meade, Maryland, white army lawyer Captain Arthur Stein testified that the military justice system discriminated against African Americans, a charge immediately and publicly denied by Meade's commanding officer, Colonel John E. Lance, Jr., and by several black senior NCOs who claimed that army discrimination "was no greater than that found in civilian society." Those who openly cooperated with the committee were also held in contempt. Lance, for example, had told Stein he was free to say "any damn thing he wants to say" to Mitchell, but after the hearing, the colonel remarked that the lawyer had been "derelict in his duty."[141] Another officer referred to blacks who had voiced to Dellums their concerns about discrimination in the military as "the dregs of the Army."[142]

Senior government officials also showed their displeasure with the Congressional Black Caucus. Their congressional colleagues on the House Armed Services Committee refused the caucus's request that one of their members be allowed to attend the Armed Services Committee's investigations into the *Kitty Hawk* and *Constellation* uprisings,[143] and Chappie James denounced the "criticism from the black side of the house," calling it "unfortunate" in light of the fact that on the issue of race, the armed forces in the past decade had "made more progress than in the whole history of the Armed Forces."[144]

The Military Strikes Back

Against the Congressional Black Caucus or the NAACP, the command structure was forced to limit its actions to issuing public statements denying military racism and to harassing service personnel who cooperated with these groups. But armed with Laird's 1969 directive, military authorities were under no such restrictions in dealing with self-confessed militants and radicals, and authorities seemed very willing to use the formidable powers at their command to ruthlessly eliminate militants from the ranks. For this reason Milton White and Mayanard Jordan purposely kept "the conflict dialectically abstract" and did not involve the Malcolm X Society in direct action or in confrontations with the air force command structure. "Mutiny, insurrection, and political disobedience wasn't our thing," White explained; but he was also a seasoned veteran of the struggle and realized that officials would use any such activity as an excuse to suppress the dissidents. "If you think Hiroshima looked bad, think of how [the military] would powder a bunch of insurrectionist niggers," he warned.[145]

White's bitter appraisal proved all too accurate. The authorities reacted to dissidents' attempts to educate their fellow servicepersons by banning the distribution of virtually all alternative literature, including most of the underground papers on the posts, and by declaring local coffeehouses off-limits to active-duty personnel. Servicepersons who attended rallies or demonstrations off base were disciplined. In at least one case, at Fort Hood, Texas, in October 1971, blacks who attended a rally sponsored by the Fort Hood United Front were first arrested by civil authorities and then charged with being AWOL by army officials.[146]

Military authorities believed the best way to eliminate radical influence from the ranks was to eliminate the radicals themselves from the services, and it was in this direction that they channeled most of their energies. Sometimes a dissident was simply transferred from a large, populous stateside base to a remote installation where he or she could do little harm. Joseph Miles found himself transferred from Fort Jackson, South Carolina, to a small radar installation in Alaska.[147] Fellow radical Ed Jurenas was sent to an equally distant outpost in that state.[148] But it was more common for authorities to use the military justice system to punish radicals or to process them out of the service than it was for them just to transfer the militants. The sentences were often quite harsh. In February 1969 navy lieutenant junior grade (jg) Susan Schnall, an African American and active member of the GI Association, was convicted of antiwar activity by court-martial, at the Presidio in San Francisco, for dropping antiwar leaflets from an airplane over that city, then disobeying a naval directive against attending antiwar functions in uniform by appearing in an antiwar parade. The twenty-five-year-old nurse and Stanford graduate was given six months at hard labor—the first woman in the navy ever to be given a sentence at hard labor—and was dismissed from the service on completion of her sentence.[149] Airmen Marty Dixon and Johny McRae were both given eighteen months of hard labor and bad conduct discharges in convictions stemming from their involvement at the Malcolm X rally and ensuing riot in South Korea in 1971.[150]

Prime targets of the military's campaign to suppress the radicals were the leadership cadres of the black leftist nationalist organizations. The American Servicemen's Union's main organizer at Fort Knox, Thomas Tuck, was court-martialed and dismissed from the army,[151] and in 1969, Andrew Pulley of GIs United was dishonorably discharged,[152] as were ASU founder Andrew Stapp and most of the members of the "Fort Jackson Eight," a group of the most prominent activists in GIs United.[153] A few of the radicals successfully defied the military's attempts to get rid of them. Miles and Rudder spent sixty-one days in the stockade but beat their dismissal charges.[154] In 1970, Stapp won a small victory when a federal judge overturned his dishonorable discharge, but he was still kept out of the army.[155]

Most of the radicals were not as fortunate as Miles, Rudder, and Stapp, and unlike these men, they were not eager to remain in uniform. The least officials could do was to make their lives miserable, and the lengthy prison sentences and bad conduct discharges attested to what could happen to them if they stayed in the services as active militants. Accordingly, a de facto compromise developed where many militants accepted a general discharge, usually under honorable conditions, and the military dropped all pending charges. Under Naval Operations Order (NAVOP) 231, issued in December 1972, the navy formally adopted a program under which seamen "who are an administrative burden to their commands because of repeated disciplinary infractions" could request general discharges under honorable conditions in the best interests of both the individual and the navy. The program was supposed to end in February 1973, but it was so successful that the navy extended it indefinitely.[156]

By February 1973 the armed forces had not totally eliminated radical influence in the services, but they had successfully contained it, and its strength was definitely in decline. Ultimately, the radicals had proved less

influential and easier to suppress than authorities had originally antici-
pated.

In April 1972, Undersecretary of the Army Kenneth E. Belieu stated in
an internal Pentagon memorandum that radical activity in that branch of
the services had been "over-estimated" and "over-rated." Only one out of
two hundred Vietnam veterans surveyed by the army a month earlier had
reported seeing an underground newspaper, at Long Binh, that he thought
might "foster racial tension" between blacks and whites. Clinton Hunt did
not recall seeing any radical literature during his tour of duty in Vietnam,
and in testimony before the House Internal Security Committee, Roland
Morrow stated that the Marine Corps "has no record of any individual
refusing to obey orders who was affiliated with a subversive or extremist
organization," adding that "there is no evidence of subversive direction in
racial incidents occurring within the Marine Corps."[157]

Contrary to the beliefs of military officials, the radicals were not responsible for aggravating the racial violence in the armed forces. The radicals
saw both black and white enlisted personnel as class allies against the real
enemy, the command structure. Far from advocating racial violence, they
counseled against it and, like the VVAW, stressed the need to be "one
people" against a "common oppressor."[158] Bobby Seale of the Panthers told
black soldiers that white GIs were also oppressed by the power structure
and that they should not "fight racism with racism."[159] The MDM took a
similar stand, declaring that "all GI brothers must unite to fight the
real enemy—the Pig!" To demonstrate their solidarity with their white
revolutionary brothers, all three of the large service organizations, the
MDM, the ASU, and GIs United, also recruited whites as members.[160]

Ironically, the emphasis on class, rather than on race, helped limit the
influence of the radical organizations. The trend in the military was toward
racial separation and solidarity, and most blacks were suspicious of all
"Chucks" and did not care to fraternize with them, whether at service clubs
or in revolutionary circles. Racial friction within the MDM, for example,
finally led that organization to disintegrate into several racially exclusive
splinter groups. At the Oleo Strut, black activist Vernon Chapman la-
mented the fact that "most of the heavy dudes have left and now we have
[only] a few people who build comradeship and relate with white radicals."
Conversely, few black radicals were involved in the Shelter Half coffeehouse
in Seattle, and Panthers spoke there only rarely as guest speakers and only
at the invitation of the Socialist Workers Party.[161]

The radical doctrines preached by many of the activists also alienated most black service personnel and occasionally led to divisions within the black military community. Fistfights broke out among black women stationed at Fort McClellan, for example, when most of them refused to join their more militant sisters in a scheduled protest. Eventually, only a few more than a hundred of the two thousand women stationed at that base attended the rally. Most often, however, black military personnel responded to the radicals and their message with disdain and apathy. Alfonza Wright, an expressed admirer of Dr. Martin Luther King, found Eldridge Cleaver and his book *Soul on Ice* to be "despicable" and thought very little in general of Stokely Carmichael, H. Rap Brown, or the Black Panthers. "I knew some Panthers back in Baltimore," he relates, "but I didn't even bother with those guys." One witness before the House Committee on Internal Security testified that the CPUSA and the SWP had little real influence over most blacks,[162] and Bob Wilkinson of the SWP admitted that the "ultraleft rhetoric" of the MDM "isolates them from the majority of GIs."[163] One black NCO informed the Congressional Black Caucus that "all black militants are no good. All they want to do is rule the world. All they want to do is make trouble."[164] And Roy Wilkins asserted in 1971 that "the overwhelming number of Negro servicemen with whom we talked are prepared to continue to fight for change within the system."[165]

Ultimately, it was the end of the draft and the war in Vietnam, the willingness of most blacks to work within the system, and the reforms instituted to eliminate prejudice and ensure equality of treatment for all personnel that did the most to eliminate racial tension and violence and radical influence from the services. Discrimination obviously had not been totally eliminated, and there was still some racially based discontent in the ranks. But like the war in Vietnam, for most African American military personnel, the worst was finally over.

7

Aftermath

Postwar Recruitment

The end of the Vietnam War also brought an end to the most severe and violent forms of racial discontent in the military, and by 1975 a relative peace had returned to the ranks. But what would never return, it seemed, was the armed forces's glowing reputation as the most racially advanced institution in America. A once well deserved reputation had been trashed by years of war, the heightened expectations of the new inductees, and the initial refusal of the military even to acknowledge that serious problems existed. It now appeared that African Americans no longer viewed military service as an honorable obligation owed to one's country or as a route to social and economic advancement.

Pentagon officials had noted this change in attitude as early as 1970 but decided it would not have a major impact on the number of black recruits. A year earlier, in 1969, President Richard Nixon had authorized the President's Commission on an All-Volunteer Armed Force—more commonly referred to as the Gates Commission after its chairman, former secretary of defense Thomas Gates—to study the problems of postwar recruitment. In its final report, released in 1970, the commission predicted that black enlistments would either remain stable or drop off slightly and concluded that "the composition of the armed forces will not be fundamentally changed by ending conscription," estimating that African Americans were unlikely to make up more than 15 to 19 percent of the military.[1]

In the years after the war, however, the Gates Commission estimates proved to be too conservative, and contrary to a perceived hostility toward the military in the black community, African American enlistments in the new "all-volunteer" army rose significantly. In the first postwar year, 1974, African Americans constituted around 16 percent of the armed forces, in line with the Gates Commission forecasts and not much different from the prewar 1964 percentage. But as the services continued the conversion to an all-volunteer force, the number of African Americans in uniform quickly rose, peaking in 1979, when blacks made up nearly one third of the enlisted strength.[2] Afterward, the numbers dropped off slightly, but as late as the 1991 Persian Gulf War, African Americans comprised more than one-quarter of the military's personnel.

After being mildly concerned in the years after Vietnam that an all-volunteer military would not be attractive to minorities, some officials expressed concern that too many African Americans were enlisting. There were legitimate concerns that, as in Vietnam, blacks would endure a disproportionate share of the casualties in the "next" war. This remained an almost chronic fear through the Persian Gulf War, when, fortunately, such dire predictions failed to come to pass. In fact, African Americans suffered fewer than expected casualties in the conflict. Though African Americans made up nearly one-quarter of the American troops deployed to the gulf, they constituted only 16.8 percent, or 63, of the 375 fatalities suffered by U.S. forces during Operations Desert Shield and Desert Storm.[3]

Another concern expressed by the military officials was that many minorities were enlisting primarily for economic, rather than patriotic, concerns and might prove untrustworthy in times of crisis. Although the Gates Commission had favored an all-volunteer force, its report also had listed the major objections to such an establishment, among which were the concerns that it could be virtually all black and dominated by individuals "motivated primarily by monetary rewards rather than patriotism."[4] In testimony before the House Armed Services Committee, Congresswoman Shirley Chisolm blasted such critics, remarking that "all this talk about a volunteer army being poor and black is not an indication of concern for the black and poor, but rather of the deep fear of the possibility of a black army. Individuals who are upset over black power rhetoric really shudder at the idea of a whole army of black men trained as professional soldiers."[5]

It is true that many of the new black enlistees were joining up for primarily economic reasons; the unemployment rate for young black males had continually remained high. Between 1973 and 1985, for example, the unemployment rate for nineteen-year-old black men fluctuated between 28 percent and 41 percent; by comparison, unemployment rates for nineteen-year-old white men over the same period fluctuated between 12 and 18 percent.[6] The picture was almost as bleak for black Vietnam veterans who left the service as it was for young black males in general. Most returned to communities where the unemployment rates were at least three times the national average. A Detroit area study of five thousand Vietnam veterans in 1973 found that one out of every four black veterans was still unemployed six months after leaving the services. Nationwide, nearly one-third of black veterans between the ages of twenty and twenty-four did not have jobs, compared to only 5.7 percent for returning white veterans.[7]

"Wished We Had Stayed in Vietnam"

Some veterans reacted by becoming bitter, feeling used and then abandoned by the nation they had served. Vietnam veteran Robert Jenkins observed, "They'll polish your shoes while you are there, but then they start their crap the minute they get back over here,"[8] and Vietnam veteran Casper Smith, echoing Jenkins's sentiments, remarked that "most of the people in Washington act like they wished we had stayed in Vietnam."[9] Bill Lawson, vice president of minority affairs for the National Association of Concerned Veterans, summed up the experiences of many African American veterans when he wrote:

> Since the enactment of the first GI Bill, the desires, needs, and problems of the minority veteran have seldom, if ever, been met to the extent of his counterpart. Drug rehabilitation in the armed service has proved, for the most part futile. Minority drug users are released back into a drug oriented . . . community. Unfavorable discharge reviews compounded by the assignment of Separation Program Numbers (SPN) have created a virtual wasteland for minority employment opportunities. Yesterday the ghetto, today a military obligation, tomorrow the ghetto.[10]

Despite Lawson's pessimistic but all too often true assessment, there was help in the form of both public and private agencies to assist the returning Vietnam veteran in securing employment. Military personnel who were nearing discharge and had less than six months of service time left could enroll in Project Transition, a four-part program of counseling, education, job training, and job placement, sponsored jointly by the Pentagon and private industry; and veterans who wished to attend college or a trade school could take advantage of the GI Bill of 1967. In addition to federal aid, most states and big cities had their own veterans affairs offices, which offered job counseling and placement among their services. Some civil rights organizations started their own programs to help returning African Americans in the transition from the military back into a civilian life. In 1967, Whitney Young, Jr., and the Urban League established the Veterans Affairs Program, aimed specifically at the newly returned black veteran. The program proved so successful that it eventually opened offices in nine major cities.[11] Black veterans also took matters into their own hands by establishing self-help and cooperative groups in conjunction with veterans agencies and academic institutions. In 1969, for example, Alfonza Wright, Kenneth Jackson, and other black veterans at the Community College of Baltimore established a veterans club aimed at job training and placement, with help from the American Association of Junior Colleges and the American Legion.[12]

Veterans who took advantage of one of these programs usually found work. Wright and Jackson's organization successfully placed many returning soldiers in construction and steel industry jobs. The Urban League found Bill Robinson a job as an account executive with a Manhattan dry-cleaning firm within days of his discharge, and the program placed twenty-one-year-old Raul Ferran in the New York-based Clarke Equipment Company as an apprentice mechanic. In all, the Urban League's program managed to find employment for 80 percent of those who applied for assistance.[13]

But for all their successes, the programs also left a lot to be desired. Because most of the programs were concentrated in urban areas, veterans who lived in rural areas seldom received any organized help. And sometimes, even moving to a larger city did little good. Casper Smith, for instance, could not work in his rural South Carolina hometown after leaving the service, so out of desperation he moved to Washington, D.C.; but the only employment he could secure there was a part-time job selling insurance. Another problem was that many veterans were unaware of the federal benefits available to them under the GI Bill and through Project Transition and various other programs, and for those who did know, even the more generous federal programs seldom offered more than limited help. The GI Bill, for instance, provided living stipends of $130 a month to single veterans and $160 a month to married ones while they attended school, an amount characterized by Otilio Mighty of the Urban League as doing "more to provide pocket money for the middle class vet . . . than it does for the average black veteran who comes from a disadvantaged background."[14] And usually, all too many of the jobs that were available were unskilled or entry-level positions that offered only minimal pay. Otilio Mighty characterized many of the jobs he could find for returning black veterans as equivalent in income to what a white without a high school diploma could hope to earn. Often the only jobs the Baltimore veterans club could find for its applicants were as caddies or janitors at a local country club, quite a humiliating comedown for men who had seen combat, commanded others, and shouldered great responsibilities while in uniform.[15]

"Things Got Better"

For many Vietnam veterans, the solution was to remain in or return to the military. In fact, it was not necessarily new enlistments but reenlistments that accounted for the overrepresentation of African Americans in the postwar armed forces. In 1972 only one in five army first-term black enlistees chose to reenlist, which reflected the antipathy African Americans felt toward the military at the end of the war. By 1981, however, more than two-thirds of the black first-term enlistees chose to "re-up" for another tour, and overall, four out of every five blacks in the military in that year decided to reenlist, most having decided to make a career out of the services. By contrast, only one out of every five white soldiers stayed in the armed forces.[16]

Financial considerations, job security, and a higher social status certainly influenced many African Americans' decision to remain in the armed forces, but there were other important factors. The end of the war in Vietnam meant a serviceperson's chances of getting killed in uniform were dramatically reduced, and this alone made a military career more attractive. Most important, many black military career personnel had become convinced that the services had indeed changed for the better with regard to issues of race and racism. Years of agitation and unrest may have damaged the service careers of numerous African Americans, but they did force the armed services to confront the problems of personal and institutional racism and to enact meaningful and enforceable reforms. "Things got better for some of us after Vietnam," recalled Allen Thomas, Jr. "The military had the ability, the power . . . it cannot control your thinking, but it can control the way you act. It was a lot better because some things were just no longer permitted."[17]

One reason the new reforms enacted toward the end of the war were so successful was that African Americans at that time were in a far better position to see that the reforms were enforced. The number of blacks in the chain of command had risen steadily, if not dramatically, in the postwar years. In fact, by the early 1980s African Americans were overrepresented in the more senior noncommissioned officer grades; African Americans constituted well over one-third of all personnel in grades E-4 to E-6, and numbered nearly one in three in grades E-7, E-8, and E-9. The number of black commissioned officers also increased, though nowhere near in proportion to the enlisted strength of African Americans. By 1989, African Americans represented 6 percent of the military's officer corps, triple the number from the Vietnam War years. In the same year, in the army blacks accounted for almost 11 percent of all officers, but in the other services the gains were more modest; blacks made up more than 5 percent of the officer corps in both the air force and the marines but still constituted less than 4 percent of the navy's commissioned officers.[18]

A sizable increase in sheer numbers of black officers certainly helped, but more important, African Americans were now in senior command and policy making positions. In 1964, Benjamin O. Davis, Jr., was the only active-duty African American general in the armed forces, and he retired before the end of the Vietnam War, in 1970. Four years later there were twelve black generals in the army, three in the air force, and, with Samuel Gravely's promotion, finally a black navy admiral. In 1979, Hazel Winifred Johnson became the first black female brigadier general in the army, and before his early death in 1978 at age fifty-eight from heart trouble, Daniel "Chappie" James, Jr., had become the first black four-star general in American history.[19] Had his promising career not been cut short, James might conceivably have become the first black chairman of the Joint Chiefs of Staff; but that honor went instead to another black Vietnam war veteran, Colin Powell, who was named to the post in 1989. Powell's assumption of the highest-ranking military post in the armed forces and his subsequent handling of the Persian Gulf War are a testament not only to Powell's own outstanding abilities but also to how much African Americans have left their mark on the postwar armed forces.

Meaningful and Normal Lives

Military service, particularly a tour of duty in Southeast Asia, also left its mark on black veterans, and often it was not for the better. Vietnam made Henry Dority "hard around the edges, skeptical, cynical," and unable to trust anyone. After he left the army, his marriage fell apart and he was unable to hold a job. By 1990 he was homeless, living in a room over the headquarters of a Vietnam Veterans of America chapter, and trying to put his life back together again.[20] Like so many veterans, Dority suffers from post-traumatic stress disorder (PTSD), a "biosomatopsychic disorder in response to catastrophic events," often caused by the stress and terror of combat. Though PTSD is a serious disorder that affects veterans of all races, it tends to strike African American veterans most frequently, with one study reporting that nearly 40 percent of all black veterans showed symptoms of stress disorder, compared to about one in five whites. Those who, like Dority, served in heavy combat were most likely to develop PTSD or other stress-related psychological disorders.

One of the more tragic cases of stress disorder involved Medal of Honor recipient Sergeant Dwight Johnson. Though his physical wounds from war soon healed, Johnson never recovered from the psychological trauma and stress of his Vietnam experiences. Shortly after receiving his nation's highest honor from President Lyndon Johnson in a White House ceremony in November 1968, Sergeant Johnson was admitted to a military hospital in Valley Forge, Pennsylvania. He was still under treatment in May 1971, when doctors allowed him a six-day pass to visit his wife and son, believing he did not represent a "threat of harm to himself or to others." Instead of seeing his family, the highly decorated but troubled veteran was shot to death by the owner of a "party" store in Detroit that Johnson allegedly had attempted to rob.[21]

Most veterans, however, went on to more meaningful and normal lives. Clinton Hunt married, settled down, and works for the post office.[22] John Brackett also married, earned a Ph.D. in history at Stanford, and is currently chairman of the Afro-American Studies Department at the University of Cincinnati.[23] Allen Thomas, Jr., retired from the army in 1978 and is currently sergeant of security for Northern Kentucky University.[24] Alfonza Wright retired from the army in 1993 and now is studying to pursue yet another career, this time as a high school guidance counselor.[25]

Regardless of their ultimate postmilitary fate, collectively the Hunts, Wrights, Powells, and Johnsons, along with the other two million black Vietnam War veterans, have left a permanent legacy—that of a more racially egalitarian military establishment. In writing about one particularly courageous black officer, Lieutenant Gary Scott, who was killed in Vietnam, Phillip L. Woodall remarked that "Gary died in vain, alright. All who died in Vietnam did so. I will not try to smother the reality of a lost cause."[26] Vietnam may have been a lost cause, but the Scotts and Johnsons did not die in vain, and the others did not serve without purpose. They forced the armed forces to live up to their promises of equality and opportunity and paved the way for other groups, such as gays and women, to claim their just place in America's military establishment. If African Americans were indeed fighting on two fronts during the Vietnam War, they at least scored a victory over racism on one front while serving with distinction and honor on the other.

Notes

Notes to Chapter 1

1. Quoted in Whitney Young, Jr., "To Be Equal," *Baltimore Afro-American,* 19 February 1966, 1.

2. Ibid.

3. Cited in Sol Stern, "When the Black GI Comes Back from Vietnam," *New York Times Magazine,* 24 March 1968, 39.

4. Thomas Johnson, "The U.S. Negro in Vietnam," *New York Times,* 29 April 1968, 1.

5. Henry I. Shaw, Jr., and Ralph W. Donnelly, *Blacks in the Marine Corps* (Washington, D.C.: U.S. Marine Corps, History and Museums Division Headquarters, 1975), 78.

6. Thomas Johnson, "Negroes in the Nam," *Ebony,* August 1968, 31–34.

7. Wallace Terry, "Bringing the War Home," *Black Scholar* 2 (November 1970): 7.

8. General William H. Westmoreland, quoted in Johnson, "U.S. Negro," 16.

9. Major Richard H. Torovsky, Jr., interview, Senior Officer Oral History Project, Company Command series, U.S. Army Military History Institute, Carlisle Barracks, Pennsylvania, 1982, 22.

10. Major John J. Ellis, interview, Senior Officer Oral History Project, Company Command series, 1982, 4–7.

11. Major Donald Dean, interview, Senior Officer Oral History Project, Company Command series, 1982, 7.

12. Daniel "Chappie" James, Jr., "Rapping with Chappie," *Air University Review* (July 1972): 13.

13. "He Taught Those of Us Who Remain How We Ought to Live," *Baltimore Afro-American,* 30 April 1966, 1.

14. Shaw and Donnelly, *Blacks in the Marine Corps,* 97; "U.S. Gives First Medal of Honor to a Negro Marine," *New York Times,* 22 August 1968, 4; and "Marine Barracks Named after Medal of Honor Winner," *Baltimore Afro-American,* 24 January 1970, 12.

15. Department of Defense, Office of the Deputy Assistant Secretary of Defense for Equal Opportunity and Safety Policy, *Black Americans in Defense of Our Nation* (Washington, D.C.: U.S. Government Printing Office, 1978), 67.

16. Rudolf J. Friedrich, "Fifty-four Black Heroes: Medal of Honor Winners," *The Crisis* (June-July 1969): 243. The actual number of African American recipients of the Medal of Honor is in dispute. Friedrich's list apparently includes some who were nominated for the award but never actually received it.

17. "Bronze Star Is Given to Soldier Slain in South Vietnam," *New York Times*, 14 October 1968, 3.

18. Department of Defense, *Black Americans*, 67–86; and Shaw and Donnelly, *Blacks in the Marine Corps*, 97–101.

19. Thomas Johnson, "Negro Veteran Is Confused and Bitter," *New York Times*, 29 July 1968, 14.

20. "Veteran Says Vietnamese Support Black Struggle," *Baltimore Afro-American*, 17 January 1970, 17.

21. Department of Defense, *Black Americans*, 75.

22. Conrad Clark, "This Is Vietnam," *Baltimore Afro-American*, 10 January 1970, 22.

23. "He Taught Those of Us Who Remain," 2.

24. "When the Black GI Comes Back," 37.

25. Lawrence M. Baskir and William A. Strauss, *Chance and Circumstance: The Draft, the War, and the Vietnam Generation* (New York: Random House, 1978), 8; and L. Deckle McLean, "The Black Man and the Draft," *Ebony*, August 1968, 62.

26. Johnson, "U.S. Negro," 16.

27. Martin Binkin, *Who Will Fight the Next War* (Washington, D.C.: The Brookings Institute, 1993), 69; Johnson, "U.S. Negro," 16; "How Negro Americans Perform in Vietnam," *U.S. News and World Report*, 15 August 1966, 62.

28. Baskir and Strauss, *Chance and Circumstance*, 8; and Roger W. Little, *Selective Service and American Society* (New York: Russell Sage Foundation, 1969), 159, for data concerning the years 1965–68.

29. Harry G. Summers, *Vietnam War Almanac* (New York: Facts on File Publications, 1985), 98.

30. Veterans Administration, *Myths and Realities: A Study of Attitudes toward Vietnam Era Veterans,* report submitted to the Senate Committee on Veteran Affairs, 96th Cong., 2d sess. (Washington, D.C.: U.S. Government Printing Office, 1980), 7.

31. Peter Karsten, ed., *The Military in America, from the Colonial Era to the Present* (New York: Free Press, 1980), 75; and Department of Defense, *Annual Report for Fiscal Year 1968* (Washington, D.C.: U.S. Government Printing Office, 1971), 74. For more data, see also; Department of Defense, *The Negro in the Armed*

Forces: A Statistical Fact Book (Washington, D.C.: Department of Defense, Office of the Deputy Assistant Secretary of Defense for Equal Opportunity and Safety Policy, 1971).

32. Shaw and Donnelly, *Blacks in the Marine Corps,* 78.

33. L. Deckle McLean, "The Black Man and the Draft," *Ebony,* August 1968, 62.

34. Thomas Johnson, "Negroes in Vietnam are Uneasy About U.S.," *New York Times,* 1 May 1968, 1.

35. Baskir and Strauss, *Chance and Circumstance,* 8.

36. Johnson, "U.S. Negro," 1

37. James Edward Hawkins, Jr., interview with the author, Cincinnati, Ohio, 9 July 1991.

38. Henry Dority, interview with the author, Cincinnati, Ohio, 26 May 1991.

39. Clinton H. Hunt, interview with the author, Cincinnati, Ohio, 21 September 1991.

40. Major Bruce B. Cary, interview, Senior Officer Oral History Project, Company Command series, 1982, 6.

41. Major Henry L. Parker, interview, Senior Officer Oral History Project, Company Command series, 1982, 6.

42. Allen Thomas, Jr., interview with the author, Highland Heights, Kentucky, 22 March 1995; Clinton Hunt interview; and Stern, "When the Black GI Comes Back," 29.

43. Hawkins interview.

44. Stern, "When the Black GI Comes Back," 2.

45. Alfonzo Wright, interview with the author, Pikeville, North Carolina, 27 December 1995.

46. Stern, "When the Black GI Comes Back," 27.

47. David Llorens, "Why Negroes Re-enlist," *Ebony,* August 1968, 88.

48. Department of Defense, *Annual Report for Fiscal Year 1968,* 15.

49. Llorens, "Why Negroes Re-enlist," 88.

50. Clark, "This Is Vietnam," 22.

51. Terry, "Bringing the War Home," 8.

52. Keith Walker, *A Piece of My Heart: The Stories of Twenty-six Women Who Served in Vietnam* (Novato, Calif.: Presidio Press, 1991), 250–252.

53. Quoted in Kathryn Marshall, *In the Combat Zone; An Oral History of American Women in Vietnam* (Boston: Little, Brown & Co., 1987), 37.

54. Major General Frederic E. Davison, interview, Senior Officer Oral History Project, Blacks in the Armed Forces series, U.S. Military History Institute, Carlisle Barracks, Pennsylvania, 1977, 26.

55. "Casualties in Viet Nam," *Baltimore Afro-American,* 26 March 1966, 5.

56. "Black Marines Die Needlessly," *Black Panther,* 26 October 1968, 3.

57. Department of Defense, *Annual Report for Fiscal Year 1968,* 38.

Notes to Chapter 2

1. "Viet Rebuke Stirs Storm," *Baltimore Afro-American*, 22 January 1966, 14. Lewis issued his remarks on behalf of the Student Nonviolent Coordinating Committee at an Atlanta press conference. For the complete text of his statement, see John Lewis, "SNCC Statement on Vietnam," *Freedomways* 6, first quarter, (winter 1966): 6–7.

2. Ralph Matthews, "Oscar DePriest Once Faced Ordeal of Julian Bond," *Baltimore Afro-American*, 19 February 1966, 14.

3. "Viet Rebuke Stirs Storm"; and L. Deckle McLean, "The Black Man and the Draft," *Ebony*, August 1968, 62. For further elaboration on both SNCC's and Dr. King's positions on the draft and the war in Vietnam, see Herbert Shapiro, "The Vietnam War and the American Civil Rights Movement," *Journal of Ethnic Studies* 16, 4 (1989): 117–41.

4. "Conyers Explains Vietnam Vote," *Baltimore Afro-American*, 12 March 1966, 14: and "Draft Test Unfair Says Adam Powell," *Baltimore Afro-American*, 21 May 1966, 1.

5. Quoted in Robert W. Mullen, *Blacks in America's Wars: The Shift in Attitudes from the Revolutionary War to Vietnam* (New York: Monad Press/Pathfinder Press, 1973), 65.

6. Richard M. Scammon, "Report from Black America," *Newsweek*, 30 June 1969, 19.

7. A good example of the militant African American stance on the war, linking opposition to the conflict with opposition to racism, black liberation, and solidarity with third world peoples, especially the National Liberation Front of Vietnam, can be seen in "Manifesto of the American Deserters Committee," *Black Panther*, 17 February 1969, 11.

8. McLean, "The Black Man and the Draft," 61–63.

9. Vietnam Veterans against the War, "Position Paper on Amnesty," manuscript (Placitas, New Mexico, 19–23 April 1973), in Citizen Soldier File 7037, box 1, file 1, Vietnam War Veterans' Archive and Manuscript Collection, Department of Manuscripts and University Archives, Ithaca, Cornell University Library, New York.

10. "Refuses Induction, Youth Gets Twenty-five Years," *Pittsburgh Courier*, 26 July 1969, 2; and "Black Draft Resister Is Sentenced," *Black Panther*, 16 August 1969, 20.

11. For examples, see "An Undying Love," *Black Panther*, 16 March 1968, 5; Eldridge Cleaver, "The Black Man's Stake in Vietnam," *Black Panther*, 23 March 1969, 16; "Editorial Policy," *Black Liberator*, March 1969, 2; "Black Antiwar Union," *Black Liberator*, September 1969, 9.

12. Department of Defense, Office of the Deputy Assistant of Defense for Equal Opportunity and Safety Policy, *Black Americans in Defense of Our Nation* (Washington, D.C.: U.S. Government Printing Office, 1978), 43.

13. Source of statistics: U.S. Army Recruiting Command, "Qualitative Distribution Report of Male Enlistments, Inductions and Rejections," DD-MM663, cited in Paul T. Murray, "Blacks and the Draft: A History of Institutional Racism," *Journal of Black Studies* (September 1971): 69.

14. Ibid., 59; and Ulysses Lee, "The Draft and the Negro," *Current History* (July 1968): 30.

15. Jack D. Foner, *Blacks and the Military in American History,* New Perspectives in American History (New York: Praeger Publishers, 1974), 11, 133–34; and Murray, "Blacks and the Draft," 64.

16. Russell F. Weigley, *History of the United States Army* (New York: Macmillan Co., 1967), 555–56; Martin Binkin and Mark J. Eitelberg with Alvin Schexnider and Marvin Smith, *Blacks and the Military,* Studies in Defense Policy (Washington, D.C.: The Brookings Institute, 1982), 26; and Murray, "Blacks and the Draft," 66–68.

17. Foner, *Blacks and the Military in American History,* 188– 90; Binkin and Eitelberg, *Blacks and the Military,* 33; and Murray, "Blacks and the Draft," 68–69.

18. Allen Thomas, Jr., interview with the author, Highland Heights, Kentucky, 22 March 1995.

19. Department of Defense, *Black Americans,* 43; "Abuse of the Draft," *Baltimore Afro-American,* 15 January 1966, 4; and "Lottery-Draft Won't Alter Race Ratio," *Pittsburgh Courier,* 24 May 1969, 3.

20. Scammon, "Report from Black America," 19.

21. Maurice Zeitlin, Kenneth G. Lutterman, and James W. Russell, "Death in Vietnam: Class, Poverty, and the Risks of War," in Maurice Zeitlin, ed., *American Society, Inc.: Studies of the Social Structure and Political Economy of the United States,* (Chicago: Rand McNally & Co., 1977), 145–46.

22. Veterans Administration, *Myths and Realities: A Study of Attitudes toward Vietnam Era Veterans,* report submitted to the Senate Committee on Veteran Affairs, 96th Cong., 2d sess. (Washington, D.C.: U.S. Government Printing Office, 1980), 6.

23. Stewart Alsop, "The American Class System," *Newsweek,* 29 June 1970, 88. In fairness, Alsop also reports that sixty graduates of the three mentioned schools volunteered and were killed in Vietnam.

24. Lee, "The Draft and the Negro," 47.

25. "The Marshall Commission Report," *Current History* (July 1968): 49.

26. Binkin and Eitelberg, *Blacks and the Military,* 33; McLean, "The Black Man and the Draft," 63–64; and Foner, *Blacks and the Military in American History,* 203. Six Southern states that had no African American representation on local draft boards in 1966 were Alabama, Arkansas, Georgia, Louisiana, Mississippi, and South Carolina.

27. "Suit Urges Negroes for Draft Boards," *New York Times,* 19 April 1968, 21.

28. "Halt Asked in Draft in Two Southern States by Liberties Union," *New York*

Times, 7 March 1967, 33; Gene Roberts, "Rights Leader Refuses to Be Inducted into Army," *New York Times,* 2 May 1967, 7; and McLean, "The Black Man and the Draft," 63–64.

29. Murray, "Blacks and the Draft," 73; Foner, *Blacks and the Military in American History,* 203; and McLean, "The Black Man and the Draft," 63.

30. Lee, "The Draft and the Negro," 47.

31. "Kluxer Fights Ouster as Draft Board Head," *Baltimore Afro-American,* 2 April 1966, 13.

32. "Goodby to Civilian Life," *Ebony,* August 1968, 46.

33. Lawrence M. Baskir and William Strauss, *Chance and Circumstance: The Draft, the War, and the Vietnam Generation* (New York: Random House, 1978), 98.

34. "Goodby to Civilian Life," 46.

35. "Marshall Commission Report," 46–49; Edward Fisk, "On Conscientious Objection to This War," *New York Times,* 5 February 1967, sec. 4, 5.

36. McLean, "The Black Man and the Draft," 64.

37. "Muslim Gets Three Year Term for Balking at Draft Exam," *New York Times,* 19 January 1967, 39.

38. Baskir and Strauss, *Chance and Circumstance,* 97; Martin Waldron, "Clay Guilty in Draft Case; Gets Five Years in Prison," *New York Times,* 21 June 1967, 1.

39. "Cassius Faces March Draft," *Baltimore Afro-American,* 19 February 1966, 1; "Board in Kentucky Refuses to Reclassify Clay as Conscientious Objector," *New York Times,* 11 January 1967, 62; and "Clay Draft Plea Denied by Board," *New York Times,* 1 February 1967, 31.

40. "Cassius Faces March Draft," 1; and "Clay Draft Plea Denied," 31.

41. "Clay Guilty in Draft Case," 1; and David E. Rosenbaum, "Ali Wins in Draft Case Appeal," *New York Times,* 29 June 1971, 1.

42. "Muhammad Ali—The Measure of a Man," *Freedomways* 7, second quarter (spring 1967): 102; and Rosenbaum, "Ali Wins," 1.

43. Baskir and Strauss, *Chance and Circumstance,* 97.

44. Roberts, "Rights Leader Refuses," 7.

45. "Move to Draft Rights Leader," *Baltimore Afro-American,* 22 January 1966, 13.

46. McLean, "The Black Man and the Draft," 64.

47. Baskir and Strauss, *Chance and Circumstance,* 99–100.

48. "Refuses Induction," 2; and "Black Draft Resister is Sentenced," 20.

49. Baskir and Strauss, *Chance and Circumstance,* 100.

50. Foner, *Blacks and the Military in American History,* 202; "Marshall Commission Report," 45; Murray, "Blacks and the Draft," 72; "Deferments in Draft," *New York Times,* 7 March 1967, 33; and "Lottery-Draft Won't Alter Race Ratio," 3.

51. Baskir and Strauss, *Chance and Circumstance,* 50–51.

52. Ibid.; and "360 Pros Reported Exempt from Draft," *New York Times,* 8 April 1967, 23.

53. "Blacks Shy Away from Nat'l Guard," *Pittsburgh Courier,* 5 April 1969, 1.

54. "Integration Lags in Md. Military," *Baltimore Afro-American,* 8 January 1966, 3.

55. Lee, "The Draft and the Negro," 47; Murray, "Blacks and the Draft," 71; and "Blacks Shy Away from Nat'l Guard," 1, 4.

56. Melvin R. Laird, *Final Report to the Congress of Secretary of Defense Melvin R. Laird* (Washington, D.C.: U.S. Department of Defense, 1973), 75.

57. Baskir and Strauss, *Chance and Circumstance,* 47; and Murray, "Blacks and the Draft," 70.

58. Baskir and Strauss, *Chance and Circumstance,* 73; and "Order of Induction," *New York Times,* 7 March 1967, 33.

59. Baskir and Strauss, *Chance and Circumstance,* 76; and David F. Addlestone, "A Background Paper on the Question of Less than Fully Honorable Military Discharges Issued during the Vietnam War," manuscript (National Veterans Law Center, Washington College of Law, American University, 27 April 1979), 2, in Flower of the Dragon file 7020, box 1, file 13, Vietnam War Veterans Archive and Manuscript Collection, Department of Manuscripts and University Archives, Cornell University Library, Ithaca, New York.

60. Baskir and Strauss, *Chance and Circumstance,* 38; Vietnam Veterans Against the War, "Report of the Vietnam Veterans Against the War Steering Committee Meeting," manuscript (Chicago, 4–8 January 1973), 7, in Vietnam Veterans Against the War/Winter Soldier Organization file 7019, box 1, file 1, Vietnam War Veterans Archive and Manuscript Collection, Department of Manuscripts and Archives, Cornell University Library, Ithaca, New York; and House Committee on Internal Security, *Investigation of Attempts to Subvert the United States Armed Forces,* 92d Cong., 2d sess. (Washington, D.C.: U.S. Government Printing Office, 1972), 6388.

61. Baskir and Strauss, *Chance and Circumstance,* 48.

62. Vietnam Veterans Against the War, "Report," 16.

63. "Seven Antidraft Pickets Are Indicted in Atlanta," *New York Times,* 18 February 1967, 16; and "Black Antiwar Union," 9.

64. Ben A. Franklin, "Protest on Vietnam Disrupts Draft Headquarters," *New York Times,* 1 April 1967, 5.

65. "Draft Cases Snag U.S. Courts," *Black Panther,* 13 September 1969, 20; and "Black Antiwar Groups to Meet," *The Guardian,* 6 April 1968, 4.

66. Johnny Woods, "Draft Resistance," *Black Liberator,* September 1969, 8.

67. Ibid., 9; and Roberts, "Rights Leader Refuses," 7.

68. "Carmichael Classified 4–F by Draft Board in the Bronx," *New York Times,* 14 March 1967, 39.

69. "Rules of the Black Panther Party," *Black Panther,* 28 September 1968, 2.

70. McLean, "The Black Man and the Draft," 63.

71. "Brass Force Black GI to Vietnam," *Black Panther,* 27 April 1969, 6.

72. "Black Soldiers in Vietnam Support the Struggle Back Home," *Black Panther,* 19 October 1968, 10.

73. Mark Allen, "The Case of Billy Dean Smith," *Black Scholar* (October 1972): 15.

74. Clinton H. Hunt, interview with the author, Cincinnati, Ohio, 21 September 1991.

75. The interviews with 1,119 African American adults were conducted in Atlanta, Birmingham, Chicago, and New York. See M. S. Handler, "Four-City Study of Negroes Finds Majority Hold Moderate Views," *New York Times*, 25 May 1967, 32.

76. Dr. John K. Brackett, interview with the author, Cincinnati, Ohio, 21 January 1992.

77. Department of Defense, Office of the Deputy Assistant Secretary of Defense for Equal Opportunity and Safety Policy, *Task Force on the Administration of Military Justice in the Armed Forces* (Washington, D.C.: U.S. Government Printing Office, 1972), 1:55.

78. James Edward Hawkins, interview with the author, Cincinnati, Ohio, 9 July 1991.

79. Ponchitta Pierce and Peter Bailey, "The Returning Vet," *Ebony*, August 1968, 150.

80. Department of Defense, *Task Force*, 1:44.

81. "Tough Chicago Gang Leader Returns from War a Hero," *Baltimore Afro-American*, 24 January 1970, 3.

82. Clyde Taylor, "Black Consciousness and the Vietnam War," *Black Scholar* (October 1973): 7.

83. William C. Westmoreland, *Report of the Chief of Staff of the United States Army, 1 July 1968 to 30 June 1972* (Washington, D.C.: Department of the Army, 1977), 10, 68.

84. Sol Stern, "When the Black GI Comes Back from Vietnam," *New York Times Magazine*, 24 March 1968, 37; and Binkin and Eitelberg, *Blacks and the Military*, 34.

85. Binkin and Eitelberg, *Blacks and the Military*, 34; and Department of Defense, *Annual Report for Fiscal Year 1968* (Washington, D.C.: U.S. Government Printing Office, 1971), 73.

86. Binkin and Eitelberg, *Blacks and the Military*, 34; Department of Defense, *Annual Report for Fiscal Year 1968*, 184; and Johnny Bowles, "A 41% Black GI Deal: Fight but Can't Re-Up," *Baltimore Afro-American*, 21 February 1970, 6.

87. Bowles, "41% Black GI Deal," 6; and Department of Defense, Assistant Secretary of Defense for Manpower and Reserve Affairs, *Project One Hundred Thousand: Characteristics and Performance of "New Standards" Men* (Washington, D.C.: U.S. Government Printing Office, 1969).

88. Whitney M. Young Jr., "When the Negroes in Vietnam Come Home," *Harpers*, June 1967, 66.

89. "Marshall Commission Report," 49; and Murray, "Blacks and the Draft," 71.

90. Foner, *Blacks and the Military in American History,* 202; and Wallace Terry, "Bringing the War Home," *Black Scholar* 2 (November 1970): 7–8.

91. Black Cadets, United States Air Force Academy, "An Answer to Wing Staff's Request," manuscript (Colorado, March, 1970), 2, in Citizen Soldier File 7033, box 8, file 54.

92. Milton White, "Malcolm X in the Military," *Black Scholar* (May 1970): 33.

93. Cited in the Honorable Ronald V. Dellums, "Institutional Racism in the Military," *Congressional Record,* 92d Cong., 2d sess. (2 March 1972), vol.118, pt.6 6740.

94. Department of Defense, *Black Americans,* 43; and William Stuart Gould, "Racial Conflict in the U.S. Army," *Race* 15, 1 (July 1973): 7.

95. Department of Defense, *Annual Report for Fiscal Year, 1968,* 74.

Notes to Chapter 3

1. Department of Defense, Office of the Deputy Assistant of Defense for Equal Opportunity and Safety Policy, *Task Force on the Administration of Military Justice in the Armed Forces* (Washington, D.C.: U.S. Government Printing Office, 1972), 1:19.

2. Ibid., 2:11–13; and National Association for the Advancement of Colored People, (NAACP), *The Search for Military Justice: Report of an NAACP Inquiry into the Problems of the Negro Serviceman in West Germany,* (New York: NAACP Special Contributions Fund, 1971), 1.

3. Department of Defense, *Task Force,* 2:13.

4. Ibid., 1:48; and Lawrence M. Baskir, and William Strauss, *Chance and Circumstance: The Draft, the War, and the Vietnam Generation* (New York: Random House, 1978), 125–26.

5. NAACP, *Search for Military Justice,* 1

6. The Honorable Louis Stokes, "Racism in the Military: A New System for Rewards and Punishment," Congressional Black Caucus Report, *Congressional Record,* 92d Cong., 2d sess. (14 October 1972), 36583, (Hereafter cited as "Black Caucus Report.")

7. NAACP, *Search for Military Justice,* 1–2; Department of Defense, *Task Force,* 1:39; and Henry I. Shaw, Jr., and Ralph W. Donnelly, *Blacks in the Marine Corps* (Washington, D.C.: U.S. Marine Corps, History and Museums Division Headquarters, 1975), 69.

8. NAACP, *Search for Military Justice,* 2.

9. Ibid., 3; Jack D. Foner, *Blacks and the Military in American History* (New York: Praeger Publishers, 1974), 208; David Llorens, "Why Negroes Re-enlist," *Ebony,* August 1968, 90; and Department of Defense, *Task Force,* 2:13.

10. Llorens, "Why Negroes Re-enlist," 90.

11. NAACP, *Search for Military Justice,* 3.

12. Morris J. MacGregor and Bernard C. Nalty, *Blacks in the United States Armed Forces: Basic Documents*, volume 11 of the Fahy Committee report (Wilmington, Del.: Scholarly Resources, 1977), 1343–45.

13. William Westmoreland, *Report of the Chief of Staff of the United States Army, 1 July 1968 to June 30 1972* (Washington, D.C.: Department of the Army, 1977), 50

14. Daniel "Chappie" James, Jr., "Rapping with Chappie,"*Air University Review* (July 1972): 14.

15. Melvin R. Laird, *Final Report to the Congress of Secretary of Defense Melvin R. Laird* (Washington, D.C.: U.S. Department of Defense, 1973), 75.

16. Westmoreland, *Report of the Chief of Staff,* 66.

17. William Bowman, Roger Little, and G. Thomas Sicilia, *The All-Volunteer Force after a Decade: Retrospect and Prospect,* (Washington, D.C.: Pergamon-Brassey, International Defense Publishers, 1984), 78.

18. Testimony of army lieutenant Joseph H. Hall, cited in the Honorable Ronald V. Dellums, "Institutional Racism in the Military," *Congressional Record,* 92d Cong., 2d sess. (2 March 1972), vol. 118, pt.6, 6739.

19. NAACP, *Search for Military Justice,* 2.

20. Hall, cited in Dellums, "Institutional Racism," 6739; and Ethel L. Payne, "Blacks Angry over Pace," *Pittsburgh Courier,* 8 May 1971, 11.

21. Hall, cited in Dellums, "Institutional Racism," 6744.

22. "Viet Hero Sees Racial Bias in Big Lie," *Baltimore Afro-American,* 26 February 1966, 20.

23. Clinton H. Hunt, interview with the author, Cincinnati, Ohio, 21 September 1991; and Alfonzo Wright, interview with the author, Pikeville, North Carolina, 27 December 1995.

24. J. Linin Allen, " 'Can't Let Viet Boys Down' Says Veteran," *Baltimore Afro-American,* 26 March 1966, 1.

25. Allen Thomas, Jr., interview with the author, Highland Heights, Kentucky, 22 March 1995; Raymond Wells, interview with the author, Cincinnati, Ohio, 11 October 1991.

26. Lionel Anderson, "Playback on Army Life," *Black Panther,* 20 September 1969, 10.

27. "Black Caucus Report," 36589; Morocco Coleman, "The Prince of Peace," letter to the editor, *Ebony,* August 1968, 17; Gene Grove, "The Army and the Negro," *New York Times Magazine,* 24 July 1966, 7; and Wallace Terry, "Bringing the War Home," *Black Scholar* 2 (November 1970): 8.

28. "Black Caucus Report," 36583; and Department of Defense, *Task Force,* 1:56.

29. Department of Defense, *Task Force,* 2:18; and NAACP, *Search for Military Justice,* 2.

30. Steven Morris, "How Blacks Upset the Marine Corps," *Ebony,* December 1969, 60.

31. Department of Defense, *Task Force,* 1:56.

32. Morris, "How Blacks Upset the Marine Corps," 60.

33. "Bias at Home," letter to the editor, *Ebony*, August 1968, 15.

34. L. Deckle McLean, "The Black Man and the Draft," *Ebony*, August 1968, 62.

35. John R. White, "Letter from Vietnam," *Black Panther*, 16 August 1969, 9.

36. Henry Dority, interview with the author, Cincinnati, Ohio, 26 May 1991; and Allen Thomas, Jr., interview with the author, Highland Heights, Kentucky, 22 March 1995.

37. Terry, "Bringing the War Home," 12; and Marshall, *In the Combat Zone: An Oral History of American Women in Vietnam* (Boston: Little, Brown & Co., 1987), 66.

38. Major Richard L. Bevington, interview, Senior Officer Oral History Project, Company Command series, U.S. Army Military History Institute, Carlisle Barracks, Pennsylvania, 1982, 4–5.

39. Major Henry L. Parker, interview, Senior Officer Oral History Project, Company Command series, 1982, 7–8.

40. Morris, "How Blacks Upset the Marine Corps," 60.

41. James Edward Hawkins, Jr., interview with the author, Cincinnati, Ohio, 9 July 1991.

42. Parker interview, 7.

43. Major Thomas Cecil, interview, Senior Officer Oral History Project, Company Command series, 1982, 19–21.

44. Edward Souders, "Racism in the Military," manuscript prepared for Safe Return (New York, January 1974), 3, in Citizen Soldier File 7033, box 8, file 59, Vietnam War Veterans Archive and Manuscript Collection, Department of Manuscripts and University Archives, Cornell University Library, Ithaca, New York.

45. "GI Transferred," *Black Liberator*, July 1969, 3. For other examples of charges of racism in assignment policies, see "Black Caucus Report," 36582–83; and Richard Halloran, "Air Force Racism Charged in Study," *New York Times*, 31 August 1971, 1.

46. Coleman, "Prince of Peace," 17.

47. Terry, "Bringing the War Home," 12.

48. *Manual for Courts-Martial, United States, 1969*, rev. ed. (Washington, D.C.: U.S. Government Printing Office, 1969), A2–1 and A2–5; and Souders, "Racism in the Military," 6.

49. *Manual for Courts-Martial*, A2–5–A2–7,

50. Department of Defense, *Task Force*, 1:68, 71.

51. Souders, "Racism in the Military," 6; *Manual for Courts-Martial*, A2–5–A2–7, and A2–26–A2–33; and Department of Defense, *Task Force*, 1:9. "Misbehavior before the enemy," as defined in Article 99 of the Uniform Code of Military Justice, includes such as infractions as a soldier exhibiting cowardice or deserting in the face of the enemy, willfully casting away arms or ammunition to avoid combat, and quitting "his place of duty to plunder or pillage."

52. NAACP, *Search for Military Justice,* 6; and Department of Defense, *Task Force,* 1:2.

53. "Black Caucus Report," 36584.

54. NAACP, *Search for Military Justice,* 6.

55. Ibid.; Curtis Daniell, "Germany: Trouble Spot for Black GIs," *Ebony,* August 1968, 127; Halloran, "Air Force Racism," 1; and "Black Caucus Report," 36584–86.

56. Hunt interview.

57. Wells interview.

58. NAACP, *Search for Military Justice,* 6.

59. "Black Caucus Report," 36583.

60. Daniell, "Germany," 127.

61. Major Bruce B. Cary, interview, Senior Officer Oral History Project, Company Command series, 1982, 8.

62. Parker interview, 19.

63. Major Thomas Peoples, interview, Senior Officer Oral History Project, Company Command series, 1982, 47.

64. Dr. John K. Brackett, interview with the author, Cincinnati, Ohio, 21 January 1992.

65. Daniell, "Germany," 127.

66. "Black Caucus Report," 36583; and Department of Defense, *Task Force,* 1:99–101.

67. "Black Caucus Report," 36583; Department of Defense, *Task Force,* 1:99–101; and Major John J. Ellis, interview, Senior Officer Oral History Project, Company Command series, 1982, 5.

68. Fort Hood United Front, *Black Organization Grows from Hearing on Racism,* pamphlet (Kileen, Texas, 15 November 1971), Citizen Soldier File 7033, box 8, file 54.

69. Department of Defense, *Task Force,* 1:99.

70. Major Michael F. Colacicco, interview, Senior Officer Oral History Project, Company Command series, 1982, 10–11.

71. "Black Caucus Report," 36583–86.

72. Ibid.

73. NAACP, *Search for Military Justice,* 2.

74. Halloran, "Air Force Racism," 1.

75. Foner, *Blacks and the Military,* 218–19.

76. Department of Defense, *Task Force,* 1:63.

77. Payne, "Blacks Angry over Pace," 11; NAACP, *Search for Military Justice,* 8; and *Manual for Courts-Martial,* Article 7, Uniform Code of Military Justice, 5–3, A2–4–A2–5.

78. NAACP, *Search for Military Justice,* 8.

79. "Black Caucus Report," 36585–86; and NAACP, *Search for Military Justice,* 8.

80. Department of Defense, *Task Force,* 1:28–29.

81. Mark Allen, "The Case of Billy Dean Smith," *Black Scholar* (October 1972): 17; and Souders, "Racism in the Military," 6.

82. Department of Defense, *Task Force,* 1:29 and 4:8.

83. NAACP, *Search for Military Justice,* 9.

84. Department of Defense, *Task Force,* 1:28–29.

85. "Air Force Jim Crow," *The Crisis* 77 (June-July 1970): 227.

86. Department of Defense, *Task Force,* 1:30.

87. Baskir and Strauss, *Chance and Circumstance,* 138–39; and Department of Defense, *Task Force,* 4:8, 151.

88. Baskir and Strauss, *Chance and Circumstance,* 10, 30–33; and Department of Defense, *Task Force,* 4:104.

89. NAACP, *Search for Military Justice,* 13; Daniell, "Germany," 127; and Department of Defense, *Task Force,* 2:60.

90. NAACP, *Search for Military Justice,* 13–14; "Two Black GIs Convicted in Rape Attempt Ask Help of Pentagon," *Chicago Tribune,* 9 June 1971, 11; and Daniell, "Germany," 127–28.

91. Enlisted personnel facing either special or general court-martial can request in writing that enlisted personnel serve on the court. See *Manual for Courts-Martial,* 2–1–2–3; and Westmoreland, *Report of the Chief of Staff,* 69.

92. Department of Defense, *Task Force,* 1:55; and Department of Defense, *Annual Report for Fiscal Year 1968* (Washington, D.C.: U.S. Government Printing Office, 1971), 6, 74.

93. Daniell, "Germany," 127.

94. Milton White, "Malcolm X and the Military," *Black Scholar* (May 1970): 34; see also Byron G. Fiman, Jonathan Borus, and Duncan M. Stanton "Black-White and American-Vietnamese Relations among Soldiers in Vietnam," *Journal of Social Issues* 31, 4 (1975): 46; and Thomas Johnson, "The U.S. Negro in Vietnam," *New York Times,* 29 April 1968, 16, for other examples.

95. Allen, "Case of Billy Dean Smith," 17; and William Stuart Gould, "Racial Conflict in the U.S. Army," *Race* 15, 1(July 1973): 9.

96. Daniell, "Germany," 127; and "Black Caucus Report," 36584.

97. "Military Prisons: About Face," *Time,* 17 May 1971, 63.

98. Department of Defense, *Task Force,* 4:57–61.

99. "Black Marines Appeal Harsh Sentences for Speaking Out Against War," *Black Panther,* 13 September 1969, 20.

100. "Blacks in Congress Will Study the Extent of Military Racism," *New York Times,* 4 November 1971, 26; and Citizen Soldier File 7033, box 8, file 55.

101. Department of Defense, *Task Force,* 4:57.

102. Daniell, "Germany," 127.

103. "Black Caucus Report," 36589; and Hawkins interview.

104. Lieutenant Charles R. Anderson, letters to family (27 August 1968), 4; (15 November 1968), 1; (7 January 1969), 5–6, in Lieutenant Charles R. Anderson File

7028, box 1, file 1, Vietnam War Veterans Archive and Manuscript Collection, Department of Manuscripts and University Archives, Cornell University Library, Ithaca, New York.

105. "Black Caucus Report," 36591.

106. Department of Defense, *Task Force,* 1:32–33.

107. Anderson, letter to family (27 August 1968), 4.

108. Wells interview.

109. "Military Prisons," 63.

110. Anderson, letters to family (15 November 1968), 1; (7 January 1969), 5–6.

111. Hawkins interview; and "Military Prisons," 63.

112. *Manual for Courts-Martial,* 13–2, 19–1, 19–3, 21–4, and 25–4; Department of Defense, *Task Force,* 1:108–10; Baskir and Strauss, *Chance and Circumstance,* 152; and NAACP, *Search for Military Justice,* 14–15.

113. Department of Defense, "Selected Manpower Statistics," cited in John W. Caknipe, "A Factor Analysis of the Metropolitan Detroit Area Vietnam Veteran: The Post Vietnam Veteran Syndrome" (Ph.D. diss., Midwestern University, 1978), 51.

114. "Black Caucus Report," 36584.

115. Caknipe, "Factor Analysis," 51; and Robert J. Brown, special assistant to President Richard Nixon, letter to the Black Legislators' Association (25 August 1971), 2, in Citizen Soldier File 7033, box 8, file 60.

116. Department of Defense, "Racial Breakdown of Discharges Issued under Other than Honorable Conditions" (1971), addendum 3 to letter from Brown to the Black Legislators' Association.

117. Vietnam Veterans Against the War, "Position Paper on Amnesty," manuscript (Placitas, New Mexico, April 1973), 5, in Vietnam Veterans Against the War/ Winter Soldier Organization File 7019, Box 1, Vietnam War Veterans Archive and Manuscript Collection, Department of Manuscripts and University Archives, Cornell University Library, Ithaca, New York; and Princeton University Educational Testing Service, *Report of the Educational Testing Service Princeton University, on Educational Assistance Programs for Veterans,* prepared for the House Committee on Veteran Affairs (Washington, D.C.: U.S. Government Printing Office, 1973), 2.

118. Daniell, "Germany," 127.

119. Department of Defense, *Task Force,* 4:156.

120. NAACP, *Search for Military Justice,* 14; and Department of Defense, *Task Force,* 1:109.

121. Allen, "Case of Billy Dean Smith," 17; Lionel Anderson, "GI Letters," *Black Panther,* 27 September 1969, 8; and Souders, "Racism in the Military," 3–6.

122. "An Interview with a Black GI," *Black Panther,* 25 May 1969, 16.

123. "GI Transferred," and "Antiwar GIs," *Black Liberator,* July 1969, 3.

124. Department of Defense, "Issuance and Review of Discharges from the

Armed Forces" (14 June 1971), addendum 1 to letter from Brown to the Black Legislators' Association, 1; NAACP, *Search for Military Justice*, 15; and Department of Defense *Task Force*, 1:109.

125. "Black Caucus Report," 36587; NAACP, *Search for Military Justice*, 15; Foner, *Blacks and the Military in American History*, 24; Department of Defense, *Task Force*, Volume I, 118, and; and Baskir and Strauss, *Chance and Circumstance*, 139.

126. Brown to the Black Legislators' Association, 1.

127. NAACP, *Search for Military Justice*, 15.

128. Department of Defense, *Task Force*, 1:118.

129. Department of Defense, "Issuance and Review of Discharges," 1–3.

130. "Black Caucus Report," 36587–88; and NAACP, *Search for Military Justice*, 15.

131. Department of Defense, "Issuance and Review of Discharges," 1–3.

132. Department of Defense, *Task Force*, 4:155–56, 1:109; "Black Caucus Report," 36592; NAACP, *Search for Military Justice*, 14; and Edward Souders to "Fellow Resisters," letter on behalf of Safe Return (August 1973), in Citizen Soldier File 7033, box 8, file 60.

133. Foner, *Blacks and the Military in American History*, 210; and "Black Caucus Report," 36587.

134. "Black Caucus Report," 36587; Foner, *Blacks and the Military in American History*, 210, 211; and Sesu Merretazon, "In Support of Incarcerated Veterans Affairs Officers within Prisons," unpublished report prepared for the Veterans Administration by the Incarcerated Veterans Assistance Organization, Inc. (Washington, D.C., June 1976), 4–5, Flower of the Dragon File 7020, box 1, file 12, Vietnam War Veterans Archive and Manuscript Collection, Department of Manuscripts and University Archives, Cornell University Library, Ithaca, New York.

135. Westmoreland, *Report of the Chief of Staff*, 69.

136. Department of Defense, *Task Force*, 1:71; NAACP, *Search for Military Justice*, 9; and Daniell, "Germany," 127.

137. Department of Defense, *Task Force*, 1:71; NAACP, *Search for Military Justice*, 9; Daniell, "Germany," 127; and "Black Caucus Report," 36583.

Notes to Chapter 4

1. William Daryl Henderson, *The Hollow Army* (New York: Greenwood Press, 1990), 77–126.

2. Charles C. Moskos, Jr., *The American Enlisted Man: The Rank and File in Today's Military* (New York: Russell Sage Foundation, 1970), 134–36.

3. Quoted in the Honorable Ronald V. Dellums, "Institutional Racism in the Military," *Congressional Record*, 92d Cong., 2d sess. (2 March 1972), vol. 118, pt. 6, 6740. For further examples, see also William Stuart Gould, "Racial Conflict in the U.S. Army," *Race* 15, 1 (July 1973): 7; and Byron G. Fiman, Jonathan F. Borus, and

Duncan M. Stanton, "Black-White and American-Vietnamese Relations among Soldiers in Vietnam," *Journal of Social Issues* 31, 4 (1975): 39.

4. "Poor Communication Seen as Cause of Marine Trouble," *Baltimore Afro-American,* 10 January 1970, 18.

5. Gene Grove, "The Army and the Negro," *New York Times Magazine,* 24 July 1966, 50; and David Llorens, "Why Negroes Re-enlist," *Ebony,* August 1968, 87.

6. "White Marine Dead following Outbreak," *Pittsburgh Courier,* 9 August 1969, 1; and Flora Lewis, "The Rumble at Camp Lejeune," *Atlantic Monthly* 225, January 1970, 35.

7. Cited in the Honorable Louis Stokes, "Racism in the Military: A New System for Rewards and Punishment," Congressional Black Caucus Report, *Congressional Record,* 92d Cong., 2d sess. (14 October 1972), 36583. (Hereafter cited as "Black Caucus Report.")

8. Raymond Wells, interview with the author, Cincinnati, Ohio, 11 October 1991.

9. Henry Dority, interview with the author, Cincinnati, Ohio, 26 May 1991.

10. Ponchitta Pierce and Peter Bailey, "The Returning Vet," *Ebony,* August 1968, 147.

11. Eleonor Clift and Thomas DeFrank, "Bush's General: Maximum Force," *Newsweek,* 3 September 1990, 38; and "Col. James Snubbed by Fla. Lounge," *Baltimore Afro-American,* 21 February 1970, 1.

12. "To My GI Brothers," *Black Panther,* 4 October 1969, 14.

13. Kathryn Marshall, *In the Combat Zone: An Oral History of American Women in Vietnam* (Boston: Little, Brown & Co., 1987), 36; and William C. Westmoreland, *Report of the Chief of Staff of the United States Army, 1 July 1968 to 30 June 1972* (Washington, D.C.: Department of the Army, 1977), 64–65.

14. Allen Thomas, Jr., interview with the author, Highland Heights, Kentucky, 22 March 1995; and "Black Caucus Report," 36583; and National Association for the Advancement of Colored People (NAACP), *The Search for Military Justice: Report of an NAACP Inquiry into the Problems of the Negro Serviceman in West Germany* (New York: NAACP Special Contributions Fund, 1971), 16–17.

15. Curtis Daniell, "Germany: Trouble Spot for Black GIs," *Ebony,* August 1968, 126.

16. "Black Caucus Report," 36583; and NAACP, *Search for Military Justice,* 16; and "Viet Hero Sees a Racial Bias in Big Lie," *Baltimore Afro-American,* 26 February 1966, 20.

17. GI Movement, *Systematic Racism Exists,* pamphlet issued by the Military and Veterans Action Committee (1972), in Citizen Soldier File 7033, box 8, file 58, Vietnam War Veterans Archive and Manuscript Collection, Department of Manuscripts and University Archives, Cornell University Library, Ithaca, New York.

18. NAACP, *Search for Military Justice,* 18; Alvin J. Schexnider, "The Develop-

ment of Nationalism: Political Socialization among Blacks in the U.S. Armed Forces" (Ph.D. diss., Northwestern University, 1973), 59.

19. "Off-Base Housing," *New Republic,* 5 August 1967, 31–33; NAACP, *Search for Military Justice,* 16; Westmoreland, *Report of the Chief of Staff,* 64; and Henry I. Shaw, Jr., and Ralph W. Donnelly, *Blacks in the Marine Corps* (Washington, D.C.: U.S. Marine Corps, History and Museums Division Headquarters, 1975), 70.

20. Department of Defense, *Annual Report for Fiscal Year 1968* (Washington, D.C.: U.S. Government Printing Office, 1971), 75.

21. "Army Denounced by Negro Major," *New York Times,* 14 October 1968, 3; "From a GI," *Black Panther,* 26 July 1969, 6; and "U.S. Army Ordered to Stop Bias against Blacks," *Pittsburgh Courier,* 9 January 1971, 1.

22. Daniell, "Germany," 126.

23. NAACP, *Search for Military Justice,* 17.

24. Shaw and Donnelly, *Blacks in the Marine Corps,* 71; "Off-Base Housing," 31; and Department of Defense, *Annual Report for Fiscal Year 1968,* 75.

25. Department of Defense, *Annual Report for Fiscal Year 1968,* 76; Westmoreland, *Report of the Chief of Staff,* 64–65; and NAACP, *Search for Military Justice,* 19.

26. Department of Defense, *Annual Report for Fiscal Year 1968,* 76.

27. Cited in Dellums, "Institutional Racism," 6743.

28. "Black Quantico Marines Tell of Housing Troubles," *Washington Post,* 16 November 1971, A8.

29. Department of Defense, Office of the Deputy Assistant Secretary of Defense for Equal Opportunity and Safety Policy, *Task Force on the Administration of Military Justice in the Armed Forces* (Washington, D.C.: U.S. Government Printing Office, 1972), 1:59.

30. Westmoreland, *Report of the Chief of Staff,* 64–65.

31. Gould, "Racial Conflict," 9.

32. Westmoreland, *Report of the Chief of Staff,* 65; and Dellums, "Institutional Racism," 6743.

33. Department of Defense, *Task Force,* 1:60; and NAACP, *Search for Military Justice,* 16–19.

34. "Black Caucus Report," 36583.

35. "No Room in the Cemetery," *Baltimore Afro-American,* 4 June 1966, 1–2.

36. "Family Sues for GI Grave," *Black Panther,* 27 September 1969, 7; "GI Lost Life in Vietnam, Won Ala. Cemetery Battle," *Baltimore Afro-American,* 3 January 1970, 1: and Glenn Stephens, "GIs Body in Cemetery He Selected," *Baltimore Afro-American,* 10 January 1970, 1.

37. Major-General Frederic E. Davison, interview, Senior Officer Oral History Project, Blacks in the Armed Forces series, U.S. Military History Institute, Carlisle Barracks, Pennsylvania, 1977, 33.

38. Steven Morris, "How Blacks Upset the Marine Corps," *Ebony,* December 1969, 57.

39. Ibid.; and Lewis, "Rumble at Camp Lejeune," 41. Many stateside defense installations did employ local African American civilian barbers.

40. "From a GI," 6; NAACP, *Search for Military Justice*, 6; and "Black Caucus Report," 36586.

41. NAACP, *Search for Military Justice*, 26; Morris, "How Blacks Upset the Marine Corps," 57–60; "Seamen Demand Jet, Soul Tunes and Juke Boxes," *Jet*, 2 September 1971, 19; Dellums, "Institutional Racism," 6741; and "Black Caucus Report," 36589.

42. Letter to the editor, *Ebony*, August 1968, 15.

43. Department of Defense, *Task Force*, 1:98.

44. NAACP, *Search for Military Justice*, 18–19; Richard Halloran, "Air Force Racism Charged in Study," *New York Times*, 31 August 1971, 1; and Dellums, "Institutional Racism," 6741.

45. "Black Caucus Report," 36589; and Wallace Terry, "Bringing the War Home," *Black Scholar* 2 (November 1970), 14.

46. For examples, see ibid., 36588; NAACP, *Search for Military Justice*, 25; and Thomas Johnson, "Negroes in the Nam," *Ebony*, August 1968, 38.

47. Gould, "Racial Conflict," 20–21; "Seamen Demand Jet," 19; Dellums, "Institutional Racism," 6741; and Westmoreland, *Report of the Chief of Staff*, 65.

48. "Marine Barracks Named after Honor Medal Winner," *Baltimore Afro-American*, 24 January 1970, 12.

49. Shaw and Donnelly, *Blacks in the Marine Corps*, 83.

50. Department of Defense, *Task Force*, 1:55, 2:60; and "The Navy's New Racial Crisis," *Newsweek*, 20 November 1972, 32–33.

51. "Black Caucus Report," 36583–90.

52. "Army Denounced," 3; and Zalin B. Grant, "Whites against Blacks in Vietnam," *New Republic*, 18 January 1969, 15.

53. "An Interview with a Black GI," *Black Panther*, 25 May 1969, 16.

54. "GI Transferred," *Black Liberator*, July 1969, 3.

55. Dr. John K. Brackett, interview with the author, Cincinnati, Ohio, 21 January 1992.

56. "GIs Complain about Bias in Armed Services," *Pittsburgh Courier*, 8 May 1971, 9.

57. Jack D. Foner, *Blacks and the Military in American History*, New Perspectives in American History (New York: Praeger Publishers, 1974), 208.

58. Ulf Nilson, "Deserters in Sweden," *Ebony*, August 1968, 121–22; and "Deserter Tells: 'Why I Left the Army,' " *Black Panther*, 13 September 1969, 20.

59. "GIs complain about bias," 9.

60. Edward Shils, "A Profile of the Military Deserter," *Armed Forces and Society* 3, 3 (May 1977): 429. For additional examples of desertion as a political act in response to racism, see "Manifesto of the American Deserters Committee," *Black Panther*, 17 February 1969, 4; and Vietnam Veterans Against the War, "Position

Paper on Amnesty," manuscript (Placitas, New Mexico, 19–23 April 1973), 5, in Citizen Soldier file 7037, box 1, file 1.

61. Shils, "Profile of the Military Deserter," 429–30; D. Bruce Bell and Beverly W. Bell, "Desertion and Antiwar Protest: Findings from the Ford Clemency Program," *Armed Forces and Society* 3, 3 (May 1977): 433–43; and Lawrence M. Baskir and William A. Strauss, *Chance and Circumstance: The Draft, the War, and the Vietnam Generation* (New York: Random House, 1978), 113–22.

62. Major Gary L. Tucker, interview, Senior Officer Oral History Project, Company Command series, U.S. Military History Institute, Carlisle Barracks, Pennsylvania, 1977, 3.

63. Major Thomas Cecil, interview, Senior Officer Oral History Project, Company Command series, 1982, 2.

64. Major Richard H. Torovsky, Jr., interview, Senior Officer oral History Project, Company Command series, 1982, 5.

65. Robert D. Heinl, Jr., "The Collapse of the Armed Forces," *Armed Forces Journal* (7 June 1971): 32.

66. James Edward Hawkins, Jr., interview with the author, Cincinnati, Ohio, 9 July 1991.

67. Baskir and Strauss, *Chance and Circumstance*, 61; and Heinl, "Collapse of the Armed Forces," 33.

68. Department of Defense, *Annual Report for Fiscal Year 1968*, 27, 156. The army was used "to assist civil authorities in insuring domestic tranquillity during three periods of trouble and tension" in 1968. Twenty-three thousand regular troops and sixteen thousand guardsmen were used to quell the uprisings.

69. Terry, "Bringing the War Home," 10; "Interview with a Black GI," 16; and "GI Gets Two Years Hard Labor," *Black Panther*, 10 January 1970, 13.

70. Johnson, "Negroes in the Nam," 40; and "Black Soldier Refuses Drill in Riot Control," *The Bond*, 16 June 1968, 3.

71. "Seamen Demand Jet," 19; and Halloran, "Air Force Racism," 1.

72. Black Cadets, United States Air Force Academy, "An Answer to Wing Staff's Request," manuscript (Colorado, March 1970), 1–3, in Citizen Soldier File 7033, box 8, file 54.

73. Thomas interview; NAACP, *Search for Military Justice*, 18; and "Brass to Press *Sumpter* Cases," *Camp News* (15 February 1973), 5, in Citizen Soldier File 7033, box 11, file 16.

74. "Black Caucus Report," 36588.

75. Morris, "How Blacks Upset the Marine Corps," 58; and Lewis, "Rumble at Camp Lejeune," 40–41.

76. Thomas Johnson, "Military Race Relations Held Explosive," *New York Times*, 18 November 1971, 12.

77. Warrant Officer John "Jackie" Breedlove, letter to parents, (7 December 1966), in Breedlove Collection File 7036, box 1, file 16, Vietnam War Veterans

Archive and Manuscript Collection, Department of Manuscripts and University Archives, Cornell University Library, Ithaca, New York.

78. "Black Caucus Report," 36589; and Johnson, "Negroes in the Nam," 38.

79. Brackett interview

80. "Lejeune Described as Worse than Mississippi," *Pittsburgh Courier,* 30 August 1969, 1.

81. Grant, "Whites against Blacks in Vietnam," 15; Terry, "Bringing the War Home," 11; and *Black Panther,* "From a GI," 6.

82. Baskir and Strauss, *Chance and Circumstance,* 137; and Thomas Johnson, "The U.S. Negro in Vietnam," *The New York Times,* 29 April 1969, 16.

83. Hawkins interview.

84. Foner, *Blacks and the Military in American History,* 213; Grant, "White against Blacks in Vietnam," 16; "Black Caucus Report," 36589; and "Air Force Jim Crow," *The Crisis* 77 (June-July 1969): 227–29.

85. Grant, "Whites against Blacks in Vietnam," 16.

86. Terry, "Bringing the War Home," 11.

87. "Requiem for Dixie," *The Crisis* (March 1969): 112.

88. "Many GIs Angry in Vietnam," *Pittsburgh Courier,* 26 April 1969, 1; "From a GI," 6; Morris, "How Blacks Upset the Marine Corps," 60; and "Black Caucus Report," 36589–90.

89. "No Dixie Flag in Armed Forces," *Baltimore Afro-American,* 19 February 1966, 3.

90. Ibid.; and "From a GI," 6.

91. GI Movement, *Systematic Racism Exists.*

92. Shaw and Donnelly, *Blacks in the Marine Corps,* 71.

93. Major Stewart H. Barnhoft, interview, Senior Officer Oral History Project, Company Command series, 1982, 6.

94. Clinton H. Hunt, interview with the author, Cincinnati, Ohio, 21 September 1991; and Alfonzo Wright, Jr., interview with the author, Pikeville, North Carolina, 27 December 1995.

95. Thomas Johnson, "Negro Expatriates Finding Wide Opportunity in Asia," *New York Times,* 30 April 1969, 18; and "U.S. Negro," 14.

96. Major Eugene J. White, Jr., interview, Senior Officer Oral History Project, Company Command series, 1982, 12.

97. Thomas Johnson, "Negro in Vietnam Uneasy about U.S.," *New York Times,* 1 May 1969, 14.

98. Grant, "Whites against Blacks in Vietnam," 16.

99. Sol Stern, "When the Black GI Comes Back from Vietnam," *New York Times Magazine,* 24 March 1968, 42; Johnson, "U.S. Negro," 16; and Johnson, "Negro Expatriates," 18.

100. GI Movement, *Systematic Racism Exists.*

101. "Viet Hero Sees Bias," 20; NAACP, *Search for Military Justice*, 18; and "Air Force Jim Crow," 229.

102. Johnson, "U.S. Negro," 16; Johnson, "Negroes in the Nam," 39; and Grant, "Whites against Blacks in Vietnam," 16.

103. Department of Defense, *Task Force*, 1:60.

104. Lewis, "Rumble at Camp Lejeune," 39; and Westmoreland, *Report of the Chief of Staff*, 62.

105. Gould, "Racial Conflict," 9.

106. Schexnider, "Development of Nationalism," 70; Morris, "How Blacks Upset the Marine Corps," 57; and Charles C. Moskos, Jr., "The American Combat Soldier in Vietnam," *Journal of Social Issues* 31, 4 (1975): 34.

107. Terry, "Bringing the War Home," 13–14; "Many GIs Angry in Vietnam," 1; and "Army Race Relations Runs into Reality," *Winter Soldier* (February 1974), 13, in Vietnam Veterans Against the War/Winter Soldier Organization File 7019, box 1, Vietnam War Veterans Archive and Manuscript Collection, Department of Manuscripts and University Archives, Cornell University Library, Ithaca, New York.

108. Robert W. Mullen, *Blacks in America's Wars: The Shift in Attitudes from the Revolutionary War to Vietnam* (New York: Monad Press/Pathfinder Press, 1973), 80; Bill Lane, "GI 'Black Power' Salutes Crimp Hope's Tour Film," *Baltimore Afro-American*, 24 January 1970, 10; Major John J. Ellis, interview, Senior Officer Oral History Project, Company Command series, 4–5; Hunt interview; and Shaw and Donnelly, *Blacks in the Marine Corps*, 74.

109. "GIs Complain about Bias," 9; Ellis interview, 4–5; Schexnider, "Development of Nationalism," 72–74; and Morris, "How Blacks Upset the Marine Corps," 57.

110. Department of Defense, *Task Force*, 1:60–61; "GIs Complain about Bias," 9; and Ellis interview, 5.

111. Lieutenant Colonel Vernon L. Conner, interview, Senior Officer Oral History Project, Company Command series, 1982, 46.

112. Department of Defense, *Task Force*, 1:60–61

113. Ibid.; "Sentence GI in Mt. Fuji Killing," *Pittsburgh Courier*, 15 May 1971, 2.

114. *NOMLAC Newsletter* 6, *Camp News* (December 1972), 16, in Citizen Soldier File 7033, box 8, file 60.

115. Shaw and Donnelly, *Blacks in the Marine Corps*, 74.

116. "GIs Complain about Bias," 9; and Department of Defense, *Task Force*, 1:61.

117. *NOMLAC Newsletter* 6, *Camp News*, 1.

118. White interview, 10.

119. Major Donald Dean, interview, Senior Officer Oral History Project, Company Command series, 1982, 7.

120. Wells interview; and "GIs Complain about Bias," 9.

121. Major William C. Long, interview, Senior Officer Oral History Project, Company Command series, 1982, 3–4; and Marshall, *In the Combat Zone,* 45.

122. Conner interview, 45.

123. Department of Defense, *Task Force,* 1:99; Halloran, "Air Force Racism," 1; and "Black GIs," *Black Liberator,* December 1969, 2.

124. Johnson, "U.S. Negro," 16.

125. Terry, "Bringing the War Home," 13–14; Schexnider, "Development of Nationalism," 66–67; Johnson, "U.S. Negro," 16; and "GIs Complain about Bias," 9.

126. "De Mau Mau," *Winter Soldier* (May 1973), 14, in Vietnam Veterans Against the War/Winter Soldier Organization File 7019, box 1.

127. "Black Caucus Report," 36589; and *NOMLAC Newsletter* 6.

128. Baskir and Strauss, *Chance and Circumstance,* 137; and Lieutenant Charles Anderson, letter to family (15 November 1968), 1, in Lieutenant Charles Anderson File 7028, box 1, file 1, Vietnam War Veterans Archive and Manuscript Collection, Department of Manuscripts and University Archives, Cornell University Library, Ithaca, New York.

129. Department of Defense, *Task Force,* 1:61–62.

130. Bobby Seale, "Letter from Chairman Bobby—No. 3," *Black Panther,* 13 September 1969, 17.

131. John R. White, "Letter from Vietnam," *Black Panther,* 16 August 1969, 9.

Notes to Chapter 5

1. Henry I. Shaw, Jr., and Ralph W. Donnelly, *Blacks in the Marine Corps* (Washington, D.C.: U.S. Marine Corps, History and Museums Division Headquarters, 1975), 72–73; "White v. Black Confrontations Are Increasing," *Pittsburgh Courier,* 23 August 1969, 14; Steven Morris, "How Blacks Upset the Marine Corps," *Ebony,* December 1969, 55; and Flora Lewis, "The Rumble at Camp Lejeune," *Atlantic Monthly* 225, January 1970, 35–37.

2. Clinton H. Hunt, interview with the author, Cincinnati, Ohio, 21 September 1991.

3. Allen Thomas, Jr., interview with the author, Highland Heights, Kentucky, 22 March 1995; and James Edward Hawkins, Jr., interview with the author, Cincinnati, Ohio, 9 July 1991.

4. "Navy Is Studying Racial Incidents," *New York Times,* 22 October 1968, 7.

5. Lawrence M. Baskir and William A. Strauss, *Chance and Circumstance: The Draft, the War, and the Vietnam Generation* (New York: Random House, 1978), 137–38, and Lewis, "Rumble at Camp Lejeune," 37.

6. Major Michael F. Colacicco, interview, Senior Officer Oral History Project, Company Command series, U.S. Army Military History Institute, Carlisle Barracks, Pennsylvania, 1982, 11.

7. Major Richard C. Anshus, interview, Senior Officer Oral History Project, Company Command series, 1982, 8.

8. Lieutenant John Paul Jones [pseud.], "Militants at Sea," *National Review,* 19 January 1973, 91.

9. "White Marine Dead Following Outbreak," *Pittsburgh Courier,* 9 August 1969, 4.

10. "Ten Bases Due Racism Probe," *Air Force Times,* 17 November 1971, 2.

11. Department of Defense, Office of the Deputy Assistant Secretary of Defense for Equal Opportunity and Safety Policy, *Task Force on the Administration of Military Justice in the Armed Forces* (Washington, D.C.: U.S. Government Printing Office, 1972), 1:61; and "Poor Communication Seen as Cause of Marine Trouble," *Baltimore Afro-American,* 10 January 1970, 18.

12. Dr. John K. Brackett, interview with the author, Cincinnati, Ohio, 21 January 1992.

13. Zalin B. Grant, "Whites against Blacks in Vietnam," *New Republic,* 18 January 1969, 16.

14. Brackett interview.

15. Bernard Weinraub, "Rioting Disquiets GI in Vietnam," *New York Times,* 8 April 1968, 35.

16. Hunt interview; and Private First Class Morocco Coleman, "The Prince of Peace," letters to the editor, *Ebony,* August 1968, 17.

17. Thomas interview; and Hawkins interview.

18. Curtis Daniell, "Germany: Trouble Spot for Black GIs," *Ebony,* August 1968, 127.

19. Department of Defense, *Annual Report for Fiscal Year 1968* (Washington, D.C.: U.S. Government Printing Office, 1971), 4–6; William C. Westmoreland, *Report of the Chief of Staff of the United States Army, 1 July 1968 to 30 June 1972* (Washington, D.C.: Department of the Army, 1977), 6–10, 48; and Charles C. Moskos, Jr., "The American Combat Soldier in Vietnam," *Journal of Social Issues* 31, 4 (1975): 30–31.

20. Moskos, "American Combat Soldier," 28–31.

21. Paul L. Savage and Richard A. Gabriel, "Cohesion and Disintegration in the American Army: An Alternative Perspective," in Peter Karsten, ed., *The Military in America, from the Colonial Era to the Present* (New York: Free Press, 1980), 418.

22. Lewis, "Rumble at Camp Lejeune," 38.

23. National Association for the Advancement of Colored People (NAACP), *The Search for Military Justice: Report of an NAACP Inquiry into the Problems of the Negro Serviceman in West Germany* (New York: NAACP Special Contributions Fund, 1971), 25; and Shaw and Donnelly, *Blacks in the Marine Corps,* 72.

24. Colacicco interview, 9–10.

25. Lieutenant Colonel Charles R. Shrader, interview, Senior Officer Oral History Project, Company Command series, 1981, 19.

26. Robert D. Heinl, Jr., "The Collapse of the Armed Forces," *Armed Forces Journal* (7 June 1971): 33.

27. Grant, "Whites against Blacks in Vietnam," 15–16; "Danang Restriction Imposed by the Navy after Racial Unrest," *New York Times*, 21 October 1968, 11; and "Navy Is Studying Racial Incidents," 7.

28. "Air Force Jim Crow," *The Crisis* 77 (June-July, 1970): 227; and the Honorable Louis Stokes, "Racism in the Military: A New System for Rewards and Punishment," Congressional Black Caucus Report, *Congressional Record*, 92d Cong., 2d sess. (14 October 1972), 36588. (Hereafter cited as "Black Caucus Report.")

29. Grant, "Whites against Blacks in Vietnam," 15–16; and "Navy Is Studying Racial Incidents," 7.

30. "Black GIs," *Black Liberator*, December 1969, 2; "Four Marines Convicted of Assault, Not Rioting," *Baltimore Afro-American*, 14 February 1970, 18; and "Memphis," *The Crisis* (March 1970): 116.

31. "Army Race Relations Runs Into Reality," *Winter Soldier* (February 1974), 12–13, in Vietnam Veterans Against the War/Winter Soldier Organization File 7019, box 1, Vietnam War Veterans Archive and Manuscript Collection, Department of Manuscripts and University Archives, Cornell University Library, Ithaca, New York.

32. Westmoreland, *Report of the Chief of Staff*, 10, 62; and "Military Race Relations Held Explosive," 18.

33. "GI's Death Sparks Riot," *Pittsburgh Courier*, 16 January 1971, 4.

34. George C. Wilson, "One Hundred Black GIs Arrested in Alabama Melee," *Washington Post*, 16 November 1971, A8.

35. "M.P. Riot on Okinawa," *Camp News* (15 February 1973), 1, in Citizen Soldier File 7033, box 11, file 16, Vietnam War Veterans Archive and Manuscript Collection, Department of Manuscripts and University Archives, Cornell University Library, Ithaca, New York.

36. Brackett interview.

37. Major Thomas Cecil, interview, Senior Officer Oral History Project, Company Command series, 1982, 28–29.

38. Wallace Terry, "Bringing the War Home," *Black Scholar* 2 (November 1970): 11.

39. Lieutenant Charles Anderson, letter to parents (15 November 1968): 4, in Lieutenant Charles Anderson File 7028, box 1, file 1, Vietnam War Veterans Archive and Manuscript Collection, Department of Manuscripts and University Archives, Cornell University Library, Ithaca, New York.

40. Lieutenant Charles Anderson, letter to parents (15 November 1968): 1, in Lieutenant Charles Anderson File 7028, box 1, file 1.

41. "Rioters at Marine Brig Set Fire to Cell Block," *New York Times*, 18 August 1968, 4; and "2D Riot Quelled at Vietnam Brig," *New York Times*, 19 August 1968, 5.

42. Lieutenant Charles Anderson, letter to parents (27 August 1968): 3–4, in Lieutenant Charles Anderson File 7028, box 1.

43. Robert Stokes, "Race Riot at Long Binh," *Newsweek,* 30 September 1968, 35; and Shrader interview, 5–6.

44. Grant, "Whites against Blacks in Vietnam," 16; Stokes, "Race Riot at Long Binh," 35; and "GI Dead, Forty-eight Hurt in Stockade Riot," *New York Times,* 30 August 1968, 6.

45. Stokes, "Race Riot at Long Binh," 35; "Riot at Long Binh Stockade Attributed to Racial Acts," *New York Times,* 4 September 1968, 2; and "Six to Face Murder Charges for GIs' Riot in Prison," *New York Times,* 1 October 1968, 3.

46. Stokes, "Race Riot at Long Binh," 35; Grant, "Whites against Blacks in Vietnam," 16; Alvin J. Schexnider, "The Development of Nationalism: Political Socialization among Blacks in the U.S. Armed Forces" (Ph.D. diss., Northwestern University, 1973), 79; and "Study Sees More Bloodshed from GI Racial Troubles," *Baltimore Afro-American,* 31 January 1970, 3.

47. "Norfolk Sailors Rebel," *Camp News* (15 February 1973), 9, in Citizen Soldier File 7033, box 11, file 16; and "Free the Camp Allen Brothers," *Winter Soldier* 3 (June 1973), 14, in Vietnam Veterans Against the War/Winter Soldier Organization File 7019, box 1.

48. Jones, "Militants at Sea," 91; and "The Navy's New Racial Crisis," *Newsweek,* 20 November 1972, 32–35.

49. Alfonzo Wright, Jr., interview with the author, Pikeville, North Carolina, 27 December 1995. Department of Defense, *Task Force,* 1: 55; "The Navy's New Racial Crisis," 32–33; and "The Less than Honorable Solution," *The Nation,* 19 February 1973, 234.

50. Jack D. Foner, *Blacks and the Military in American History,* New Perspectives in American History (New York: Praeger Publishers, 1974), 239–45; and Jones, "Militants at Sea," 33.

51. Foner, *Blacks and the Military,* 239–45; Jones, "Militants at Sea," 33; "The Navy's New Racial Crisis," 32–35; and "Norfolk Sailors Rebel," 5.

52. Herbert R. Northrup, Steven M. DiAntonio, John A. Brinker, and Dale F. Daniels, *Black and Other Minority Participation in the All-Volunteer Navy and Marine Corps,* Studies of Negro Employment, vol. 8 (Philadelphia: University of Pennsylvania, Wharton School, Industrial Research Unit, 1979), 18–20; "The Navy's New Racial Crisis," 35; and "Less than Honorable Solution," 234.

53. Northrup et al., *Black and Other Minority Participation,* 20; "The Navy's New Racial Crisis," 35; Vice Admiral Samuel L. Gravely, Jr., interview, Senior Officer Oral History Project, Blacks in the Armed Forces series, U.S. Army Military History Institute, Carlisle Barracks, Pennsylvania, 1977, 13; and "Air Force Jim Crow," 227.

54. William Stuart Gould, "Racial Conflict in the U.S. Army," *Race* 15, 1 (July 1973): 9.

55. Heinl, "Collapse of the Armed Forces," 32.

56. Shrader interview, 5–7.

57. Major Bruce B. Cary, interview, Senior Officer Oral History Project, Company Command series, 1982, 7–8.

58. Cecil interview, 5.

59. Terry, "Bringing the War Home," 11

60. Major Richard Barnes, interview, Senior Officer Oral History Project, Company Command series, 1982, 6.

61. Major Henry L. Parker, interview, Senior Officer Oral History Project, Company Command series, 1982, 3.

62. Anderson, letter to parents (27 August 1968), 4.

63. Major Thomas Peoples, interview, Senior Officer Oral History Project, Company Command series, 1982, 4–5.

64. Lieutenant Colonel Vernon L. Conner, Senior Officer Oral History Project, Company Command series, 1985, 6.

65. Major Richard L. Bevington, interview, Company Officer Oral History Project, Company Command series, 1982, 2.

66. Cecil interview, 27.

67. "GIs Complain about Bias in Armed Services," *Pittsburgh Courier*, 8 May 1971, 9.

68. Baskir and Strauss, *Chance and Circumstance*, 143; Mark Allen, "The Case of Billy Dean Smith," *Black Scholar* (October 1972): 16; Eugene Linden, "Fragging and Other Withdrawal Symptoms," *Saturday Review*, January 1972, 12–17; and James Olson, ed., *Dictionary of the Vietnam War* (New York: Peter Bedrick Books, 1987), 160.

69. "Melvin X. Smith," *Winter Soldier* (January 1974), 15, in Vietnam Veterans Against the War/Winter Soldier Organization File 7019, box 1; and "Melvin X. Smith Faces Hearing," *Winter Soldier* (February 1974), 12–13, Vietnam Veterans Against the War/Winter Soldier Organization File 7019, box 1.

70. "Sentence GI in Mt. Fuji Killing," *Pittsburgh Courier*, 15 May 1971, 2; and Allen, "Case of Billy Dean Smith," 16.

71. House Committee on Internal Security, *Investigation of Attempts to Subvert the United States Armed Forces*, 92d Cong., 2d sess. (Washington, D.C.: U.S. Government Printing Office, 1972), part 2, 6993.

72. Baskir and Strauss, *Chance and Circumstance*, 134–35; and Cecil interview, 30.

73. Conner interview, 6–8.

74. Raymond Wells, interview with the author, Cincinnati, Ohio, 11 October 1991.

75. Heinl, "Collapse of the Armed Forces," 33.

76. Dale Reich, *Good Soldiers Don't Go to Heaven* (Whitewater, Wisc.: Garden of Eden Press, 1979), 23.

77. Hunt interview.

78. Hawkins interview.

79. Colacicco interview, 10.

80. Major O. J. Golphenee, interview, Senior Officer Oral History Project, Company Command series, 1982, 9.

81. Gould, "Racial Conflict," 9–10; and Morris, "How Blacks Upset the Marine Corps," 62.

82. Terry, "Bringing the War Home," 11.

83. Cecil interview, 2.

84. Brackett interview.

85. John R. White, "Letter from Vietnam," *Black Panther*, 16 August 1969, 9.

86. "Three Black GIs Murdered," *The Bond*, 16 June 1968, 1.

87. For examples, see Terry, "Bringing the War Home," 9–11; "Air Force Jim Crow," 227–28; "Black Caucus Report," 36587–88; and "Probe Racial War Crimes, Jackson," *Chicago Sun-Times*, 28 April 1971, 14.

88. Jones, "Militants at Sea," 90–93; and Heinl, "Collapse of the Armed Forces," passim.

89. Westmoreland, *Report of the Chief of Staff*, 10, 62.

90. Shaw and Donnelly, *Blacks in the Marine Corps*, 72; Lewis, "Rumble at Camp Lejeune," 26, 38; and "White v. Black Confrontations," 14.

91. "Study Sees More Bloodshed," 3.

92. Shaw and Donnelly, *Blacks in the Marine Corps*, 73.

93. Byron G. Fiman, Jonathan F. Borus, and M. Duncan Stanton, "Black-White and American-Vietnamese Relations among Soldiers in Vietnam," *Journal of Social Issues* 31, 4 (1975): 39.

94. Thomas Johnson, "Negroes in the Nam," *Ebony*, August 1968, 36.

95. Keith Walker, *A Piece of My Heart: The Stories of Twenty-six American Women Who Served in Vietnam* (Novato, Calif.: Presidio Press, 1985), 257; and Major William G. Riederer, interview, Senior Officer Oral History Project, Company Command series, 1982, 6.

96. Grant, "Whites against Blacks in Vietnam," 16.

97. Henry Dority, interview with the author, Cincinnati, Ohio, 26 May 1991.

98. Major Cecil F. Davis, interview, Senior Officer Oral History Project, Company Command series, 1982, 4.

99. Hawkins interview.

100. Major Richard H. Torovsky, Jr., interview, Senior Officer Oral History Project, Company Command series, 1982, 5–6.

101. Major Patrick Carder, interview, Senior Officer Oral History Project, Company Command series, 1982, 4.

102. Major Maxwell V. Terrian, interview, Senior Officer Oral History Project, Company Command series, 1982, 3–4.

103. Hawkins interview.

104. Anshus interview, 10.

105. Major Robert Arnold, interview, Senior Officer Oral History Project, Company Command series, 1982, 6.

106. Cary interview, 7.

107. Wells interview.

108. "Black Caucus Report," 36589.

109. Major Steven N. Townsend, interview, Senior Officer Oral History Project, Company Command series, 1982, 8.

110. Arnold interview, 3.

111. Barnes interview, 13.

112. Colacicco interview, 9–11.

113. Ibid.; and Major Donald Dean, interview, Senior Officer Oral History Project, Company Command series, 1982, 7.

114. Major James Love, interview, Senior Officer Oral History Project, Company Command series, 1982, 2.

115. Bevington interview, 2.

116. Dority interview.

117. Lieutenant Colonel Joseph DeFrancisco, interview, Senior Officer Oral History Project, Company Command series, 1982, 6.

118. Cary interview, 7.

119. Major John J. Ellis, interview, Senior Officer Oral History Project, Company Command series, 1982, 4.

120. Major Henry Koren, Jr., interview, Senior Officer Oral History Project, Company Command series, 1982, 2.

121. Major Michael Yap, interview, Senior Officer Oral History Project, Company Command series, 1982, 4.

122. Love interview, 6.

123. Peoples interview, 2–4, 26–30.

124. Cecil interview, 29.

125. Bevington interview, 26.

126. Major Eugene J. White, Jr., interview, Senior Officer Oral History Project, Company Command series, 1982, 8.

127. Major Gary L. Tucker, interview, Senior Officer Oral History Project, Company Command series, 1982, 4.

128. Cecil interview, 3.

129. Westmoreland, *Report of the Chief of Staff,* 66; Northrup et al., *Black and Other Minority Participation,* 22; and Melvin R. Laird, *Final Report to the Congress of Secretary of Defense Melvin R. Laird* (Washington, D.C.: U.S. Department of Defense, 1973), 74.

130. Major James B. Hollis, interview, Senior Officer Oral History Project, Company Command series, 1982, 3.

131. Major Clay Melton, interview, Senior Officer Oral History Project, Company Command series, 1982, 3

132. Cecil interview, 30.

133. Barnes interview, 13–14.

134. Peoples interview, 30–31.

135. "Black Caucus Report," 36592; Shaw and Donnelly, *Blacks in the Marine Corps*, 74–75; and NAACP, *Search for Military Justice*, 5.

136. Morris J. MacGregor and Bernard C. Nalty, *Blacks in the United States Armed Forces: Basic Documents*, vol. 13 of the Fahy Committee report (Wilmington, Del.: Scholarly Resources, 1977), 439 (hereafter cited as "Fahy Committee Report"); and Department of Defense *Task Force*, 1: 55.

137. Alex Poinsett, "The Negro Officer," *Ebony*, August 1968, 137.

138. "Fahy Committee Report," 439; and Department of Defense *Task Force*, 1: 55.

139. "Fahy Committee Report," 439.

140. Shaw and Donnelly, *Blacks in the Marine Corps*, 74–75; Department of Defense *Task Force*, 1: 55; and Poinsett, "The Negro Officer," 139.

141. "Fahy Committee Report," 439; and Department of Defense *Task Force*, 1: 55.

142. Poinsett, "The Negro Officer," 136–38; and Department of Defense, *Annual Report for Fiscal Year 1968*, 74.

143. "Fahy Committee Report," 439; and Department of Defense, Office of the Deputy Assistant Secretary of Defense for Equal Opportunity and Safety Policy, *Black Americans in Defense of Our Nation* (Washington, D.C.: U.S. Government Printing Office, 1978), 114.

144. "No Admirals," *Newsweek*, 30 September 1968, 35; and Poinsett, "The Negro Officer," 36.

145. Westmoreland, *Report of the Chief of Staff*, 65.

146. "Fahy Committee Report," 439.

147. " 'Chappie' James Gets General's Star," *Baltimore Afro-American*, 10 January 1970, 2; and Department of Defense, *Black Americans*, 115.

148. "Fahy Committee Report," 439.

149. "Black Navy Officer Talks of Vietnam," *Pittsburgh Courier*, 19 July 1969, 2; and Poinsett, "The Negro Officer," 140.

150. "A Black Admiral for U.S. Navy," *Pittsburgh Courier*, 8 May 1971, 1.

151. "Fahy Committee Report," 439; "Marines Count Over Two Hundred Black Officers," *Pittsburgh Courier*, 29 March 1969, 16; "Marine Fighter Squadron Honored," *Pittsburgh Courier*, 5 April 1969, 2; and Shaw and Donnelly, *Blacks in the Marine Corps*, 71–78

152. Poinsett, "The Negro Officer," 138.

153. Westmoreland, *Report of the Chief of Staff*, 65.

154. Poinsett, "The Negro Officer," 138.

155. "Black Caucus Report," 36585.

156. Westmoreland, *Report of the Chief of Staff,* 65; Foner, *Blacks and the Military in American History,* 240; and Daniel "Chappie" James, Jr., "Rapping with Chappie," *Air University Review* (July 1972): 12.

157. Foner, *Blacks and the Military in American History,* 66, 130; and Poinsett, "The Negro Officer," 137.

158. Shaw and Donnelly, *Blacks in the Marine Corps,* 82; Foner, *Blacks and the Military in American History,* 170–71; and "Black Admiral for U.S. Navy," 1.

159. Poinsett, "The Negro Officer," 137; and "Black Admiral for U.S. Navy," 1.

160. Poinsett, "The Negro Officer," 138; NAACP, *Search for Military Justice,* 5; and "Black Admiral for U.S. Navy," 11.

161. Major General Frederic E. Davison, interview, Senior Officer Oral History Project, Blacks in the Armed Forces series, 1977, 24; and "Black General Ends Tour in Vietnam," *Pittsburgh Courier,* 7 June 1968, 1.

162. "Marine Fighter Squadron Honored," 2.

163. "Colonel Tests AF's Hottest Combat Jet," *Ebony,* May 1968, 44.

164. Department of Defense, *Black Americans,* 115.

165. James, "Rapping with Chappie," 12

166. "Black Caucus Report," 36592.

167. "No Admirals," 35; and Davison interview, 26.

168. "Marine Fighter Squadron Honored," 2.

169. Poinsett, "The Negro Officer," 136.

170. "No Admirals," 35.

171. Department of Defense, *Black Americans,* 5.

172. Gravely interview, 13.

173. "Black General Ends Tour," 1.

174. "Lt. General Benjamin O. Davis, Jr.," *Ebony,* August 1968, 58.

175. "Black Caucus Report," 36592.

176. Milton White, "Self-Determination for Black Soldiers," *Black Scholar,* November 1970, 42.

177. Thomas interview; Hawkins interview.

178. Grant, "Whites against Blacks in Vietnam," 15

179. Gould, "Racial Conflict," 9.

180. Westmoreland, *Report of the Chief of Staff,* 63.

181. Shaw and Donnelly, *Blacks in the Marine Corps,* 22, 72; and Lewis, "Rumble at Camp Lejeune," 36.

182. Shaw and Donnelly, *Blacks in the Marine Corps,* 72; and House Armed Services Committee, *Inquiry into the Disturbances at Marine Corps Base, Camp Lejeune, N.C. on July 20, 1969* (Washington, D.C.: U.S. Government Printing Office, 1969), 5050–59.

183. Westmoreland, *Report of the Chief of Staff,* 62–63.

184. Foner, *Blacks and the Military in American History,* 218–19; and Richard Halloran, "Air Force Racism Charged in Study," *New York Times,* 31 August 1971, 1.

185. "White v. Black Confrontations," 14; and Foner, *Blacks and the Military in American History,* 228.

Notes to Chapter 6

1. Henry I. Shaw, Jr., and Ralph W. Donnelly, *Blacks in the Marine Corps* (Washington, D.C.: U.S. Marine Corps, History and Museums Division Headquarters, 1975), 73.

2. "The Navy's New Racial Crisis," *Newsweek,* 20 November 1972, 36.

3. William C. Westmoreland, *Report of the Chief of Staff of the United States Army, 1 July 1968 to 30 June 1972* (Washington, D.C.: Department of the Army, 1977), 8, 62.

4. Russell F. Weigley, *History of the United States Army,* (New York: Macmillan Company, 1967), 555.

5. Morris J. MacGregor and Bernard C. Nalty, *Blacks in the United States Armed Forces: Basic Documents,* vol. 13 of the Fahy Committee report (Wilmington, Del.: Scholarly Resources, 1977), xvii.

6. Jack D. Foner, *Blacks and the Military in American History,* New Perspectives in American History (New York: Praeger Publishers, 1974), 219–20; and "Military Prisons: About Face," *Time,* 17 May 1971, 63.

7. Westmoreland, *Report of the Chief of Staff,* 66.

8. Ibid., 67; and Herbert R. Northrup, Steven M. DiAntonio, John A. Brinker, and Dale F. Daniels, *Black and Other Minority Participation in the All-Volunteer Navy and Marine Corps,* Studies of Negro Employment, vol. 8 (Philadelphia: University of Pennsylvania, Wharton School, Industrial Research Unit, 1979), 1.

9. Foner, *Blacks and the Military in American History,* 235–37; Daniel "Chappie" James, Jr., "Rapping with Chappie," *Air University Review* (July 1972): 20; and Westmoreland, *Report of the Chief of Staff,* 65.

10. George M. Boyd, "A Look at Racial Polarity in the Armed Forces," *Air University Review* (September-October, 1970): 45.

11. Northrup et al., *Black and Other Minority Participation,* 22; and Melvin R. Laird, *Final Report to the Congress of Secretary of Defense Melvin R. Laird* (Washington, D.C.: U.S. Department of Defense, 1973), 74.

12. Shaw and Donnelly, *Blacks in The Marine Corps,* 74–75.

13. Westmoreland, *Report of The Chief of Staff,* 63–67.

14. Boyd, "A Look at Racial Polarity," 45–46.

15. Richard Halloran, "General Combats Racial Irritants," *New York Times,* 2 September 1971, 3.

16. Foner, *Blacks and the Military in American History*, 239–42; and Northrup et al., *Black and Other Minority Participation*, 22.

17. Department of Defense, Office of the Deputy Assistant Secretary of Defense for Equal Opportunity and Safety Policy, *Task Force on the Administration of Military Justice in the Armed Forces* (Washington, D.C.: U.S. Government Printing Office, 1972): 1, 20.

18. Robert D. Heinl, Jr., "The Collapse of the Armed Forces," *Armed Forces Journal* (7 June 1971): 33; Shaw and Donnelly, *Blacks in the Marine Corps*, 72–73; and Flora Lewis, "The Rumble at Camp Lejeune," *Atlantic Monthly* 225, January 1970, 38.

19. Harris was a supporter of Maulana Karenga's US movement and, as a civilian, had twice been arrested during the Watts uprising; see Wallace Terry, "Bringing the War Home," *Black Scholar* 2 (November 1970): 14.

20. Shaw and Donnelly, *Blacks in The Marine Corps*, 76–77.

21. James, "Rapping with Chappie," 13–14.

22. Richard Halloran, "Air Force Racism Charged in Study," *New York Times*, 31 August 1971, 1.

23. "The Navy's New Racial Crisis," 36; and Foner, *Blacks and the Military in American History*, 222.

24. Cited in the Honorable Ronald V. Dellums, "Institutional Racism in the Military," *Congressional Record*, 92d Cong., 2d sess. (2 March 1972), vol. 118, pt. 2, 6739–40.

25. Department of Defense, *Task Force*, 2: 5.

26. Foner, *Blacks and the Military in American History*, 219–20, 242; and "The Navy's New Racial Crisis," 36.

27. William Stuart Gould, "Racial Conflict in the U.S. Army," *Race* 15, 1 (July 1973): 9.

28. Heinl, "Collapse of the Armed Forces," 30; and Boyd, "A Look at Racial Polarity," 46.

29. Boyd, "A Look at Racial Polarity," 46; James, "Rapping with Chappie," 13; and Vice Admiral Samuel L. Gravely Jr., interview, Senior Officer Oral History Project, Blacks in the Armed Forces series, U.S. Army Military History Institute, Carlisle Barracks, Pennsylvania, 1977, 13.

30. Boyd, "A Look at Racial Polarity," 43–46.

31. Westmoreland, *Report of the Chief of Staff*, 62.

32. House Armed Services Committee, *Inquiry into the Disturbances at Marine Corps Base, Camp Lejeune, N.C. on July 20, 1969* (Washington, D.C.: U.S. Government Printing Office, 1969), 5052.

33. Phillip S. Foner, ed., *The Black Panthers Speak* (Philadelphia: J.B. Lippincott Co., 1970), xiv–xv.

34. James Edward Hawkins, Jr., interview with the author, Cincinnati, Ohio, 9 July 1991.

35. Zalin B. Grant, "Whites against Blacks in Vietnam," *New Republic*, 18 January 1969, 15; and Terry, "Bringing the War Home," 10, 14.

36. Henry Dority, interview with the author, Cincinnati, Ohio, 26 May 1991.

37. Milton White, "Malcolm X in the Military," *Black Scholar* (May, 1970): 33; and House Committee on Internal Security, *Investigation of Attempts to Subvert the United States Armed Forces*, 92d Cong., 2d sess. (Washington, D.C.: U.S. Government Printing Office, 1972), part 2, 6568.

38. Terry Klug, "Statement by Terry Klug after Ft. Dix Acquittal," *Black Panther*, 10 January 1970, 13; and Heinl, "Collapse of the Armed Forces," 30.

39. Peoples Justice Committee, "Black Organization Grows from Hearing on Racism," flier (15 November 1971), in Citizen Soldier File 7033, box 8, file 54, Vietnam War Veterans Archive and Manuscript Collection, Department of Manuscripts and University Archives, Cornell University Library, Ithaca, New York.

40. White, "Malcolm X in the Military," 33; and Milton White, "Self-Determination for Black Soldiers," *Black Scholar* 2 (November 1970): 40.

41. House Committee on Internal Security, *Investigation of Attempts to Subvert*, 6542; and "The Peace GIs," *Newsweek*, 21 April 1969, 35.

42. House Committee on Internal Security, *Investigation of Attempts to Subvert*, 6568; and "The Fort Jackson Eight," *Black Panther*, 4 May 1969, 9.

43. White, "Malcolm X in the Military," 32–33.

44. "Two against the War Bring Militant Message to Philadelphia," *Workers World*, 16 December 1967, 2; Charles Hightower, "GI Conference November 13 to Put Brass on Trial," *Black Panther*, 20 September 1969, 8.

45. House Committee on Internal Security, *Investigation of Attempts to Subvert*, 6731.

46. Bob Wilkinson, "GIs and the Antiwar Movement," *Young Socialist Discussion Bulletin* 14 (December, 1970): 17, reprinted in House Committee on Internal Security, *Investigation of Attempts to Subvert*, 6625; see also White, "Self-Determination for Black Soldiers," 46.

47. House Committee on Internal Security, *Investigation of Attempts to Subvert*, 6437.

48. Foner, *Black Panthers Speak*, xv; and Bobby Seale, "Black Soldiers as Revolutionaries to Overthrow the Ruling Class," *Black Panther*, 20 September 1969, 2.

49. House Committee on Internal Security, *Investigation of Attempts to Subvert*, 7091; and "White Marine Dead Following Outbreak," *Pittsburgh Courier*, 9 August 1969, 1.

50. House Committee on Internal Security, *Investigation of Attempts to Subvert*, 6387, 6487, 6544, 7296.

51. "Only Four Attend Antiwar Rally of Black Caucus," *Baltimore Afro-American*, 3 January 1970, 16. As the newspaper article's title suggests, the rally, which

was held at St. Thomas Episcopal Church, did not attract much attention in the black community. Speakers attributed the lack of interest to the "reluctance of blacks to participate in what they are said to regard as primarily a white movement."

52. House Committee on Internal Security, *Investigation of Attempts to Subvert*, 6516.

53. "Fort Dix Repression," *Black Panther*, 26 July 1969, 18.

54. "Four Anti-War GIs Thrown into Ft. Jackson Stockade," *Black Panther*, 6 April 1969, 15; and "An Interview with a Black GI," *Black Panther*, 25 May 1969, 16. Other leftist nationalist publications also provided extremely favorable coverage of the ASU's, and GIs United's activities. For examples, see, "GI Transferred," *Black Liberator*, July 1969, 3; and "GIs United against Vietnam," *Black Liberator*, August, 1969, 4.

55. House Committee on Internal Security, *Investigation of Attempts to Subvert*, 6384, 6484, 6542, 6624.

56. Ibid., 6555, 6571; and "Two against the War," 2.

57. Movement for a Democratic Military (MDM), *MDM Factsheet* (Chicago, May 1970); and Stephanie Allan, "MDM," *Daily World*, 14 March 1970, M-3, both reprinted in House Committee on Internal Security, *Investigation of Attempts to Subvert*, 6622–24.

58. Pacific Counseling Service, circular (8 May 1970), reprinted in House Committee on Internal Security, *Investigation of Attempts to Subvert*, 6619.

59. Vietnam Veterans Against the War, "Report of the Vietnam Veterans Against the War Steering Committee Meeting," Manuscript (Chicago, 4–8 January 1973), 17, in Vietnam Veterans Against the War/Winter Soldier Organization File 7019, box 1, file 1, Vietnam War Veterans Archive and Manuscript Collection, Department of Manuscripts and University Archives, Cornell University Library, Ithaca, New York.

60. Flower of the Dragon, "Flower of The Dragon/Vietnam Veterans Against the War: Position Paper on Vietnam," manuscript (Placitas, New Mexico, April 1973), 19–20, in Flower of the Dragon File 7020, box 1, Vietnam War Veterans Archive and Manuscript Collection, Department of Manuscripts and University Archives, Cornell University Library, Ithaca, New York.

61. House Committee on Internal Security, *Investigation of Attempts to Subvert*, 6493–94, 6500, 6544–68, 7099, 7499.

62. Mack Smith, "Smash the Bosses' Armed Forces," *Progressive Labor*, September 1970, 7, reprinted in House Committee on Internal Security, *Investigation of Attempts to Subvert*, 6653–57.

63. House Committee on Internal Security, *Investigation of Attempts to Subvert*, 6616–17.

64. Ibid., 6541.

65. Allan, "MDM," M-3; and "GI Wounded in Attack on Antiwar Group," *GI*

Press Service, 22 May 1970, 2, both reprinted in House Committee on Internal Security, *Investigation of Attempts to Subvert*, 6622.

66. Al Greengold, "War, Revolution and GIs," *Young Socialist Discussion Bulletin*, 14 (18 December 1970): 9–10.

67. House Committee on Internal Security, *Investigation of Attempts to Subvert*, 6568.

68. Taylor Branch, *Parting of the Waters: America in the King Years* (New York: Simon & Schuster, 1988), 209–10.

69. Heinl, "Collapse of The Armed Forces," 32; and House Committee on Internal Security, *Investigation of Attempts to Subvert*, 6638, 7082–85, 7296.

70. Peoples Justice Committee, "Black Organization Grows from Hearing on Racism."

71. House Committee on Internal Security, *Investigation of Attempts to Subvert*, 6679–80, 6732.

72. "Brass Bans Paper—GIs Seek Injunction," *Black Panther*, 27 September 1969, 9; and "Peace GIs," 35.

73. "GI Transferred," 3; and "Antiwar GIs," *Black Liberator*, August, 1968, 4.

74. "GI Sentenced for Distribution of Anti-War Leaflets," *Black Panther*, 26 July 1969, 18.

75. House Committee on Internal Security, *Investigation of Attempts to Subvert*, 6980.

76. "Brass Bans Paper," 9.

77. Smith, "Smash the Bosses' Armed Forces," 29.

78. House Committee on Internal Security, *Investigation of Attempts to Subvert*, 7070.

79. "The Peace GIs," 35.

80. Ibid.; and House Committee on Internal Security, *Investigation of Attempts to Subvert*, 6638, 6980, 7082–84.

81. Smith "Smash the Bosses' Armed Forces," 29. Smith claimed he started *EM-16*, despite the fact that Fort Knox already had two underground papers, because the other two GI presses "had a rotten political line." *In Formation* largely appealed to liberals, and *FTA*, while somewhat more radical, was still "revisionist" and catered to "Hippie Types" and "ex-students" more interested in getting out of the army than in changing it.

82. House Committee on Internal Security, *Investigation of Attempts to Subvert*, 7082–84.

83. Ibid., 6542.

84. Klug, "statement by Terry Klug," 13.

85. Kenneth Dupre, "Statement of Kenneth Dupre," *Black Panther*, 10 January 1970, 13.

86. "The Peace GIs," 35; and House Committee on Internal Security, *Investigation of Attempts to Subvert*, 6569–71.

87. Robert W. Mullen, *Blacks in America's Wars: The Shift in Attitudes from the Revolutionary War to Vietnam* (New York: Monad Press/Pathfinder Press, 1973), 83; and George C. Wilson, "One Hundred Black GIs Arrested in Alabama Melee," *Washington Post*, 16 November 1971, A8.

88. Peoples Justice Committee, "Black Organization Grows from Hearing on Racism."

89. GI Movement, *Systematic Racism Exists*, pamphlet issued by the Military and Veterans Action Committee (1972), in Citizen Soldier File 7033, box 8, file 58.

90. House Committee on Internal Security, *Investigation of Attempts to Subvert*, 6731–38, 7641.

91. Ulf Nilson, "Deserters in Sweden," *Ebony*, August 1968, 121–22.

92. First Lieutenant Patrick Graves, diary entry (10 August 1965), 55, in Patrick Graves File 7047, box 1, Vietnam War Veterans Archive and Manuscript Collection, Department of Manuscripts and University Archives, Cornell University Library, Ithaca, New York.

93. "ASU Chairman Addresses Korean Youth Conference," *Workers World*, 13 July 1971, 5.

94. For examples of the cartoons, see, *Black Panther*, 26 October 1968, 3; and *Black Panther*, 20 September 1969, 2.

95. "NLF Begins Ninth Year," *Black Panther*, 4 January 1969, 7.

96. "Long Live Ho Chi Minh," *Black Panther*, 19 May 1969, 11.

97. "Contingent in Solidarity with the Vietnamese People," *Black Liberator*, November 1969, 1.

98. "Long Live Ho Chi Minh," 11.

99. "To the Courageous Vietnamese People, Commemorating the Death of Ho Chi Minh," *Black Panther*, 13 September 1969, 16.

100. "Hanoi Sends Condolences to Group Led by Dr. King," *New York Times*, 9 April 1968, 37. The Vietnam Youth Federation Central Committee also sent its condolences; see "On the Death of Dr. Martin Luther King," *Black Panther*, 4 May 1968, 3.

101. Ho Chi Minh, "Appeal of President Ho Chi Minh," *Black Panther*, 23 August 1969, 19.

102. Diane Nash Bevel, "Journey to North Vietnam," *Freedomways* 7, second quarter (spring 1967): 118; and Diane Nash Bevel, "Black Woman Views Genocidal War in Vietnam," *Black Liberator*, May 1969, 2.

103. House Committee on Internal Security, *Investigation of Attempts to Subvert*, 7427.

104. Bevel, "Black Woman Views Genocidal War," 2.

105. House Committee on Internal Security, *Investigation of Attempts to Subvert*, 7426–28.

106. "Two GIs Freed by Vietnam Face 'Helping Enemy' Charge," *Baltimore Afro-American*, 8 January 1966, 13.

107. Bobby Seale, "Bring It Home," *Black Panther,* 3 January 1970, 5.

108. Charles C. Moskos, Jr., *The American Enlisted Man: The Rank and File in Today's Military,* (New York: Russell Sage Foundation, 1970), 130; and Martin Binkin and Mark J. Eitelberg, *Blacks and the Military,* Studies in Defense Policy (Washington D.C.: Brookings Institute, 1982), 118.

109. Raymond Wells, interview with the author, Cincinnati, Ohio, 11 October 1991.

110. "GIs Complain about Bias in Armed Services," *Pittsburgh Courier,* 8 May 1971, 9.

111. Nilson, "Deserters in Sweden," 121–22.

112. "Veteran Says Vietnamese Support Black Struggle," *Baltimore Afro-American,* 17 January 1970, 19.

113. "This Paper Can Save Your Life," Vietcong propaganda leaflet, reprinted in House Committee on Internal Security, *Investigation of Attempts to Subvert,* 6806.

114. "Two GIs Freed," 13.

115. Nilson, "Deserters in Sweden," 122.

116. Hawkins interview.

117. House Committee on Internal Security, *Investigation of Attempts to Subvert,* 6382, 6978, 7061. Ichord added, however, that the racial problems facing the armed forces were complex and not simply the result of radical subversion.

118. House Armed Services Committee, *Inquiry,* 5059.

119. House Committee on Internal Security, *Investigation of Attempts to Subvert,* 6545, 6616, 7058.

120. Major Donald Dean, interview, Senior Officer Oral History Project, Company Command series, U.S. Army Military History Institute, Carlisle Barracks, Pennsylvania, 1982, 7.

121. Lieutenant Colonel Charles R. Shrader, interview, Senior Officer Oral History Project, Company Command series, 1981, 9.

122. Major Richard L. Bevington, interview, Senior Officer Oral History Project, Company Command series, 1982, 4–5.

123. Major John J. Ellis, interview, Senior Officer Oral History Project, Company Command series, 1982, 4.

124. House Committee on Internal Security, *Investigation of Attempts to Subvert,* 6937–38; and House Armed Services Committee, *Inquiry,* 5051–52.

125. Foner, *Blacks and the Military in American History,* 248–53; and "Fleet Racism Whitewash," *Camp News* (15 February 1973), 7.

126. Lieutenant John Paul Jones [pseud.], "Militants at Sea," *National Review,* 19 January 1973, 91–92.

127. House Committee on Internal Security, *Investigation of Attempts to Subvert,* 6943–52, 7061–90.

128. Ibid., 6952; and Secretary of Defense Melvin Laird, "Guidelines for Handling Dissident and Protest Activities among Members of the Armed Forces,"

Department of Defense directive 1325.6 (12 September 1969), 1–3, in Citizen Soldier File 7033, box 8, file 59.

129. White, "Self-Determination for Black Soldiers," 46.

130. Laird, "Guidelines for Handling Dissident and Protest Activities," 1.

131. White, "Malcolm X in the Military," 33.

132. "Air Force Jim Crow," *The Crisis* 77 (June-July, 1970): 227–29; and Foner, *Blacks and the Military in American History,* 232.

133. National Association for the Advancement of Colored People (NAACP), *The Search for Military Justice: Report of an NAACP Inquiry into the Problems of the Negro Serviceman in West Germany* (New York: NAACP Special Contributions Fund, 1971), 19; and "GIs Complain," 11.

134. "Military Race Relations Held Explosive," *New York Times,* 18 November 1971, 18; and the Honorable Louis Stokes, "Racism in the Military: A New System for Rewards and Punishment," Congressional Black Caucus Report, *Congressional Record,* 92d Cong., 2d sess. (14 October 1972), 36582. (Hereafter cited as "Black Caucus Report.")

135. "Chisolm Blasts Hard at Defense Spending," *Pittsburgh Courier,* 12 April 1969, 2.

136. "Two Black GIs Convicted of Rape Ask Help of Pentagon," *Chicago Tribune,* 9 June 1971; and Joel Dreyfuss, "Shirley Aids Black GI's Fight," *Washington Post,* 11 August 1971, 9.

137. "Free the Camp Allen Brothers," *Winter Soldier* 3 (June 1973), 14, in Vietnam Veterans Against the War/Winter Soldier File 7019, box 1.

138. Erwin Knoll, "Representative Ron Dellums: Black, Radical, and Hopeful," *The Progressive,* June 1971, 14.

139. Ibid., 18; and Hank Burchand, "Dellums Urges Troops to Resist Vietnam War," *Los Angeles Times,* 14 April 1971, 22.

140. "Black Caucus Report," 36582; and Fort Hood United Front, "Congressional Hearings on Racism," flier (23 October 1971), in Citizen Soldier File 7033, box 8, file 55; and Derrick Morrison, "Black Caucus Exposes Military Racism," *The Militant,* 3 December 1971, 24.

141. Richard M. Cohen, "Army Lawyer at Fort Meade Charges Discrimination at Base," *Washington Post,* 16 November 1971, A8.

142. Knoll, "Representative Ron Dellums," 15.

143. Foner, *Blacks and the Military in American History,* 249; and "Fleet Racism Whitewash," 7.

144. James, "Rapping with Chappie," 12.

145. White, "Malcolm X in the Military," 33.

146. Peoples Justice Committee, "Black Organization Grows from Hearings on Racism."

147. "GI Transferred," 3.

148. House Committee on Internal Security, *Investigation of Attempts to Subvert,* 7245–46, 7250.

149. "Jailed Black Marines Appealing Sentences," *Pittsburgh Courier,* 15 March 1969, 1; "More GIs Face Court Martials," *Pittsburgh Courier,* 22 March 1969, 1; and "Navy Nurse Convicted after Antiwar March," *New York Times,* 1 February 1969, 14.

150. GI Movement, *Systematic Racism Exists.*

151. "Interview with a Black GI," 16.

152. Ben A. Franklin, "War Resistance by GIs Is Urged," *New York Times,* 14 November 1969, 11.

153. "The Peace GIs," 35; and "Army Cancels Court Martials," *Pittsburgh Courier,* 31 May 1969, 2.

154. "GI Transferred," 3.

155. Heinl, "Collapse of the Armed Forces," 33.

156. NOMLAC *Newsletter* 6 (undated), in Citizen Soldier File 7033, box 8, file 60.

157. House Committee on Internal Security, *Investigation of Attempts to Subvert,* 7058, 7323; and Clinton H. Hunt, interview with the author, Cincinnati, Ohio, 21 September 1991.

158. Flower of the Dragon, "Flower of the Dragon/Vietnam Veterans Against the War: Position Paper on Vietnam."

159. Seale, "Black Soldiers as Revolutionaries," 2.

160. House Committee on Internal Security, *Investigation of Attempts to Subvert,* 6568, 6751; and "The Peace GIs," 34.

161. House Committee on Internal Security, *Investigation of Attempts to Subvert,* 6391, 6411, 6623.

162. Alfonzo Wright, Jr., interview with the author, Pikeville, North Carolina, 27 December 1995; and House Committee on Internal Security, *Investigation of Attempts to Subvert,* 6717.

163. Wilkinson, "GIs and the Antiwar Movement," 17.

164. "Black Caucus Report," 36591.

165. NAACP, *Search for Military Justice,* 19.

Notes to Chapter 7

1. Thomas Gates, *Report of the President's Commission on an All-Volunteer Armed Force* (Washington, D.C.: U.S. Government Printing Office, 1970), 15–16, 149.

2. William Bowman, Roger Little, and Thomas G. Sicilia, *The All-Volunteer Force after a Decade: Retrospect and Prospect* (Washington, D.C.: Pergamon-Brassey, International Defense Publishers, 1984), 76; and Martin Binkin and Mark

J. Eitelberg with Alvin Schexnider and Marvin Smith, *Blacks and the Military,* Studies in Defense Policy (Washington, D.C.: The Brookings Institute, 1982), 43.

3. "War Death Data Allays Blacks' Fears," *Cincinnati Enquirer,* 18 December 1991, 2.

4. Gates, *Report of the President's Commission,* 16.

5. "Testimony of Shirley Chisolm before the House Armed Services Committee," *The Congressional Digest* (May 1971), 156.

6. Binkin and Eitelberg, *Blacks and the Military,* 72–73.

7. John W. Caknipe, "A Factor Analysis of the Metropolitan Detroit Area Vietnam Veteran: The Post Vietnam Veteran Syndrome," (Ph.D. diss., Midwestern University, 1978), 5–6, 48.

8. Ponchitta Pierce and Peter Bailey, "The Returning Vet," *Ebony,* August 1968, 146.

9. Thomas Johnson, "Negro Veteran Is Confused and Bitter," *New York Times,* 29 July 1968, 1.

10. Bill Lawson, "Minority Veterans Haven't Forgotten Their Obligation to America, but America Has Forgotten Its Obligation to the Minority Veteran," *National Association of Concerned Veterans Newsletter* (September 1973): 4.

11. Pierce and Bailey, "The Returning Vet," 146–48.

12. Alfonzo Wright, Jr., interview with the author, Pikeville, North Carolina, 27 December 1995; and Earl Arnett, "Veterans Seek Place in Civilian Society," *Baltimore Sun,* 15 November 1969, 1.

13. Wright interview; Arnett, "Veterans Seek Place," 1; Pierce and Bailey, "The Returning Vet," 147; and Sol Stern, "When the Black GI Comes Back From Vietnam," *New York Times Magazine,* 24 March 1968, 42.

14. Quoted in Pierce and Bailey, "The Returning Vet," 147.

15. Wright interview.

16. Bowman, Little, and Sicilia, *All-Volunteer Force,* 76–79.

17. Allen Thomas, Jr., interview with the author, Highland Heights, Kentucky, 22 March 1995.

18. Department of Defense, Office of the Deputy Assistant Secretary of Defense for Equal Opportunity and Safety Policy, *Black Americans in Defense of Our Nation* (Washington, D.C.: U.S. Government Printing Office, 1991), 89.

19. J. Alfred Phelps, *Chappie: The Life and Times of Daniel James, Jr.* (Novato, Calif.: Presidio Press, 1991), 322.

20. Henry Dority, interview with the author, Cincinnati, Ohio, 26 May 1991.

21. "Medal of Honor Winner Is Slain in Holdup Try," *Pittsburgh Courier,* 8 May 1971, 4.

22. Clinton H. Hunt, interview with the author, Cincinnati, Ohio, 21 September 1991.

23. Dr. John K. Brackett, interview with the author, Cincinnati, Ohio, 21 January 1992.

24. Thomas interview.

25. Wright interview.

26. Phillip L. Woodall, letter to R. Boyce Pennington (2 November 1981), in Phillip Woodall File, box 85, Vietnam War Veterans Archive and Manuscript Collection, Department of Manuscripts and University Archives, Cornell University Library, Ithaca, New York.

Bibliography

Archive and Manuscript Collections

Senior Officer Oral History Project, U.S. Army Military History Institute, Carlisle Barracks, Pennsylvania.

INTERVIEWS USED FROM COMPANY COMMAND SERIES

Major Richard C. Anshus
Major Robert Arnold
Major Richard Barnes
Major Stewart H. Barnhoft
Major Richard L. Bevington
Major Patrick Carder
Major Bruce B. Cary
Major Thomas Cecil
Major Michael F. Colacicco
Lieutenant Colonel Vernon L. Conner
Major Cecil F. Davis
Major Donald Dean
Lieutenant Colonel Joseph DeFrancisco
Major John J. Ellis
Major O. J. Golphenee

Major James B. Hollis
Major Henry Koren, Jr.
Major William C. Long
Major James Love
Major Clay Melton
Major Henry L. Parker
Major Thomas Peoples
Major William G. Riederer
Lieutenant Colonel Charles P. Shrader
Major Maxwell V. Terrian
Major Richard H. Torovsky, Jr.
Major Steven N. Townsend
Major Gary L. Tucker
Major Eugene J. White, Jr.
Major Michael Yap

INTERVIEWS USED FROM BLACKS IN THE ARMED FORCES SERIES

Major General Frederic E. Davison   Vice Admiral Samuel L. Gravely, Jr.

Vietnam War Veterans Archive and Manuscript Collection, Department of Manuscripts and University Archives, Cornell University Library, Ithaca, New York

Addlestone, David F. "A Background Paper on the Question of Less than Fully Honorable Military Discharges Issued during the Vietnam War." Manuscript. National Veterans Law Center, Washington College of Law, American University, 27 April 1979.

Anderson, Lieutenant Charles R. Letters to parents. 27 August 1968; 15 November, 1968; 25 November 1968; 7 January 1967.

Black Cadets, United States Air Force Academy. "An Answer to Wing Staff's Request." Manuscript. Colorado, March 1970.

Breedlove, John "Jackie," Letter to parents. 7 December 1966.

Brown, Robert J., special assistant to President Richard Nixon. Letter to the Black Legislators' Association. 25 August 1971.

Flower of the Dragon. "Flower of the Dragon/Vietnam Veterans Against the War; Position Paper on Vietnam." Manuscript. Placitas, New Mexico, April 1973.

Fort Hood United Front. *Black Organization Grows from Hearing on Racism.* Pamphlet. Killeen, Texas, 15 November 1971.

GI Movement. *Systematic Racism Exists.* Pamphlet issued by the Military and Veterans Action Committee. 1972.

Graves, First Lieutenant Patrick. Diary entry for 10 August 1965.

Merretazon, Sesu. "In Support of Incarcerated Veterans Affairs Officers within Prisons." Unpublished report prepared for the Veterans Administration by the Incarcerated Veterans Assistance Organization, Inc., Washington, D.C., June 1976.

Peoples Justice Committee. "Black Organization Grows from Hearing on Racism." Flier. 15 November 1971.

Souders, Edward. Letter to "Fellow Resisters" on behalf of Safe Return. August 1973.

———. "Racism in the Military." Manuscript prepared for Safe Return. New York, January 1974.

Vietnam Veterans Against the War. "Report of the Vietnam Veterans Against the War Steering Committee Meeting." Manuscript. Chicago, Illinois, 4–8 January 1973.

———. "Position Paper on Amnesty." Manuscript. Placitas, New Mexico, 19–23 April 1973.

Dissertations

Caknipe, John W. "A Factor Analysis of the Metropolitan Detroit Area Vietnam Veteran: The Post Vietnam Veteran Syndrome." Ph.D. diss., Midwestern University, 1978.

Schexnider, Alvin J. "The Development of Nationalism: Political Socialization among Blacks in the U.S. Armed Forces." Ph.D. diss., Northwestern University, 1973.

Published Studies and Primary Sources

Howe, Steven. *Homelessness in Ohio: A Study of People in Need, Hamilton County Report*. Cincinnati: University of Cincinnati, Institute for Policy Research, 1985.

National Association for the Advancement of Colored People, *The Search for Military Justice: Report of an NAACP Inquiry into the Problems of the Negro Serviceman in West Germany*. New York: NAACP Special Contributions Fund, 1971.

Princeton University Educational Testing Service. *Report of the Educational Testing Service Princeton University, on Educational Assistance Programs for Veterans*. Prepared for the House Committee on Veterans Affairs. Washington, D.C.: U.S. Government Printing Office, 1973.

United States Government Studies and Publications

U.S. Congress. House. Armed Services Committee. *Inquiry into the Disturbances at Marine Corps Base, Camp Lejeune, N.C., on July 20, 1969*. Washington, D.C.: U.S. Government Printing Office, 1969.

———. House. Dellums, the Honorable Ronald V. "Institutional Racism in the Military." *Congressional Record*. 118, pt. 6. 92d Cong., 2d sess., 2 March 1972.

———. House. Committee on Internal Security. *Investigation of Attempts to Subvert the United States Armed Forces*. 92d Cong., 2d sess. Washington, D.C.: U.S. Government Printing Office, 1972. Part 2.

———. House. Stokes, the Honorable Louis. "Racism in the Military: A New System for Rewards and Punishment." The Congressional Black Caucus Report. *Congressional Record*, 92d Cong., 2d sess., 14 October 1972.

Department of Defense. *Annual Report for Fiscal Year 1968*. Washington, D.C.: U.S. Government Printing Office, 1971.

———. *The Negro in the Armed Forces: A Statistical Fact Book*. Washington, D.C.: Department of Defense, Office of the Deputy Assistant Secretary of Defense for Equal Opportunity and Safety Policy, 1971.

———. Assistant Secretary of Defense for Manpower and Reserve Affairs. *Project One Hundred Thousand: Characteristics and Performance of "New Standards" Men*. Washington, D.C.: U.S. Government Printing Office, 1969.

———. Office of the Deputy Assistant Secretary of Defense for Equal Opportunity and Safety Policy. *Task Force on the Administration of Military Justice in the Armed Forces*. 5 vols. (Washington, D.C.: U.S. Government Printing Office, 1972.

———. Office of the Deputy Assistant Secretary of Defense for Equal Opportunity and Safety Policy. *Black Americans in Defense of Our Nation*. Washington, D.C.: U.S. Government Printing Office, 1978 and 1991.

Gates, Thomas. *Report of the President's Commission on an All-Volunteer Army Force*. Washington, D.C.: U.S. Government Printing Office, 1970.

Laird, Secretary of Defense Melvin R. *Final Report to the Congress of Secretary of Defense Melvin R. Laird.* Washington, D.C.: U.S. Department of Defense, 1973.

———. "Guidelines for Handling Dissident and Protest Activities among Members of the Armed Forces." Department of Defense directive 1325.6. 12 September 1969.

MacGregor, Morris J., and Bernard C. Nalty. *Blacks in the United States Armed Forces: Basic Documents.* Fahy Committee Report. 13 vols. Wilmington, Del.: Scholarly Resources, 1977.

Shaw, Henry I., Jr., and Ralph W. Donnelly. *Blacks in the Marine Corps.* Washington, D.C.: U.S. Marine Corps, History and Museums Division Headquarters, 1975.

Manual for Courts-Martial, United States 1969. Rev. ed. Washington, D.C.: Government Printing Office, 1969.

Veterans Administration. *Myths and Realities: A Study of Attitudes toward Vietnam Era Veterans.* Report submitted to the Senate Committee on Veteran Affairs, 96th Cong., 2d sess. Washington, D.C.: U.S. Government Printing Office, 1980.

Westmoreland, General William C. *Report of the Chief of Staff of the United States Army, 1 July 1968 to 30 June 1972.* Washington, D.C.: Department of the Army, 1977.

Books

Baskir, Lawrence M., and William A. Strauss. *Chance and Circumstance: The Draft, the War, and the Vietnam Generation.* New York: Random House, 1978.

Binkin, Martin. *Who Will Fight the Next War.* Washington, D.C.: The Brookings Institute, 1993.

Binkin, Martin, and Mark J. Eitelberg with Alvin Schexnider and Marvin Smith. *Blacks and the Military.* Washington, D.C.: The Brookings Institute, 1982. Studies in Defense Policy.

ʾraestrup, Peter. *The Big Story.* Boulder, Colo.: Westview Press, 1977.

ʾch, Taylor. *Parting of the Waters: America in the King Years.* New York: ʾn & Schuster, 1988.

William, Roger Little, and G. Thomas Sicilia., *The All-Volunteer Force ʾecade: Retrospect and Prospect.* Washington, D.C.: Pergamon-Brassey, ʾnal Defense Publishers, 1984.

Self-Destruction: The Disintegration and Decay of the United States ʾg the Vietnam Era. New York: W. W. Norton & Co., 1981.

ʾd G., and George Hill, *Blacks in the American Armed Forces 1776– ʾography.* Westport, Conn.: Greenwood Press, 1985.

Blacks and the Military in American History. New York: Praeger ʾ74. New Perspectives in American History.

Foner, Phillip S., ed. *The Black Panthers Speak.* Philadelphia: J. B. Lippincott Co., 1970.

Henderson, William Daryl. *The Hollow Army.* New York: Greenwood Press, 1990.

Herr, Michael. *Dispatches* New York: Avon Books, 1978.

Herring, George C. *America's Longest War: The United States and Vietnam.* New York: Alfred A. Knopf, 1979.

Karnow, Stanley. *Vietnam: A History.* New York: Viking Press, 1983.

Karsten, Peter, ed. *The Military in America, from the Colonial Era to the Present.* New York: Free Press, 1980.

Leckie, William H. *The Buffalo Soldiers: A Narrative of the Negro Cavalry in the West.* Norman: University of Oklahoma Press, 1967.

Lindenmeyer, Otto. *Black and Brave: The Black Soldier in America.* New York: McGraw-Hill Book Co., 1970. Black America.

Little, Roger W. *Selective Service and American Society.* New York: Russell Sage Foundation, 1969.

Marshall, Kathyrn. *In the Combat Zone: An Oral History of American Women in Vietnam.* Boston: Little, Brown & Co., 1987.

Moskos, Charles C., Jr. *The American Enlisted Man: The Rank and File in Today's Military.* New York: Russell Sage Foundation, 1970.

Mullen, Robert W. *Blacks in America's Wars: The Shift in Attitudes from the Revolutionary War to Vietnam.* New York: Monad Press/Pathfinder Press, 1973.

Northrup, Herbert R., Steven M. DiAntonio, John A. Brinker, and Dale F. Daniels. *Black and Other Minority Participation in the All-Volunteer Navy and Marine Corps,* vol. 8, Studies of Negro Employment Series. Philadelphia: University of Pennsylvania, Wharton School, 1979.

Olson, James, ed. *Dictionary of the Vietnam War.* New York: Peter Bedrick Books, 1987.

Parson, Erwin Randolph, et al. *Report of the Working Group on Black Vietnam Veterans.* Washington, D.C.: Readjustment Counseling Service, 1984.

Phelps, J. Alfred. *Chappie: The Life and Times of Daniel James, Jr.* Novato, Calif.: Presidio Press, 1991.

Polenberg, Richard. *One Nation Divisible: Class, Race and Ethnicity in the United States Since 1938.* New York: Penguin Books, 1980.

Reich, Dale. *Good Soldiers Don't Go to Heaven.* Whitewater, Wis.: Garden of Eden Press, 1979.

Santoli, Albert. *Everything We Had.* New York: Ballantime Books, 1981.

Sevy, Grace, ed. *The American Experience in Vietnam.* Norman: University of Oklahoma Press, 1989.

Sheehan, Neil, ed. *The Pentagon Papers: The Secret History of the Vietnam War.* New York: Bantam Books/New York Times, 1971.

Summers, Harry G. *Vietnam War Almanac.* New York: Facts on File Publications, 1985.

Walker, Keith. *A Piece of My Heart: The Stories of Twenty-six American Women Who Served in Vietnam.* Novato, Calif.: Presidio Press, 1985.
Wallace, Terry. *Bloods: An Oral History of the Vietnam War by Black Veterans.* New York: Random House, 1984.
Walton, George. *The Tarnished Shield: A Report on Today's Army.* New York: Dodd, Mead & Co., 1973.
Weigley, Russell F. *History of the United States Army.* New York: Macmillan Co., 1967.
Zeitlin, Maurice, ed. *American Society, Inc.: Studies of the Social Structure and Political Economy of the United States.* Chicago: Rand McNally & Co., 1977.

Articles

"Abolish the Draft! Enact the 'Freedom Budget'!" *Freedomways* 6, fourth quarter (fall 1966).
"Air Force Jim Crow." *The Crisis* 77, (June-July 1970).
Allen, Mark. "The Case of Billy Dean Smith." *Black Scholar* (October 1972).
Alsop, Stewart. "The American Class System." *Newsweek* 29 June 1970.
Bell, D. Bruce, and Beverly W. Bell. "Desertion and Antiwar Protest: Findings from the Ford Clemency Program." *Armed Forces and Society* 3, (May 1977).
Bevel, Diane Nash. "Journey to North Vietnam." *Freedomways* 7, second quarter (spring 1967).
"Bias at Home," Letter to the editor. *Ebony,* August 1968.
Boyd, Major George M. "A Look at Racial Polarity in the Armed Forces." *Air University Review* (September-October 1970).
Burroughs, Eric, "Leaflet To North Vietnam," *Freedomways* 6, fourth quarter (fall 1966).
Clift, Eleonor, and Thomas DeFrank. "Bush's General: Maximum Force." *Newsweek,* 3 September 1990.
Coleman, Private First Class Morocco. "The Prince of Peace." Letter to the editor. *Ebony,* August 1968.
"Colonel Tests AF's Hottest Combat Jet." *Ebony,* May 1968.
Daniell, Curtis. "Germany: Trouble Spot for Black GIs," *Ebony,* August 1968.
Davison, Lieutenant General Michael S. "The Negro as Fighting Man." *The Crisis* (February 1969).
Fairclough, Adam. "Martin Luther King Jr. and the War in Vietnam." *Phylon* 45, 1 (1984).
Fiman, Byron G., Jonathan Borus, and Duncan M. Stanton. "Black-White and American-Vietnamese Relations among Soldiers in Vietnam." *Journal of Social Issues* 31, 4 (1975).
Friederich, Rudolf J. "Fifty-four Black Heroes: Medal of Honor Winners." *The Crisis* (June–July 1969).

"Goodby to Civilian Life." *Ebony*, August 1968.

Gould, William Stuart. "Racial Conflict in the U.S. Army." *Race* 15, 1 (July 1973).

Grant, Zalin B. "Whites Against Blacks in Vietnam." *New Republic*, 18 January 1969.

Greengold, Al. "War Revolution and GIs." *Young Socialist Discussion Bulletin* 14 (18 December 1970).

Grove, Gene. "The Army and the Negro." *New York Times Magazine*, 24 July 1966.

"Gunning Down the Vietnamese." *Freedomways* 9, fourth quarter (fall 1969).

Hare, Nathan. "We Are All Soldiers." *Black Scholar* 2 (November 1970).

Heinl, Colonel Robert D., Jr. "The Collapse of the Armed Forces." *Armed Forces Journal* (7 June 1971).

"How Negro Americans Perform in Vietnam." *U.S. News and World Report*, 15 August 1966.

James, Brigadier General Daniel "Chappie," Jr. "Rapping with Chappie." *Air University Review.* (July 1972).

Johnson, Thomas. "Negroes in the Nam." *Ebony*, August 1968.

Jones, Lieutenant John Paul [psuedo.]. "Militants at Sea." *National Review*, 19 January 1973.

Katz, William Loren, "The Afro-American's Response to U.S. Imperialism." *Freedomways* 11, third quarter (summer 1971).

King, Martin Luther, Jr. "A Time to Break Silence." *Freedomways* 7, second quarter (spring 1967).

Knoll, Erwin. "Representative Ron Dellums: Black, Radical, and Hopeful." *The Progressive*, June 1971.

Kramer, Aaron. "To the People of Vietnam." *Freedomways* 7, first quarter (winter 1967).

Ladinsky, Jack. "Vietnam, the Vets, and the VA." *Armed Forces and Society* 2 (spring 1976).

Lee, Ulysses. "The Draft and the Negro." *Current History* (July 1968).

"The Less Than Honorable Solution." *The Nation*, 19 February 1973.

Lewis, Flora. "The Rumble at Camp Lejeune." *Atlantic Monthly* 225, January 1970.

Lewis, John, chairman, Student Nonviolent Coordinating Committee (SNCC). "Statement on Vietnam." *Freedomways* 6, first quarter (winter 1966).

Linden, Eugene. "Fragging and Other Withdrawal Symptoms." *Saturday Review*, January 1972.

Llorens, David. "Why Negroes Re-enlist." *Ebony*, August 1968.

"Lt. General Benjamin O. Davis, Jr." *Ebony*, August 1968.

"The Marshall Commission Report." *Current History* (July 1968).

McLean, L. Deckle. "The Black Man and the Draft." *Ebony*, August 1968.

"Memphis." *The Crisis* (March 1970).

"Military Prisons: About Face." *Time*, 17 May 1971.

Morris, Steven. "How Blacks Upset the Marine Corps." *Ebony*, December 1969.

Moskos, Charles C., Jr. "The American Combat Soldier in Vietnam." *Journal of Social Issues* 31, 4 (1975).

"Muhammad Ali—The Measure of a Man." *Freedomways* 7, second quarter (spring 1967).

Murray, Paul T. "Blacks and the Draft: A History of Institutional Racism." *Journal of Black Studies* (September 1971).

"The Navy's New Racial Crisis." *Newsweek*, 20 November 1972.

Nilson, Ulf. "Deserters in Sweden." *Ebony*, August 1968.

"No Admirals." *Newsweek*, 30 September 1968.

"Off-Base Housing." *New Republic*, 5 August 1967.

"The Peace GIs." *Newsweek*, 21 April 1969.

"The Pentagon's 'Secret Papers.' " *Freedomways* 11, second quarter (spring 1971).

Pierce, Ponchitta and Peter Bailey. "The Returning Vet." *Ebony*, August 1968.

Pilisuk, Marc. "The Legacy of the Vietnam Veteran." *Journal of Social Issues* 31, 4 (1975).

Poinsett, Alex. "The Negro Officer." *Ebony*, August 1968.

"Requiem for Dixie." *The Crisis* (March 1969).

Scammon, Richard M. "Report From Black America." *Newsweek*, 30 June 1969.

"Seamen Demand Jet, Soul Tunes on Juke Boxes." *Jet*, 2 September 1971.

Shapiro, Herbert. "The Vietnam War and the American Civil Rights Movement." *Journal of Ethnic Studies* 16, 4 (1989).

Shields, Patricia M. "Enlistment during the Vietnam Era and the 'Representation' Issue of the All-Volunteer Force." *Armed Forces and Society* 7, 1 (fall 1980).

Shils, Edward. "A Profile of the Military Deserter." *Armed Forces and Society* 3, 3 (May 1977).

Smith, Mack. "Smash the Bosses' Armed Forces." *Progressive Labor*, September 1970.

Stern, Sol. "When the Black GI Comes Back from Vietnam." *New York Times Magazine*, 24 March 1968.

Stokes, Robert. "Race Riot At Long Binh." *Newsweek*, 30 September 1968.

Taylor, Clyde. "Black Consciousness and the Vietnam War." *Black Scholar* (October 1973).

Terry, Wallace. "Bringing the War Home." *Black Scholar* 2 (November 1970).

White, Command Sergeant Major Milton. "Malcolm X in the Military." *Black Scholar* (May 1970).

———. "Self-Determination for Black Soldiers." *Black Scholar* 2 (November 1970).

Whitney, Craig R. "A Bitter Peace: Life in Vietnam." *New York Times Magazine*, 30 October 1983.

Wilkinson, Bob. "GIs and the Antiwar Movement." *Young Socialist Discussion Bulletin* 14 (December 1970).

Young, Whitney M., Jr. "When the Negroes in Vietnam Come Home." *Harpers,* June 1967.

Newspapers 1962–1978

Air Force Times
Baltimore Afro-American
Baltimore Sun
Black Liberator
Black Panther
The Bond
Camp News
Chicago Sun-Times
Chicago Tribune

Cincinnati Enquirer
Daily World
Los Angeles Times
The Militant
New York Times
Pittsburgh Courier
Washington Post
Winter Soldier
Workers World

Interviews with the Author

Brackett, Dr. John K. Cincinnati, Ohio, 21 January 1992.
Dority, Henry. Cincinnati, Ohio, 26 May 1991.
Hawkins, James Edward, Jr. Cincinnati, Ohio, 9 July 1991.
Hunt, Clinton H. Cincinnati, Ohio, 21 September 1991.
Thomas, Allen, Jr. Highland Heights, Kentucky, 22 March 1995.
Wells, Raymond. Cincinnati, Ohio, 11 October 1991.
Wright, Alfonzo, Jr. Pikeville, North Carolina, 27 December 1995.

Index

Index